Sinascape

Sinascape

Contemporary Chinese Cinema

Gary G. Xu

ROWMAN & LITTLEFIELD PUBLISHERS, INC.
Lanham • *Boulder* • *New York* • *Toronto* • *Plymouth, UK*

ROWMAN & LITTLEFIELD PUBLISHERS, INC.

Published in the United States of America
by Rowman & Littlefield Publishers, Inc.
A wholly owned subsidiary of The Rowman & Littlefield Publishing Group, Inc.
4501 Forbes Boulevard, Suite 200, Lanham, Maryland 20706
www.rowmanlittlefield.com

Estover Road, Plymouth PL6 7PY, United Kingdom

British Library Cataloguing in Publication Information Available

Library of Congress Cataloging-in-Publication Data
Xu, Gary G., 1968–
    Sinascape : contemporary Chinese cinema / Gary G. Xu.
      p.   cm.
    Includes bibliographical references and index.
    ISBN-13: 978-0-7425-5449-8 (cloth : alk. paper)
    ISBN-10: 0-7425-5449-X (cloth : alk. paper)
    ISBN-13: 978-0-7425-5450-4 (pbk. : alk. paper)
    ISBN-10: 0-7425-5450-3 (pbk. : alk. paper)
    1. Motion pictures—China.   I. Title.
    PN1993.5.C4X8 2007
    791.430951—dc22
                                                            2006021950

Printed in the United States of America

♾™ The paper used in this publication meets the minimum requirements of American
National Standard for Information Sciences—Permanence of Paper for Printed Library
Materials, ANSI/NISO Z39.48-1992.

To My Wife, Chiawen, and Our Children, Troy and Juliann

Contents

Illustrations

Acknowledgments

As I explain in the introduction, this is a book about the complex network of transnational film production and consumption centered on China. The book could not have been completed without help from those who constitute this network: filmmakers, filmgoers, transcultural intellectuals with intimate knowledge of the mutual influence between cinematic visuality and globalization, and colleagues who endeavor to bring the actual cinema experience into conventional textual analyses of films. For sharing with me the excruciating yet exhilarating experience of filmmaking, I thank Ang Lee, Tsai Ming-liang, Wang Xiaoshuai, Zhu Tianwen, Peggy Chiao, and Roy Lee. For challenging me to rethink the filmgoing experience and cinematic visuality, I thank my University of Illinois students at both my undergraduate and graduate film seminars. For inspiring me intellectually, guiding me professionally, or simply being a supportive friend, Karen Kelsky, Nancy Abelmann, Nancy Blake, Yomi Braester, Cai Zong-qi, David Desser, Poshek Fu, Liu Kang, Ann Kaplan, Sheldon Lu, Tonglin Lu, Shao Dan, Wang Ban, and Slavoj Zizek. I thank Wang Yanjie for compiling the bibliography. I thank various research arms of the University of Illinois for support: the Campus Research Board for one semester of teaching relief, the Center for East Asian and Pacific Studies for a summer research grant, and the Illinois Program for Research in the Humanities for a reading group grant. I thank my editor, Jessica Gribble, and all the supporting staff at Rowman & Littlefield for making the publication of this book possible.

My teacher David Der-wei Wang read the entire manuscript and offered invaluable suggestions for revision. I am most grateful for his guidance, support, and friendship. My father, Xu Caishi (1941–2001), who was my most enthusiastic reader, could not live to see the publication of this book, but he is with me at every moment of my professional development. My mother, Jin Yanyu, and my sister, Xu Zheng, have given me the strongest research support: they routinely find and send me indispensable books and videos from China. My weekly phone conversations with them sustain me in numerous ways. My deepest gratitude is to my wife, Chiawen, and our children, Troy and Juliann, whose infinite love gives meaning to everything I do, including the writing of this book. To them, I dedicate this book.

—⁊⁊⁊—

Introduction

China's (Cinematic) Century

The notion of the twenty-first century as "China's century" has become increasingly popular with the American news media. *Newsweek*, for instance, made "China's century" the special topic for its May 9, 2005, issue. Inside the magazine is a profusion of "factoids" about the twenty-first-century global power shift to China. Outside, gracing its cover, are three superimposed images: the Great Wall of China, the Shanghai Television Tower (the so-called Pearl of the Orient), and the film star Zhang Ziyi. Zhang Ziyi's close-up is the most prominent image among the three. The symbolic meanings of the first two images are obvious: the Great Wall represents China's past (the glorious civilization and long history), and the Pearl of the Orient symbolizes China's present (the successful economic reforms and massive urbanization projects). The implications of the third image, however, are not as unequivocal. Zhang Ziyi is known to the American audience for her roles in such martial arts blockbusters as *Crouching Tiger, Hidden Dragon* (*Wo hu cang long* [2000]), *Hero* (*Yingxiong* [2004]),[1] and *House of Flying Daggers* (*Shi mian mai fu* [2004]). She also appears in Wong Kar-wai's internationally acclaimed *2046* (2005) and stars in Rob Marshall's visually sumptuous *Memoirs of a Geisha* (2005). She *is* the face of early twenty-first-century transnational Chinese cinema[2] and, to an extent, of the quintessential Oriental woman. But why did *Newsweek* feature a film star in its report on China's economic and political rise? Why not Deng Xiaoping (1904–1997), the "designer" of China's reforms? Or Hu Jintao, who is presently at the helm? Or Li Yanhong, whose NASDAQ-traded

1

Baidu, also known as "China's Google," made him an instant billionaire and symbol of the new Internet bubble inflated by China-related hype?

The answer simply may lie in Zhang's star power and beauty. It is also possible that *Newsweek* uses Zhang's image to represent the future of China, which, after all, is in the hands of the post-Mao generations. To a great extent, Zhang is representative of the turn-of-the-millennium generation: youthful, energetic, confident, cosmopolitan, and entrepreneurial. Featuring Zhang's image also certainly has to do with the increasing visibility of Chinese cinema, which could be considered part and parcel of China's economic activities. Still, these possibilities do not warrant the visual prominence given to a film star on the cover of the special issue about the rise of China as a whole. Unless, of course, Chinese cinema is implicitly understood as *the* most important component of China's rise.

The hypothesis that Chinese cinema is most crucial to China's rise in the twenty-first century arises because the electronic image is what made China's rise fundamentally different from the rises of Europe and of the United States during the past four centuries. The notion "China's century," unlike any other previous economic-political temporalities, gains popularity through fast-spread electronic images of change. "China's century" is more a media-fanned speculation than an actual socioeconomic experience. China's actual developments are undeniable; the developments, however, can be either ex-aggerated or downplayed, depending on different political and ideological agendas. Through selected images, for instance, China could be presented or perceived as a peace-loving nation geared toward economic developments or as an emerging military superpower that bullies neighbors such as Japan and India and threatens world peace. The very notion of "China's rise," in fact, is often associated with "China's threat" or "China's challenge to the U.S. monopoly."[3] We must understand that the effect of China's rise on the world has more to do with the ways in which different political and ideological agendas manipulate the *representations* of the rise than with the rise itself.

"China's century" is media-based. But I want to further emphasize that cin-ema is at the core of the media. By highlighting Chinese cinema as one of the most crucial aspects of China's rise, I hope to draw attention to the changes of the mode of production in the twenty-first century. Unlike the previous power shifts, which benefited from the automation-driven industrial revolutions and from territorial colonization, the new century's power shift is closely related to the increasing dominance of cinema as a mode of production and to the colonization of the virtual space. Whoever can increase production through revolutionizing the cinematic mode of production will have the most power in the twenty-first century. By "cinematic mode of production," I mean that cinema has become a factory in which the spectator works in order to produce surplus value. *To see is to labor*: cinema has become a transnational industry, and hand labor is increasingly being replaced by eye labor in postmodern conditions. Viewing and sense-making based on cinematic narratives are required for commercials to be effective; to sell or accept a product, one must tell a compelling story and establish a visual code based on careful studies of consumer psychology. Chains of demand and supply begin with the urge to consume when one looks at the silver screen or into the computer monitor. Cultures and ethnicities become global commodities through cross-cultural spectatorship.[4] Most important, the cinematic mode of production in the twenty-first century is about producing free-floating signs, such as digitized images that are deliverable through the Internet or global wireless networks, "dematerialized" and detached from film stock or storage devices such as the DVD. These signs are not limited to filmic images. Brand names, intellectual properties, personal identities and other important personal data, biological information, and gene sequences are all ideally producible, transportable, or transferable without being actually attached to a concrete material form. I use "cinematic mode of production" to refer to what is at stake with productions of free-floating signs: copyright, digital encryption, and ownership of virtual space. The narrative cinema provides important cases for the study of this new mode of production, and the latter in turn helps one understand the narrative cinema of the twenty-first century.

From 1985 to 1990, the U.S. film industry experienced tremendous growth, a near-doubling of revenue from $21.5 billion to $40 billion. The annual growth rate after 1990 has also been consistently close to 7 percent, more than twice as fast as the annual U.S. GDP growth, which rarely surpassed 3 percent for each of the past fifteen years.[5] All predictions point to more growth of the film industry and its peripheral industries, which together are called "copyright industries," as I explain in chapter 2. These copyright industries will continue to grow more rapidly than other industrial sectors do and therefore become increasingly more important to the overall U.S. economy. So far, there are no reliable statistics available for the burgeoning Chinese film industry. But the increasing importance of cinema to the overall Chinese economy is evident in the big-budget filmmaking represented by *Hero* and *House of Flying Daggers* and in Zhang Yimou's being designated the director for the opening ceremony of the 2008 Beijing Olympics. As I explain in chapter 1 of this book, these films are essential for the promotion of contemporary China as a "society of great prosperity." Backed by private investment, they also reflect the trend of China's transition to privatization in all economic spheres. How to protect the free-floating filmic images and, by extension, all digitized intellectual properties through implementation of copyright laws and through political or military maneuvers is arguably the biggest challenge both the United States and China face in the twenty-first century.

If "China's century" is indeed about the U.S.-China rivalry, then the competition will always come down to the production and circulation of images: films; brand names; and biological, ethnic, cultural, and national identities, etc. But we must also note that the national boundaries between cinematic images are increasingly blurred by globalization. As Sean Smith puts it in his article on Chinese cinema for a *Newsweek* special issue:

> Without Chinese cinema, there would be no *Matrix* franchise. There would be no *Rush Hour* with Jackie Chan and no Quentin Tarantino flicks. Without Chinese filmmakers there would be no Bruce Lee movies and no Jet Li movies; there would be no *Face/Off*, no *Ice Storm*, no *Farewell My Concubine*.[6]

Through attracting mainland Chinese, Hong Kong, and Taiwanese film industry talent, remaking Chinese films, or coproducing films with Chinese companies, Hollywood absorbs the best of Chinese cinema and makes the distinction between American and Chinese films more arbitrary than ever. If "China's century" is media-based with a focus on Chinese cinema, and since Chinese cinema is increasingly Hollywoodized and Hollywood has been penetrated by Chinese cinema, we have an interesting corollary: "China's century" equals "Hollywood's century." The two notions, China's century and Hollywood's global dominance, complement each other, pointing to the importance of the cinematic mode of production to the new century in the midst of unprecedented globalization.

The ambiguities of "China's century" constitute the main frame of reference for this book, which studies contemporary Chinese cinema as an inherently transnational network. The picture of transnational production and consumption of cinema is further complicated when we understand Chinese cinema not as a coherent whole but as the filmmaking practices and films of mainland China, Taiwan, Hong Kong, and the Chinese diaspora. Tensions abound in this cinema of different regions, nations, cultures, and even languages. "Chinese-language film," a term adopted by Sheldon Lu and Emilie Yeh for describing the heterogeneous and multidialect Chinese cinema, might be more appropriate.[7] For the sake of brevity and for the lack of better terms (even "Chinese-language film" sounds more homogeneous than heterogeneous), I settle for the term "Chinese cinema." This cinema is inherently heterogeneous, transnational, *and* political; its domination by the cinematic mode of production, or its involvement in intense international intellectual property and copyright battles, is intricately linked to global politics at the turn of the millennium. The very notion of "China's century" is part and parcel of the U.S.-dominated global politics, in which the United States explicitly seeks to strengthen American hegemony and to push for global marketization and homogenization. To examine "China's century" as cinema's century just might provide a counterpolitics that keeps hegemonic global politics at bay. This is the ultimate goal of my project.

The most direct objective of this book is to help readers understand contemporary Chinese cinema. The understanding cannot simply come from a linear historical narrative within the Chinese context, because contemporary Chinese cinema is the outcome of both the historical development of Chinese film industry and transnational cultural practices. It also cannot be solely based on universal notions of "poetics of cinema," which tend to depoliticize and to essentialize. Only through combining textual, historical, and aesthetic analyses with political critiques can we truly appreciate and critique the popularity and cinematic innovations of contemporary Chinese cinema. This is why I choose to closely read individual films in this book. Close readings allow me to examine the global appeal of contemporary Chinese cinema and understand the ways in which Chinese films historicize, criticize, reveal, or reinforce various aspects of global politics.

Establishing Shot

Before I proceed to individual directors and films, it is necessary to draw a broad picture of film production and consumption in contemporary China. To avoid both generalization and trivialization, I begin my narrative with four vignettes. In cinematographic terms, I choose to unveil my scene with an establishing shot, which is taken not by a single camera but by several cameras from different angles. The vignettes taken by these cameras are not meant to be added up into a whole picture; instead, they are location marks that, collectively, provide an initial visual or narrative orientation based on which an overall view becomes possible. They are also ethnographic fragments intended for establishing a cultural and historical context in which Chinese cinema can be better understood.

Vignette I

During a recent return to China, I visited an old friend in Nanjing. A writer, my friend is known for his private book collection, part of which was inherited from his father and grandfather. Both his father and grandfather are prominent figures in twentieth-century Chinese literary history. Stepping into that new apartment in a high-rise built for college professors, artists, and writers, I expected to see books everywhere. Instead of books, however, I saw a VCD and DVD film collection large enough to fill the media section of an American public library. The titles include everything from the Lumière brothers to Eisenstein, from the French New Wave and Italian Neorealism to Dogma 95, from 1930s Chinese Leftist films to contemporary Hong Kong kung fu flicks, and from Chinese Sixth Generation directors to pioneers of New Taiwan cinema. I was speechless, amazed by my friend's enthusiasm for novel visuality. After all, my friend, along with most Chinese intellectuals, had previously privileged the form of writing over all the other forms of representation. My friend was very proud of his collection. He kept asking me to estimate how much all those videos would cost in the United States.

"Hundreds of thousands of dollars?" I guessed, knowing only that the figure must have been astronomical.

"Less than ten thousand Renminbi (around $1,100)!" my friend bragged. "They are all pirated copies!"

I thought so. That all the videos were pirated did not surprise me. Who would want to spend a big chunk of their monthly paycheck on a legitimate DVD of *The Lord of the Rings* when all three installments of Peter Jackson's epic are sold in a boxed set for less than two dollars? What surprised me was my friend's euphoric tone. After all, he himself suffered tremendous financial and other intangible losses from rampant piracy of his books. He often found pirated versions of his books in the same stores where he bought his videos. The symbiosis of the pirate and the pirated was both ironic and fascinating to me. When I bade him farewell, my friend mentioned how his daughter wanted to become a film director. "With all these world cinema classics readily available, it is not difficult to imagine the possibility of having a group of China's own world-class masters of cinema in the near future," he concluded.

Vignette II
During my seven-week stay in China in the summer of 2004, I was frequently amazed by the ingenuity of some of the latest cell phone models sported by gadget-craving Chinese yuppies. Phones could dance on tables or do numerous other tricks, and all the ringtones were individualized and acoustically pleasant. Once, at a restaurant, several phones rang at the same time. But the ringtones were surprisingly identical; they all sounded the same as the unique ringtone in the immensely popular film *Cell Phone* (*Shouji* [2003]). The film was directed by Feng Xiaogang, China's perennial box office champion.

I did not think much about that restaurant episode until I read an article about Wang Zhongjun, *Cell Phone*'s producer. Easily one of the most powerful men in the Chinese film industry, Wang owns the film production and distribution company Huayi Brothers, which is the investor behind almost all of Feng Xiaogang's films. Huayi has also recruited Stephen Chow, the famous Hong Kong comedian and director whose film *Kung Fu Hustle* (*Gong fu*) opened on 2,500 American screens in May 2005. To my amazement, the writer of the article reveals that Wang had a cell phone experience similar to mine. Wang was ecstatic when he heard the identical ringtones in a restaurant, because it proved that one of his business strategies had succeeded: it was his idea to make a film about cell phones in order to market cell phone–related products, including the distinctive ringtone. He wanted a "theme ringtone," not a "theme song." The exclusive right to offer the ringtone was sold to Motorola.

Feng Xiaogang is Wang's cash cow. A Beijing native, Feng single-handedly created mainland China's "New Year films" (*hesui pian*), following a cinema tradition that Hong Kong filmmakers pioneered for taking advantage of the celebratory mood of the winter holidays. Unlike in the United States, where summer is the most important season for the box office, in China the month-long winter holiday season from Christmas to the Chinese New Year is more lucrative. A typical example of success is Jackie Chan's *Rumble in the Bronx*, which conquered mainland audiences in December 1995. Feng's series of light comedies has been able to compete with Jackie Chan and has broken multiple box office records in China. These films include *Be There or Be Square* (*Bujian busan* [1998]), *Big Shot's Funeral* (*Dawan* [2002]), *Cell Phone* (2003), and *A World without Thieves* (*Tianxia wuzei* [2004]). Stephen Chow's *Kung Fu Hustle*, in which Feng has an acting part, competed with Feng's *A World without Thieves* in the 2005 New Year market. At the very beginning of Chow's film, Feng, playing a mafia boss, walks out of a police station and is surprised by the emptiness of the film theater across the street: "Movie houses should have been packed at this hour! I will never go into the movie business!" Feng's performance in *Kung Fu Hustle* is consistent with his directing style: making references to his own work and poking fun at filmmaking. Both *A World without Thieves* and *Kung Fu Hustle* were megahits in China.

Hollywood has always been interested in Feng, but Columbia Asia's major investment in *Big Shot's Funeral*, starring Donald Sutherland, proved to be a financial disaster. The film was criticized for being "neither here nor there"; it lampoons Western products such as Coca-Cola so relentlessly and explicitly that it becomes "offensive to Western audiences."[8] But, as Wang Zhongjun confessed in the article about him, Feng's excessive embedding of global name brands in his films was not his artistic or ideological choice. It was part of a business decision: Wang had signed countless endorsement deals, forcing Feng to find ways to showcase those name brands. Lampooning was Feng's unique method to call attention to the featured products without sacrificing cohesion.

Wang Zhongjun was in the United States in the early 1990s. According to the article, he studied communications at the University of Michigan from 1989 to 1995. He allegedly saved $100,000 from working at Chinese restaurants and used the money to start his own business upon his return to China. He is thus lauded as a model "returned overseas student." Initially an advertising firm, Huayi Brothers did not enter the film industry until 2000. The government's regulatory scheme was still rigid; private investors were allowed only to coproduce films with state-owned film studios, and they were forbidden to distribute their own films. To circumvent the regulations, Wang Zhongjun bought 40 percent of the internally traded stocks of Xi'an Film Studio's distribution arm. As soon as regulations on private investment in the film industry relaxed in 2003, Wang began to buy shares of Xi'an Film Studio and gradually gained control of the entire studio. It is worth noting that this small provincial studio is where Zhang Yimou and Chen Kaige began their audacious film experiments. By producing such films as *Big Parade* (*Da yue bing* [1986]) and *Red Sorghum* (*Hong gao liang* [1988]), which helped launch Chen Kaige's and Zhang Yimou's illustrious film careers, Xi'an Film Studio became the cradle of the new Chinese cinema. By selling itself to Wang Zhongjun, this studio again leads Chinese cinema into a new era of private ownership. "Within ten years, Chinese companies will begin to purchase Hollywood studios. It does not matter who the first buyer is. It could be us, or someone else. What matters is the increase in power of China's private media corporations," Wang boldly predicts.[9]

Vignette III
On April 19, 2005, the Shanghai No. 2 Intermediate People's Court sentenced Randolph Hobson Guthrie III and Cody Abram Thrush, two American citizens, to two and a half years in prison. Both will be expelled from China after serving their sentences. The two were convicted of selling pirated DVDs over the Internet to the United States and Europe.

That Americans were caught selling pirated DVDs from China is not a surprise. Every day, at every place frequented by Westerners such as Beijing's Sanlituan bar district and Shanghai's Hengshan Road, street hawkers of bootlegged DVDs converge on passersby, especially Westerners. The quality of these DVDs is usually excellent, and the DVDs all have English subtitles. The American college students I led to China on a study tour would often come back to the hotel with bags full of DVDs. With a complete set of *Sex and the City* costing only ten dollars, it is not difficult to imagine the profit potential. What is surprising about the case against Guthrie and Thrush is the number of DVDs they sold: 130,000 copies in a short span of seven months, between November 3, 2003, and July 1, 2004. Each copy was sold for three dollars, thus explaining their website's name: threedollarDVDs.com. They reaped a net profit of $117,000.

Vignette IV

One day, in spring 2004, sitting in my home in the United States, I received a phone call from Peggy Chiao, who had an urgent request: to translate a screenplay from Chinese to English in six days. She needed the translation to court potential Western investors at various international film festivals. Written by Wang Xiaoshuai, the screenplay was titled "Eleven Flowers" and bore Wang's childhood memories about being forced to relocate from Shanghai to the remote mountainous area in Guizhou Province. The screenplay went through several rewrites after I translated it. It eventually evolved into the film *Shanghai Dreams* (*Qing hong*). Directed by Wang Xiaoshuai himself, the film won the Prix du Jury at the 2005 Cannes International Film Festival.

The conversation with Peggy Chiao left a lingering impression on me. The impression was not about the script but about the location from which she made the call. "Guess where I am?" she asked.

"Taipei?" I guessed. Although I knew how frequently she traveled, I naturally assumed that she would spend more time in Taipei than anywhere else. After all, Peggy Chiao was called the "godmother of new Taiwan cinema" for a reason. A USC-trained film critic, Chiao heads the Taiwan Film Center, writes film reviews and scripts, and serves as executive producer for many renowned Taiwanese films. She has been instrumental in the promotion of Taiwanese New Wave cinema to the world.

But my guess was wrong. Peggy Chiao was calling from a restaurant in Shanghai. "Every Taiwanese film person is in Shanghai right now!" she claimed. "Guess whom I just ran into? Rene Liu!" Also from Taiwan, Rene Liu (Liu Ruoying) is a megastar in Taiwan, Hong Kong, and mainland China. Most recently, she costars with Andy Lau in Feng Xiaogang's 2005 "New Year hit" *A World without Thieves*.

Indeed, Peggy Chiao and almost every major Taiwanese filmmaker are working more closely with mainland China's film talents than ever before. Besides *Shanghai Dreams*, Peggy Chiao has also been involved in numerous other collaborations with her mainland colleagues. For instance, she cowrote with Wang Xiaoshuai the screenplay for *Beijing Bicycle* (*Shiqi sui de dan che*). She was also the executive producer. The film won the Silver Bear at the 2001 Berlin International Film Festival. I have a detailed discussion of this film in chapter 3 of this book.

What I intend to provide in these four vignettes is a glimpse into the complex network of transnational film production and consumption. As a transnational intellectual based in the United States, I have a position in this network. My awareness of my position gives this book an intrinsic self-reflexivity. There is a position for every reader of this book as well. Filmmakers, critics, teachers, writers, consumers of pirated or legitimate DVDs, business people, art film buffs, and average American filmgoers can all find where they are in this network and judge their relations with contemporary Chinese cinema. As a critic, my comprehensive understanding of this cinema consists of the following observations based on these vignettes and on my research: (1) a shift from literary culture to visual culture is taking place in twenty-first-century China; (2) Chinese state regulation of the film industry is generally moving toward the direction of marketization, privatization, pan-Sinicization, and globalization; and (3) rampant piracy has threatened the film industry, but it also has unexpected consequences that have shaped Chinese cinema and will dictate the direction of Chinese cinema's future development. I explain these three observations in more detail below.

The Turn to the Visual

A new paradigm of cultural production and consumption is taking shape in China. The paradigm shift is twofold. On the one hand, electronic images are now dominating people's daily lives. TV, the Internet, and pirated VCDs and DVDs allow unprecedented access to electronic images that include photographs, video games, flash animations, films, and so on. On the other hand, the plethora of electronic images makes it difficult to differentiate a few good and useful images from a large quantity of junk. Chinese intellectuals step in at this juncture to solve the dilemma: they consume the electronic images with "better" taste so as to point the way and, ultimately, to establish cultural capital for themselves as the newly arisen middle class in twenty-first-century China.

This shift began around the mid-1990s. The national shock and trauma of the June 4 Tiananmen Incident of 1989 had been forgotten or at least deeply hidden. International societies had fully extended their arms again to embrace an economically open China, eager to gain a share of China's exploding market. Privatization of state-run enterprises was gaining momentum. Shanghai was quickly replacing Shenzhen and the other Special Economic Zones as the model of economic reforms and the harbinger of China's transition to financial capitalism. Urbanization through real estate speculation was demolishing traces of previous lives, replacing them with ersatz and marketable "cultural heritage sites." And well-educated professionals, including teachers, writers, artists, and producers of electronic images, had begun to earn a living better than they ever enjoyed. These cultural workers, living in new apartments and possessing a high degree of mobility, became trendsetters and thus model consumers. They made suggestions, publicly or privately, on how to behave like a "white collar," how to enjoy the metropolitan culture, and how to lead a happy and healthy personal life, whether in a nuclear family or as a "single aristocrat."[10] The symbolic capital and the monetary capital finally came together for Chinese intellectuals.

The rupture in the patterns of cultural production and consumption is highly visible. In the 1980s, serious literary magazines were still immensely popular, although their popularity was undergoing a steady decline. Writers, such as Wang Meng, Liu Xinwu, and Zhang Jie, enjoyed their status as national celebrities. Wang Shuo, however, simultaneously brought the fame of the writer to its peak and demystified writing through what he called the "electrification/electrocution" (*chudian*) of literature in adapting his novels into TV series and films.[11] National debates about "root-seeking literature" and humanism developed into what Jing Wang terms "high culture fever,"[12] namely, a widespread enthusiasm for narrative fiction and philosophical topics. This enthusiasm indirectly fueled the student energies behind the June 4 Tiananmen movement.

Even during the Cultural Revolution (1966–1976), when books were mostly banned and writing often incurred political persecution, the symbolic capital associated with literature was still important to Chinese intellectuals. This is amply demonstrated in *Balzac and the Little Chinese Seamstress* (2002), Dai Sijie's breakout film based on his eponymous best-selling French-language novel. The film tells how the "intellectual youths," in order to maintain their cultural superiority over illiterate peasants during their "sent-down" years, not only eagerly read foreign novels but also repeatedly yell out such exotic names as Balzac, Flaubert, and Dumas. The two students from the city explicitly claim that they intend to change the little seamstress from a local beauty to an accent-free and foreign-fiction-reading modern girl. Their literacy also earns them an enviable "political" assignment: go watch a North Korean film and then narrate the sentimental plot of the film to the peasants. Those who experienced the Cultural Revolution can easily relate to this unique way of treating film as literature and reading "literary screenplays" (*dianying wenxue juben*) instead of watching the actual films.

Dai Sijie's overt motif of "sentimental education," borrowed from Flaubert and set in the most improbable circumstance, speaks volumes about the nature of the obsession with literature in socialist and Republican China. The obsession is part of the legacy of Chinese modernity, enthusiastically pursued and woven into a complex discourse by Chinese intellectuals in responding to nineteenth-century Western territorial colonialism and twentieth-century cultural neocolonialism that continued to emphasize the differences between a modernized West and a primitive East.[13] This discourse, based on desires to empower the nation and imaginations of an exotic and advanced West, has a double bind. On the one hand, Chinese intellectuals claim the same sophistication and cosmopolitanism enjoyed by their contemporary Western counterparts, implying a potential challenge to the colonial strategy of "othering" the primitive. On the other hand, the claim of cultural cosmopolitanism always paradoxically harbors an inferiority complex and reinforces the belatedness of "other modernities," by which such a claim becomes subordinated to the logic of othering.[14]

Since Chinese literature is the major vehicle for the discursive practice of Chinese modernity, the postsocialist shift to the visual can be regarded as "postmodern." The very abandonment of the elite status of literature contains implicit criticism of modernity's desire for the sublime, the advanced, and the progressive. I thus agree with Sheldon Lu's claim that postsocialist Chinese visual culture is based on postmodernist politics, which "eclipses certain Enlightenment values that are absent in China" on the one hand and "resists the hegemony of the Eurocentric teleology of temporality and modernity by looking for alternative narratives" on the other.[15]

To briefly summarize, the turn to the visual has to do with Chinese intellectuals' rise as the new middle class, China's transformation to a consumer society, the abandonment of the discourse of modernity, and the postmodern condition.

Regulating Chinese Cinema in the New Century

The shift to the visual has also been aided by recent developments in China's state regulation of the film industry. The rigid, state-controlled, and inefficient big-studio system is going through rapid changes at the turn of the millennium, because regulation is loosening its tight grip and encouraging a shift toward marketization, privatization, pan-Sinicization, and globalization. These shifts are liberating, for they challenge the conservative communist ideology and stimulate artistic creativities, but they are also complicit with global politics centered on neoliberal marketization and cultural homogenization. Unwilling to simplify the issues or draw easy conclusions, I provide here a brief time line of regulatory changes implemented by China's State Administration for Radio,

Film and Television's (SARFT) Film Bureau during the first several years of the twenty-first century:

In June 2002, province-based film distribution and exhibition companies were consolidated into thirty-seven cinema chains. Together, these cinema chains include 1,100 theaters and around 2,000 screens. In the United States, there were 2,000 theaters with a total of 35,500 screens around the same time.

In 2003, new rules were enacted to allow private and overseas companies greater access to film distribution. Wang Zhongjun was able to take advantage of the new rules. Kodak and Warner Brothers were among the first group of companies to form alliances with local film distributors and film theaters. In cities that include Shanghai and Nanjing, *Huana yingcheng* (Warner Brothers Theater City) began to open for business in the summer of 2004 and draw large audiences into state-of-the-art multiplexes.

On September 28, 2003, the Rules for the Administration of Sino-Foreign Cooperative Film Production were modified by SARFT. The new rules took effect on December 23, 2003. Compared to the old rules, several changes were made in order to encourage more coproductions: the SARFT approval time limit has fallen from thirty days to ten; and there is no longer a 50 percent cap on overseas (meaning foreign countries, Hong Kong, Macao, and Taiwan) personnel as leading and supporting cast members for a coproduction.

On October 1, 2003, the Closer Economic Partnership Agreement (CEPA) became effective. The agreement was signed between the PRC's central government and the governments of the Hong Kong and Macao special administrative regions. It was intended to stimulate Hong Kong's and Macao's stagnant economies by opening up the mainland market in cinema, television, and telecommunications. Hong Kong films were no longer restricted by quota. Almost overnight, Chinese theaters were flooded with Hong Kong films.

On January 8, 2004, SARFT issued another ruling, "Several Opinions on Accelerating the Development of the Film Industry." It is a document for the future, indicating the direction of Chinese cinema's development in the new century. Significant details include the following: a film rating system will soon be introduced, and Sino-foreign joint ventures (JVs) for coproductions may soon be allowed. Presently, coproductions are limited to a project basis and contractual JVs must be dissolved after the completion of the project. Foreign investors should be allowed to take up to a 75 percent stake (compared to the previous 49 percent) in Sino-foreign equity JVs (EJVs) in certain trial cities; since January 1, 2004, investors from Hong Kong and Macao have been able to take up to a 75 percent stake in both EJVs and cooperative JVs (CJVs) for the construction and/or refurbishment of cinemas.

On October 15, 2004, Warner Brothers announced that it had received SARFT approval to establish China's first film production JV in cooperation with the state-owned China Film Group and privately run Hengdian Group. Hengdian owns a big studio set for filming Chinese imperial periods. American audiences are familiar with this set: it turns into the magnificent Qin palace featured in *Hero*. The new company, Warner China Film, produces, markets, and distributes Chinese-language feature films, television movies, and animated shows. Warner Brothers holds 30 percent of the new venture, with China Film Group holding a 40 percent share and Hengdian Group holding the remaining 30 percent.

In June 2005, the three-year contracts of the thirty-seven cinema chains expired. Film distribution and exhibition companies were encouraged to form partnerships across provincial boundaries. A new round of reshuffling began. Private companies and foreign companies became the most powerful players in the new wave of consolidation.[16]

Understanding these regulations is crucial to understanding many aspects of contemporary Chinese cinema. The "underground" films produced by young Chinese directors are often lauded in the West as being politically subversive. Most of these films, however, are not at all politically sensitive. They were "banned" in China because they violated certain regulations: some, fully backed by non-Chinese investors, did not apply for coproduction permits; some, in the case of *Suzhou River* (2000), which is discussed in chapter 3 of this book, went into postproduction in Germany before the studio informed SARFT. If these incidents had happened in the West, we would have called these practices "illegal" and asked no more questions. But when banning occurs to Chinese filmmakers, the image of political dissidence fuels the "banned" directors' popularity in the West. China's regulations, of course, have adverse effects on free expression and artistic imaginations. But don't all regulations, in various degrees, contain free spirits through bureaucracy and forced obedience?

Because of the recent loosening of restrictions on the Chinese film industry, Taiwanese film luminaries, many of whom are U.S. passport holders and thus "foreigners," increasingly flock to China. These talents include Peggy Chiao, Rene Liu, and Chen Kuo-fu (director of *Double Vision* [2003] and executive producer of numerous mainland Chinese films), among many others. Coproductions between Hong Kong and mainland studios also increased. Without the 50 percent personnel limit, mainland films produced by such obscure studios as Inner Mongolia Film Studio can now employ personnel entirely of Hong Kong origin, from director, screenwriter, and cinematographer to male and female leads. With Hong Kong films flooding the new Warner Brothers multiplexes, it is no longer easy to draw the boundaries distinguishing the mainland, Hong Kong, Taiwan, and foreign countries from each other in the Chinese film industry. This is "pan-Sinicization" through regulatory changes. The pan-China interconnectedness and the reliance on the mainland market often force self-censorship on the part of Hong Kong and Taiwanese filmmakers. Private investors, in the meantime, are slowly but surely chipping away at the state-controlled film industry. Savvy businessmen like Wang Zhongjun may not get what they want directly, but the opening up of multiple coproduction venues gives them plenty of room to maneuver. Wang, for instance, could very well acquire a Hollywood studio in the near future and return to China to form JVs. The boundaries between Hollywood and Chinese cinema will only be further blurred.

The most significant regulatory change is probably the implementation of a rating system. The Chinese officials are clearly aware of the positive changes to Korean cinema after a rating system was adopted in Korea in the late 1990s. Censorship will become less rigid, creativity will soar, films will become more commercial, and importation of foreign films will grow easier. Twenty-first-century Chinese cinema's development will largely depend on the sophistication and effectiveness of the rating system.

Consequences of Piracy

The regulatory changes reveal a disproportionate emphasis on attracting foreign and private investment. There is little attention, on the legal level, to the rampant piracy. China's jailing of Guthrie and Thrush was a highly symbolic and politically significant act, meant to show the American Congress and the powerful Motion Picture Association of America that the Americans are more responsible for piracy than the Chinese. Other than a few sporadic cases, there have not been substantial regulatory moves or legal action against piracy. There are many reasons for this general lack of interest in fighting piracy. In chapter 1, I discuss in detail how piracy could be seen as potentially beneficial to the Chinese film industry in particular and to the copyright industry in general. Here I only briefly outline several consequences of piracy that are not as disastrous to Chinese cinema as appearances might suggest, consequences with which Chinese filmmakers have learned to live. These consequences, to a great extent, have helped shape Chinese cinema of the early twenty-first century along the direction demanded by the "market economy with Chinese characteristics":

1. Piracy serves as a form of local protectionism. Hollywood blockbusters are the major targets of piracy. The more Chinese audiences watch pirated Hollywood films on home video and over the Internet, the less negative impact

Hollywood imports have on China's national film industry. Although China's official entry into the WTO in 2002 requires China to fully open its cinema market, piracy has prevented Chinese theaters from being flooded with Hollywood films.

2. Piracy forces out independent filmmakers and pushes for industrial concentration of resources on a few megastars such as Zhang Yimou, Chen Kaige, Feng Xiaogang, and Stephen Chow.

3. Piracy gives Chinese authorities and American corporations alike the perfect excuse for urbanization based on real estate developments around multiplex film theaters. The expansion of Nanjing's new city around *Huana yingcheng* (Warner Brothers Theater City) is a fitting example. According to a *Los Angeles Times* article on April 27, 2005, new theaters like those of Warner Brothers in China "give Hollywood a weapon in fighting rampant foreign film piracy." "You have to create a 'want to see-be seen' location—that is something the pirates cannot offer," Millard Ochs, president of Warner Brothers International Cinemas, said in an interview.[17]

4. Piracy has helped create a strange yet functional symbiosis between the Chinese film and television industries. Piracy makes most Chinese films unprofitable, but television series (soap operas, comedy sitcoms, martial arts melodramas, etc.) based on pirated films are immensely popular and profitable. It is not that TV series are not pirated. In fact, the piracy of TV series on condensed DVDs, which hold ten times more data than regular DVDs, is even more ruthless and brutal than the piracy of films. One disc, holding a twenty-installment series, costs only two dollars. But most Chinese audiences still prefer free TV programming to cheap pirated DVDs. TV stations regularly pay the series producers up front; whether the series is later pirated is no longer the producer's concern. An interesting phenomenon is generated by this difference between the TV and film industries. A film director makes an excellent film first, which is quickly pirated and thus attracts no interest from state-controlled distribution chains. The director then makes an eponymous TV series based on the film, often using the same cast. The film has already served to advertise the TV series. TV stations purchase the series, and the director reaps healthy financial gains. Examples abound, such as Chen Kaige's film *Together* (*He ni zai yiqi* [2000]), which was quickly made into a twenty-installment TV series with the same title and more than recouped Chen's investment in the film.[18]

Sinascape

The turn to the visual, the flexible regulations that promote marketization, privatization, pan-Sinicization, and globalization, and the counterintuitively productive piracy are interlocking components of sinascape. In this book, the neologism "sinascape" simultaneously means three things:

1. Sinascape is the network called "Chinese cinema," a complex web of transnational film production and consumption centered on and in China. I have attempted to give a visual or narrative orientation to the readers of this book, an orientation that allows everyone, including myself, to establish a position in relation to this network. As a network, Chinese cinema is relational, alive and full of constant changes; it is not a cold, objective, and irrelevant "thing" waiting for us to discover or learn about it. Rather, it is part of the world around everyone; it needs to be fully engaged in order to be truly understood.

2. Sinascape is the filmic representation of China's social, political, and economic changes in the early twenty-first century. The representation can be direct, such as the *realistic* and *realist* cinematographic portrayal of contemporary China and Chinese-speaking areas. Examples include Chen Kaige's *Together*, all of Feng Xiaogang's films, Lou Ye's *Suzhou River*, Wang Xiaoshuai's *Beijing Bicycle*, and Fruit Chan's *Hollywood Hong Kong*. The representation can be indirect, such as revelations and reflections of the times, of the collective psyche, and of the political tensions of twenty-first-century China in subject matters unrelated to the contemporary. Examples include Zhang Yimou's *Hero* and *House of Flying Daggers*, Stephen Chow's *Kung Fu Hustle*, and Jiang Wen's *Devils on the Doorstep*. These films all have hidden messages inside their period dramas, as I elaborate in chapters following the introduction. The representation can also be both direct and indirect, such as images situated in shifting time and space and as memories, fictions, fantasies, and imaginations that nevertheless *refract* the contemporary. Examples include Wong Kar-wai's *2046* and Tsai Ming-liang's *Goodbye, Dragon Inn*. My book's discussion of sinascape is mostly based on analyses of these three forms of representation.

3. Sinascape is part of the "mediascape," referring to the image-based, media-manipulated, and transnational nature of "China's century." "Mediascape" is a term coined by Arjun Appadurai, who has drawn a scheme of "imagined worlds" through which he analyzes the global flow of cultures in multiple directions. The imagined worlds have five dimensions: ethnoscape, mediascape, technoscape, financescape, and ideoscape. The use of the suffix *–scape* for all five dimensions, Appadurai contends, "allows us to point to the fluid, irregular shapes of these landscapes, shapes that characterize international capital as deeply as they do international clothing styles." The common suffix also "indicate[s] that these [terms] are not objectively given relations that look the same from every angle of vision but, rather, that they are a deeply perspectival construct, inflected by the historical, linguistic, and political

situatedness of different sorts of actors: nation-states, multinationals, diasporic communities, as well as subnational groupings and movements (whether religious, political, or economic), and even intimate face-to-face groups, such as villages, neighborhoods, and families."[19] That these "scapes" are unstable perspectival constructs echoes what I describe as the relational "network" of Chinese cinema. "Mediascape" is particularly appropriate for describing the mediated nature of this network.

I disagree, however, with Appadurai when he uses mediascape to describe transnational cultural production as being postnational and deterritorialized. Appadurai is correct in understanding transnationalism in terms of the "situatedness of different sorts of actors," namely, the role of agency in conducting, creating, and adapting to the multiple cultural flows. My position and the positions of the readers of this book in the network of Chinese cinema are exactly this "situatedness," which, in Michael Peter Smith's words, "concretely connects macro-economic and geopolitical transformations to the micro-networks of social action that people create, move in, and act upon in their daily lives."[20] When analyzing the paradigm shift in the postsocialist Chinese cultural industry, for example, we need to look closely at the ways in which Chinese filmmakers cope with state regulations and create every possible margin for independent voices. The margins are still inevitably infiltrated and sometimes even deliberately left intact by China's system of macro sociopolitical controls. But the fissures and gaps between the macro control and the micromechanism of individual imaginations and representations of China's postsocialist transformations are often visible enough for forming meaningful and radical critique of the dominant ideology and of the film industry itself.

Appadurai's theoretical framework of the "scapes," however, has an inherent contradiction. Despite his stated emphasis on agency and micropolitics, the five dimensions of transnationalism are too fluid and too encompassing to reflect the ruptures at local levels. Appadurai's totalizing concepts imply an elitist perspective, which centers on the thinking and imagination of jet-flying intellectuals unbound by national borders and unconstrained by economics. Legal and illegal immigrants harassed by the police and the Department of Homeland Security, political dissidents facing persecutions, sweatshop laborers and migrant workers—these groups are also "transnational," but their transnationality cannot be fully explained in the five "scapes." It is true that, facilitated by the ubiquitous global electronic images, visions of a better life might form a possible grassroots resistance against transnationalism and/or globalization. But these groups must first and foremost deal with everyday concerns and pressures imposed by their own governments and by the governments of their host countries. National powers have become more sophisticated than ever and are playing an increasingly important role in these "transnational" groups' daily lives. If we want to understand what these transnational subalterns experience everyday, we simply cannot render national borders and sovereignty irrelevant under Appadurai's rubric of a "deterritorialized" and "postnational" transnationalism.

One of the premises of this book is that national boundaries have not been weakened but rather reinforced in the turn-of-the-millennium production of electronic images. I have repeatedly pointed out how the boundaries between Chinese cinema and Hollywood are increasingly blurred. But the blurring does not contradict what I mean by the strengthening of national boundaries; behind the assimilation of the film industries are national powers at work, jostling for position in order to control the twenty-first-century copyright industry. My understanding of transnationalism is similar to that of Aihwa Ong, who contends that "the art of government has been highly responsive to the challenge of transnationality" in terms of containing and manipulating specific needs of ethnically marked class groupings within articulations of sovereignty.[21] The examples Ong cites are some ingenious methods adopted by Chinese and Southeast Asian governments for creating an ethnically coherent "Chineseness" that is seemingly unrestrained by the state. The concept of a "state-free" citizenship enhances the role of the nation in mobilizing capitals from outside the country and in constructing an "Asian" ethos most suitable for capitalist efficiency and pragmatism. Better controlled and more efficiently exploited, the "flexible citizenship," as termed by Ong, nevertheless poses threats to Eurocentric visions of a unidirectional transnational mobility.

I want to push Ong's argument one step further by asking why transnationalism triggers imaginations of a deterritorialized and postnational world while state machines have become more sophisticated than ever. Is transnationalism simply border crossing, or even border eliminating? Isn't transnationalism about representations of border crossing under the demand of profit-seeking nations that are more competitive, not collaborative, with each other even if collaborations are deemed essential? "Sinascape," as a part of the mediascape, is coined to specifically address these questions. It describes twenty-first-century Chinese cinema as media-based contact zones, where ideologies clash, where new identities emerge through both border crossings and resistance against globalization, and where visual innovations and progressive visions become possible.

To summarize: sinascape is reality, referring to the Chinese film industry as a transnational network; it is representation, including films of and about China; it is also an analytical metaphor, probing mediation, transnationalism,

nationalism, and global politics of the twenty-first century. Through sinascape, I analyze six crucial developments in contemporary global politics that are specifically related to the Chinese film industry and to Chinese films:

1. Proliferation of the copyright industry;
2. Representation of violence and violence of representation;
3. Manipulation of reality through mediation and simulacra;
4. Relentless demolition driven by modernization and urbanization;
5. Erasure of individual memories by linear and masculinist history; and
6. Domination of the socioeconomic and political life by the cinematic mode of production.

The first and the sixth have to do with the film industry, the second and the third are related to the filmic representation, and the fourth and the fifth are helpful to the strengthening of the analytical metaphor. Each of the following six chapters in this book corresponds to one of these themes.

Chapter 1 of *Sinascape: Contemporary Chinese Cinema* analyzes Zhang Yimou's recent blockbusters *Hero* and *House of Flying Daggers* in the context of the proliferation of the copyright industry. It discusses in detail Zhang's visual innovations, linking them to cross-cultural spectatorship and to postsocialist China's obsession with ethnic harmony, historical greatness, and Chinese cultural authenticity. One of the key issues in Zhang's global cultural enterprises is intellectual copyright. Drawing attention to the U.S. Congress's enactment of the Digital Millennium Copyright Act (DMCA), I contend that at the heart of "China's century" is the Sino-American battle for copyright hegemony and for world market domination.

Chapter 2 discusses Jiang Wen's film *Devils on the Doorstep* (*Guizi lai le* [2000]), focusing on how Jiang relies on black-and-white cinematography to represent the national trauma of World War II and to critique state violence. I pay particular attention to how this film was received in China and in Japan. Through reflections on Chinese historical narratives of national defense, Jiang's film reveals the violence of cinematic representation and helps us understand the recent tension between China and Japan.

Chapter 3 focuses on the representations of Beijing and Shanghai in Wang Xiaoshuai's *Beijing Bicycle* and Lou Ye's *Suzhou River*. Although both films present spectacular cityscapes symbolic of China's economic takeoff, their real focus is on the invisible presence of the "floating population" of migrant laborers. While *Beijing Bicycle* explicitly links urban prosperity to the classical capitalist scenario of surplus value extraction, *Suzhou River* goes one step further by playing with the notion "my camera doesn't lie" and highlighting the intricate relationship between realism as a mode of representation and value extraction under postsocialist conditions.

Chapter 4 begins with a brief reading of Stephen Chow's film *Kung Fu Hustle*, revealing the ways in which Chow is indebted to Shaw Brothers cinema. From the intertextual site of "Pigsty Alley" that Chow borrows from a 1973 Shaw Brothers film, *The House of Seventy-Two Tenants*, I proceed to discussions of the old Shaw theaters as both physical sites of Southeast and East Asian modernization and symbolic sites of the politics of demolition. After a historical account of Shaw Brothers' practice of building theaters throughout Southeast Asia, this chapter reveals the link between Tsai Ming-liang, a Malaysian-Taiwanese director, and the old theaters owned by Shaw Brothers. Through an analysis of King Hu's *Dragon Inn* (*Long men ke zhan* [1967]) and Tsai's *Goodbye, Dragon Inn* (*Busan* [2003]), I discuss how Tsai makes use of the history of world cinema and how he reconstructs the old theater in defiance of the global politics of demolition and Hollywoodization.

Chapter 5 analyzes Taiwanese director Hou Hsiao-hsien's search for the collective memory of transnational urban youth. Since smell, such as that of flowers, perfume, and nightlife, is an important motif in Hou's film *Millennium Mambo* and in his screenwriter Zhu Tianwen's novels, I begin with a cross-disciplinary examination of the relationship between memory and smell. For Hou's protagonists, their olfactory memories are not so much of generic knowledge (memories acquired through semantic definitions) as of episodic memory (remembrance through association); they remember odors based on the time and place where the odors occur for the first time. Hou implies through his breathtaking cinematography that episodic memory, paradoxically due to its nature of spontaneity and contingency, is the only reliable mode of remembrance in the twenty-first century.

Chapter 6 discusses how, as Hong Kong's Fruit Chan has consistently explored in his films, cinema becomes the dominant mode of production. To reflect on transnational cinematic fantasies made in and about Hong Kong, Fruit Chan uses a special technique that I call "double sequencing": the same sequence occurs twice in the film without either one being privileged over the other; both "take one" and "take two" coexist, illuminating the illusive nature of reality. Chan hints that transnational cinema as a mode of production is destructive of human relations yet potentially liberating.

The last chapter, "Postscript," begins with my conversation with Roy Lee, Hollywood's "king of remakes," who is behind the early-twenty-first-century Hollywood trend of remaking films from China, Hong Kong, Taiwan, Japan, and Korea. By analyzing such hits as *The Ring* series and *The Grudge*, I provide an explanation of the popularity of East Asian remakes. Linking Hollywood's global strategy to outsourcing, I consider the gains and losses for East Asian film industries from this trend. One of the consequences, I contend, is the further consolidation and transnationalization of East Asian cinemas.

Notes

1. The year in parentheses or brackets after a film title refers to the film's North American premiere, which could have come after the Chinese premiere. In the case of *Hero*, it was released in China in 2002 but not in the United States until 2004. There is a discussion of this delay in chapter 2.

2. The term "transnational Chinese cinema" first appears in Sheldon Lu, ed., *Transnational Chinese Cinemas: Identity, Nationhood, Gender* (Honolulu: University of Hawaii Press, 1997). In coining this term, Lu draws attention to an interesting phenomenon of contemporary Chinese cinema: its international circulation is made possible only by emphasizing its rootedness in Chinese and/or Oriental culture. Being inherently "transnational" means that contemporary Chinese cinema is simultaneously "international" and "Chinese," namely, crossing borders while maintaining or even strengthening its original national and territorial attachment. Zhang Ziyi's popularity best demonstrates this transnational nature of contemporary Chinese cinema.

3. For instance, a *New York Times* editorial on May 6, 2005, titled "A Rising China," is filled with Cold War rhetoric that urges Washington to "handle" and "contain" an increasingly powerful China.

4. See Jean and John Comaroff's introduction to their edited volume, *Millennial Capitalism and the Culture of Neoliberalism* (Durham: Duke University Press, 2000).

5. Shujen Wang, "Recontextualizing Copyright: Piracy, Hollywood, the State, and Globalization," *Cinema Journal* 43 (Fall 2003): 28.

6. Sean Smith, "Invasion of the Hot Movie Stars," *Newsweek*, May 9, 2005, 37.

7. See Sheldon Lu and Emilie Yeh, eds., *Chinese-Language Film: Historiography, Poetics, Politics* (Honolulu: University of Hawaii Press, 2005).

8. Stephen Short, "Neither Here nor There," *Time Asia*, March 18, 2002.

9. Li Xia, "Yong san jia mache da tianxia: piaofang guanjun beihou de laoban Wang Zhongjun" (Conquering the world in a three-horse carriage: Wang Zhongjun, the boss behind box office champions), *Dongfang qiyejia* (*Oriental Entrepreneurs*), May 12, 2005.

10. There are numerous books written by and about Chinese intellectuals on how to be a cosmopolitan consumer. A recent example is a story on Qian Wenzhong, a Sanskrit professor at Shanghai's prestigious Fudan University. Qian brags about how he becomes rich and what brand names he consumes: Rolex, Callaway, LV, and so on. See the Netease.com website (http://news.163.com/05/0822/13/1ROUU2B20001124T.html) (accessed January 9, 2006).

11. Films adapted from Wang Shuo's novels include *The Troubleshooters* (*Wan zhu* [1988]); *Half Water, Half Brine* (*Yiban shi haishui, yiban shi huoyan* [1989]); *In the Heat*

of the Sun (*Yangguang canlan de rizi* [1994]); *Gone Forever with My Love* (*Yong shi wo ai* [1994]); *The Dream Factory* (*Jiafang yifang* [1997]); *Father* (*Baba* [2000]); *A Sigh* (*Yisheng tanxi* [2000]); and *I Love You* (*Wo ai ni* [2003]). Scripted or coscripted by Wang and directed by renowned directors such as Xia Gang, Jiang Wen, Zhang Yuan, and Feng Xiaogang, these films were mostly hits.

12. See Jing Wang, *High Culture Fever: Politics, Aesthetics, and Ideology in Deng's China* (Berkeley: University of California Press, 1996).

13. See Rey Chow, *Primitive Passions* (New York: Columbia University Press, 1995).

14. For a thorough discussion of how modernity continues to be contested in Chinese filmic representations, see Tonglin Lu, *Confronting Modernity in the Cinemas of Taiwan and Mainland China* (Cambridge: Cambridge University Press, 2001).

15. Sheldon H. Lu, *China, Transnational Visuality, Global Postmodernity* (Stanford: Stanford University Press, 2001), 69.

16. See the Chinese government's official website (http://english.gov.cn/2005-08/12/content_22063.htm) for more detailed information on recent regulatory changes (accessed January 9, 2006).

17. Lorenza Munoz, "Modern Movie Houses Are Sprouting Overseas," *Los Angeles Times*, April 27, 2005.

18. See the People's Net (*renmin wang*) website (http://www.people.com.cn/GB/yule/1081/2536801.html) for reports on the commercial success of the TV series *Together* (accessed January 9, 2006).

19. Arjun Appadurai, *Modernity at Large: Cultural Dimensions of Globalization* (Minneapolis: University of Minnesota Press, 1996), 33.

20. Michael Peter Smith, *Transnational Urbanism: Locating Globalization* (New York: Blackwell, 2001), 6.

21. Aihwa Ong, *Flexible Citizenship: The Cultural Logics of Transnationality* (Durham, NC: Duke University Press, 1999), 7.

CHAPTER ONE

——⁓——

The Right to Copy and the Digital Copyright: *Hero, House of Flying Daggers*, and China's Cultural Symptoms

On December 20, 2002, the long-awaited and much-hyped film *Hero* (*Yingxiong*) had its Chinese premiere in the city of Shenzhen. This was a watershed event for Chinese cinema, which officially entered the era of big-budget production, global distribution, and copyright competition.

Directed by Zhang Yimou and starring Jet Li, Tony Leung, Maggie Cheung, and Zhang Ziyi, *Hero* exceeded $27 million in total production costs. This record amount of investment for a single film came from a private company owned by Zhang Weiping, who had been Zhang Yimou's longtime collaborator. The film's music was composed by Tan Dun, who won the 2001 Academy Award for Best Original Score in *Crouching Tiger, Hidden Dragon* (*Wo hu cang long* [2000]). Its costumes were designed by Wada Emi, winner of the 1985 Academy Award for Best Costume Design for Akira Kurosawa's epic *Ran*. The big budget and the star-studded cast triggered a media frenzy. Talks about winning the Oscars began even before the shooting of the film commenced. The media hype was further fueled by the shroud of mystery and secrecy that prevented the film's production process and plot from being leaked to the public until the premiere.

Zhang Weiping later revealed that the secrecy was part of a carefully orchestrated PR and antipiracy campaign. The campaign reached its peak at the film's premiere in Shenzhen. The stiff antipiracy measures were unprecedented: the audiences were closely searched, their cameras and camcorders confiscated, the seats individually designated, the size of the audience for each screen strictly limited, and a large number of security guards deployed.[1] Besides the tight security at the premiere, all the distributed copies were individually monitored. The suicide of a Lanzhou theater distribution manager after signing in a copy of *Hero* added more twists to the detective fiction and soap opera around the release of *Hero*. The measures were well justified: video piracy was so rampant that DVD copies of a new film often appeared on store shelves before the film's premiere. The U.S. Chamber of Commerce has estimated that U.S. companies lose between $2.5 billion and $3.8 billion annually in China to piracy.[2] Piracy has destroyed China's own film industry; only a few big names, including Zhang Yimou and Feng Xiaogang, can blossom because they have the resources to fight it.

Hero did not disappoint, in international recognition, box office, or piracy prevention. The film was nominated for the 2003 Academy Award for Best Foreign Film. It grossed more than $100,000 on the first day of nationwide screening—this record box office take, according to Zhang Weiping, was already a largely reduced figure reported by tax-evading theaters. The gross total was estimated at $45 million. The first pirated copy did not appear on the market until three days after the nationwide screening. "All we needed was the first weekend," Zhang said. *Hero* fared even better in the United States. After much delay by Disney's Miramax, *Hero*'s exclusive global distributor, it was finally released on August 20, 2004, in the United States, during the traditional "cool-down" period immediately after the summer blockbuster season.[3] *Hero* topped the chart for two consecutive weekends and grossed $52 million. It did not break the Chinese-language film record set by *Crouching Tiger, Hidden Dragon*, which grossed $128 million, but, given the circumstances, both Zhang Yimou and Zhang Weiping were satisfied.

Hero's success paved the way for *House of Flying Daggers* (*Shi mian mai fu* [2004]), which is another martial arts melodrama directed by Zhang Yimou. *House of Flying Daggers* went through the same routine in China: media hype, tight antipiracy measures, and a grandiose opening ceremony. It opened in China in July 2004 and in the United States in December of the same year. Its total U.S. gross was $11 million, far less than *Hero*'s, but its worldwide gross reached $90 million, indicating that it was more popular in Europe and in Japan than *Hero* was. Both *Hero* and *House of Flying Daggers* made almost every "best films of 2004" list. *Time* magazine, for instance, combines the two films and ranks them as the No. 1 film of 2004.[4] *House of Flying Daggers* was nominated for the Best Cinematography Academy Award.

Both films, however, were severely criticized and ruthlessly ridiculed in China. The Chinese media and Internet bulletin boards were overwhelmingly negative about the films despite cheering for Zhang's victory in the American market. The films were criticized for everything including overt resemblance to *Couching Tiger, Hidden Dragon*; shameless imitation of the bamboo grove fight scene in King Hu's *A Touch of Zen* (*Xia nu* [1971]); melodramatic expressions; artificiality; implausibility; lack of immediate social concerns; and an ambivalence toward violence in Zhang Yimou's attempt to write a revisionist history of Qin Shihuang, the first Emperor of Qin (259–210 BC).[5] The timing for *Hero*'s release was particularly awkward. When the American invasion of Iraq became imminent and antiwar sentiments were running high throughout the world, Zhang Yimou's favorable portrayal of Qin Shihuang was suspected of being a paean to George W. Bush and American "warmongers." The central theme of the film, that conquering the world is the best way to stop violence in separate regions of the world, seems eerily resonant of the purported American neoconservative strategy of preemptive strikes.

I personally witnessed the opposite reactions of Chinese and American audiences to *House of Flying Daggers*. I first saw the film in a state-of-the-art multiplex theater in Beijing in summer 2004. The audience was impatient, openly laughing at the film. "Stupid!" yelled an audience member sitting behind me when Zhang Ziyi woke up for the third time after being fatally wounded. People groaned at the sudden—and implausible—change of season when snow began to fall on the spectacular autumn foliage. They jeered at Andy Lau's Cantonese accent and Takeshi Kaneshiro's Taiwanese accent (Takeshi is Taiwanese-Japanese),[6] when the two actors conversed in an awkward mixture of semicolloquial Chinese and semiclassical Chinese. When I walked out of the theater, I heard everyone complaining, "What a waste of money!" The ticket price was 50 Renminbi, about $6. Priced like a Hollywood import, it was expensive for a Chinese film. The ticket price for the premiere, held at Beijing's Great Hall of the People (seat of supreme political power in China), was even higher, ranging from 1,000 to 5,000 yuan (approximately $125 to $625) apiece.

It was a completely different scene when I watched the film in an American theater in January 2005. The viewers were focused and deeply moved; they thrilled to the visual beauty and the acrobatic moves, and they sighed when the heroes and heroine died. They gave the film a standing ovation when the credits began to roll. "Amazing!" commented the lady standing beside me.

How should we understand the opposite reactions to the films in China and the United States? Zhang Yimou also saw the discrepancies. His answer is that audiences of both sides need to be educated: the Chinese audience needs to appreciate Chinese blockbusters in the same way it worships imports from Hollywood. No one would complain about Hollywood films' shallowness because the audience's focus is only on the visual spectacle, and the American audience needs to become accustomed to subtitled Chinese films in order to absorb authentic Chinese culture.[7] These comments are important: they form the necessary point of departure from which we can begin to understand the fundamental changes to Chinese cinema in the twenty-first century. What Zhang reveals in these comments is that Chinese blockbusters are created by copying the Hollywood formula: shallow in content and weak in plot but fast in pace and spectacular in visual effects; he also indicates the importance of cultural authenticity to the cross-cultural spectatorship and to successful imitation of and competition with Hollywood big-budget filmmaking. These indications lead us to one of the key issues in "China's century": a fight for intellectual property between China and the United States. China's aspiration to develop its own name brands begins with cultural icons such as Zhang Yimou and Zhang Ziyi, with big-budget films, and with the constructed Chinese cultural authenticity that is copyrightable, marketable, and profitable.

To understand these issues, I first examine in this chapter the nature of the copyright competition. I will then provide a close reading of *Hero*. Representing the future direction of Chinese cultural production, *Hero* reveals many *cultural symptoms* of twenty-first-century China, such as an obsession with history and with historical greatness, insistence on Chinese cultural authenticity, and imagination of Chinese ethnic homogeneity and harmony. These cultural symptoms should not be placed solely within the Chinese context. They are produced through cross-cultural spectacles and cross-ethnic representations; they are also reflections of the copyright competition.

Cinema as a Copyright Industry

According to Shujen Wang, an expert on copyright issues, there are two classifications of copyright industries. One is the core copyright industries, including motion pictures, recording, music publishing, print media, computer software, and broadcasting. The other is the total copyright industries, including both the core industries and portions of other industries that create, distribute, or depend on copyrighted works. These include retailing, toys, and computer manufacturing.[8] Most of today's high-tech industries are copyright industries: they either produce digitized copyrighted works, including films such as George Lucas's *Star Wars: Episode III—Revenge of the Sith* (2005), or create means by which copyrighted materials are manufactured, circulated, or safeguarded.

Realizing the importance of the copyright industries in the new century, the U.S. Congress passed the Digital Millennium Copyright Act (DMCA) in 1998. Interpreting and enforcing this act require legal expertise. For the purpose of understanding the significance of this act to transnational Chinese cinema, I first of all call attention to the very naming of this act and of the new millennium: "digitization" separates the new and old millennia; it also is most crucial to the copyright industry of the new millennium. Because of digitization, the copyright competition will be associated less with the physical and the material than with the abstract and the symbolic—the symbols, languages, and "signifiers," the arbitrary systems of meaning based on which the human being "makes sense of" everything. Culture as collective accumulation of these systems of meaning is thus more important to the copyright competition than ever. Culture itself, as Jean and John Comaroff have repeatedly argued, is becoming increasingly commodified through claiming symbolic authenticity and ownership of copyright.[9]

The other crucial issue delineated in the act is encryption versus circumvention. It is necessary to create encryptions so as to protect the digital copyright, and it is therefore illegal to either circumvent the encryption or manufacture equipment that facilitates the encryption circumvention. The logic of creating encryptions in one form or another to prevent circumvention has interesting implications. Technological advancements create secure encryption, but the encryption will sooner or later be broken by pirates. This will spur the creation of a higher-level encryption. Technology most possibly would not advance without piracy. As much as computer viruses are important to the advancement of computer technology, the circumventions are potentially productive to the copyright industry. In other words, piracy sometimes is necessary for the development of the film industry.

The fear of piracy, or the necessity of encryption, has propelled Zhang Yimou to create the spectacular colors and the multilayered sound effects that can be appreciated only in state-of-the-art multiplexes. Besides the technical details, Zhang Yimou has also repeatedly expressed his desire to make *Hero* a truly personal project that bears his distinctive traits. Only by being individually different can this film be nonduplicable, he figures. These distinctive traits are either visualized understandings of the uniqueness and authenticity of Chinese culture or his personal desires refracted through visual language. As such, these traits are "cultural symptoms" that are both collective and personal, both consciously and unconsciously presented, reflecting the demands as well as dilemmas of the copyright competition.

The term "cultural symptom" comes from Marjorie Garber's analysis of contemporary American culture. A symptom is first of all different from a syndrome, which describes a collective experience that can be but is not strictly related to illness. "A syndrome is a symptom in the public sphere," Garber writes.[10] While a symptom can also be public and representative of an entire "culture," it often dwells on the private and the particular, containing both psychological and clinical experiences that require diagnosis and interpretation in specific cultural contexts. On the one hand, therefore, symptoms are manifestations of problems faced by individuals in their everyday life, manifestations to which many can relate. On the other hand, symptoms often present a challenge to singular and universal cultural identification because they are the deviate and the different.

By describing the cultural symptoms manifested in *Hero*, I intend to draw attention to both the public and the private, or both the industrial and the representational, in contemporary Chinese cultural practices. *Hero* is, first of all, a *Chinese* film; it is thus a representation of certain aspects of China and a reflection of anxieties related to contemporary Chinese society. But it is also a film made by an auteur whose own psychic making—from a desperate feeling of entrapment by history to urges of oedipal patricide—has left visible marks on the film. There are symptoms in the film that cannot be safely contained and explained in historicist narrative or in terms of industrialized film production, symptoms that give the film an individualistic darkness. The existence of these symptoms ultimately generates a discomfort in those who seek an explicit Oriental tale of tradition and honor, of beautiful scenery and exotic customs.

From the Great Ruler to the Great Wall: Zhang Yimou's Historical Predicament

Hero begins with the arrival of Nameless (Jet Li) at the magnificent Qin palace. Nameless brings with him three weapons that once belonged to Sky (Donnie Yen), Broken Sword (Tony Leung), and Flying Snow (Maggie Cheung), thereby announcing the deaths of the three assassins most feared by Qin Shihuang (Chen Daoming). The feat earns Nameless the privilege of drinking within ten steps of the emperor. Their conversation inevitably centers on the ways in which the three assassins were killed. Spectacular scenes of martial arts fighting are staged according to Nameless's reminiscences. The emperor, however, is not convinced by the story. Instead, he presents his own theory and points out Nameless's complicity with the assassins. He believes that the assassins made the ultimate sacrifice in order to ensure Nameless's success. The previous scenes of fighting are thus restaged, with enough changes in choreography and in colors of the clothes to sustain the audience's interest. During the conversation, Nameless becomes increasingly affected by Qin Shihuang's charisma. Despite having absolute confidence in his ultimate strike that can kill anyone within ten steps, Nameless feels hesitant. He begins to understand why, under the most favorable circumstance several years ago, Broken Sword

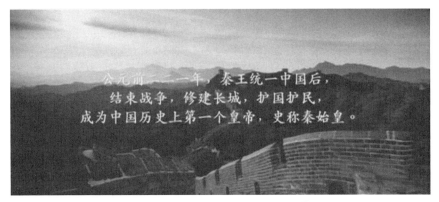

Figure 1.1.   The First Emperor's Great Wall, *Hero*.

did not kill the emperor. And Broken Sword's farewell words, "*tianxia*," now make perfect sense. Meaning "all under the heavens," *tianxia* points to Qin Shihuang's ambition and ability to unify the "warring states" and even expand beyond China proper. These words also convey a Taoist principle that preaches the wholeness and greatness of nature, to which the human world bears resemblance. Thinking of the people under the heavens, Nameless decides to abort his assassination and lets the imperial guards kill him. His rationale is that a temporary bout of violence, no matter how extreme, will eventually end separate long-term conflicts among the warring states. The closing scene of the film is a panoramic shot of the Great Wall (fig. 1.1), on which are superimposed scripts that praise Qin Shihuang's historical achievement in unifying China, simplifying the Chinese language, protecting the Chinese people, and building the Great Wall.

Hero is loosely based on the historical tale of an assassin named Jing Ke, who was able to gain access to Qin Shihuang by showing him the head of one of his enemies and a map that would give Qin Shihuang access to a large territory. Jing Ke failed because Qin Shihuang was a skilled swordsman and was able to defend himself. The tale was originally recorded in the "Grand Historian" Sima Qian's (c. 145–c. 85 BC) *Shiji* (*The Record of History*), which made the figure of Jing Ke synonymous with loyalty, revenge, and tragic heroism. Nameless, in certain ways, is reminiscent of Jing Ke, but Sima Qian's criticism of the cunning and atrocities of imperial rulers is nonexistent in Zhang Yimou's film. The hero in *Hero* is not Nameless but rather Qin Shihuang, who is seen as masculine, perceptive, articulate, calculative, disciplined, fearless, and understanding. The charisma of Qin Shihuang is unmistakable.

Zhang is not alone in showing fascination with "great rulers." A widespread phenomenon in postsocialist Chinese popular culture is the staging of histori-cal royal figures on television and film screens. Television series are represented by *Princess Pearl* (*Huanzhu Gege* [1998]), which transfixed all of China in front of TV sets during the summer of 1998. These TV series are mostly melodramas and light comedies focusing on imperial court struggles of the Qing Dynasty (1644–1911). Emperors Kangxi (1662–1722) and Qianlong (1736–1795) are the most popular. Both emperors are traditionally ranked among the great-est rulers in Chinese history, for they were able to expand China's territory and maintain prosperity and stability for relatively long periods. In China's official discourse, the Han, the Manchu, and other ethnic minorities were assimilated into a single Chinese identity during the Qing Dynasty. Kangxi's and Qianlong's territorial expansions, especially their annexation of Taiwan, are significant to the Chinese government, which regards the reunification of China and Taiwan as its ultimate historical task. This partially explains the government's encouragement of the production and consumption of the "historical" TV dramas despite these dramas' lighthearted treatment of the sacred subject of history.

The popularity of great imperial figures is also related to China's economic prosperity. In China, the turn of the millennium has been called *shengshi* (the age of great prosperity), the same term used to describe the early Tang Dynasty and the reigns of Kangxi and Qianlong. It is widely believed that this contemporary *shengshi* has yet to peak in prosperity and will last a long time, at least for the entire twenty-first century. Hence, the widespread notion of "China's century," which seemingly is under the blessing of an integrated world economy, has taken root. This *shengshi* is considered different from the previous ones, which were always shadowed by a feeling of doom based on a belief in historical vicissitudes and dynastic cycles.

The attraction of Qin Shihuang is similar to that of Kangxi and Qianlong. A notorious tyrant, Qin Shihuang in contemporary Chinese culture is neverthe-less identified as someone who, besides the aforementioned achievements of unifying the Chinese and building the Great Wall, simplified and standardized the Chinese language and currency. On the movie screen alone, there have been numerous productions about Qin Shihuang since 1995. Most renowned are *The Emperor's Shadow* (*Qin song* [1996]) and *The Emperor and the Assassin* (*Jing ke ci qin wang* [1999]). Directed by Zhang Yimou's fellow Fifth Gener-ation directors, Zhou Xiaowen and Chen Kaige, respectively, these films pit individuals against the inevitability and irreversibility of history. In doing so, they create a Shakespearean epic style and spectacular crowd scenes befitting the big screen.

Chinese critic Dai Jinhua points out that Fifth Generation directors' fixation on history and historical figures comes from their "historical predicament," which consists of the desire "to represent an individual experience of shock as legitimate historical experience."[11] Having spent most of their adolescent years during the Cultural Revolution, the Fifth Generation directors experienced political persecution, hunger, sexual frustration, disillusion, and trauma. Their initial goal in filmmaking, therefore, was to capture their unique experience of suffering and youthful struggles. But their personal experience was too traumatic to be directly and publicly confronted. They chose to retreat into history, to replace personal angst with traditional notions of history, such as posthumous greatness, historical progress, or individuals' antagonistic yet dialectic relationship with history. Hence arose the term "the son's generation," referring to the directors' dilemma of choosing between their revolutionary heritage and their desire to differ from their fathers' generation.

In Zhang Yimou's films, the lure of history is manifested in the visual depiction of the contrast between men's revolution and the earth's unassuming antiquity, as shown in one film for which he was the cinematographer (*Yellow Earth* [*Huang tu di*] [1984]). That same lure is evident in the criticism of patriarchal repression during the early Republican period (*Raise the Red Lantern* [*Da hong deng long gao gao gua*] [1991]), the patricidal urge intertwined with sexual transgressions (*Ju Dou* [1990]), and concern with modernization and rural education in the reform era (*Not One Less* [*Yi ge dou bu neng shao*] [1999]).[12] All these films are related to Zhang's conflict between the need to legitimize his own traumatic experiences by representing history and the unwillingness to follow the communist linear narrative of modern Chinese history.

One way to solve his dilemma, with which Zhang Yimou experimented in *The Road Home* (*Wo de fu qin mu qin* [1999]) and *Happy Times* (*Xingfu shiguang* [2000]), is to deliberately efface the temporal setting of historical moments. Instead of drowning personal lives in the grand narrative of history by linking them explicitly to historical events, Zhang embeds the historical moments in personal lives. This strategy gives the audience an impression: historical events do not necessarily dominate personal lives; there are unforgettable moments in even the most mundane life that transcend specific historical events. One can only infer the temporal setting from close examinations of personal tragedies in these films. In *The Road Home*, for instance, Father is suddenly summoned back to the city without being given any explanation. Father's departure devastates Mother and triggers the most emotional moment—Mother's falling ill—in the film. A figure loosely based on Zhang's own father, Father has been labeled a rightist and stripped of his teaching post, an ordeal that is only hinted at in the film. The historical trauma of the Antirightist Movement in 1957

Figure 1.2. *Titanic* **Poster,** *The Road Home.*

is nowhere to be seen in the film, which drowns all heavy feelings in its *timelessness*, its beautiful and dreamy colors, its coming-of-age motif, and its overt sentimentality.

The timelessness in *The Road Home* is temporarily disrupted when the camera gives prominence to the *Titanic* movie poster (fig. 1.2) on the wall of Mother's home. The temporal frame is clearly indicated as the contemporary and post-Father era, which, in contrast to the "timeless" past in vibrant colors, is shot in black and white. This poster represents a reality check, a signal of the intrusion of Hollywood and global capital into the reclusive villages of China. It is also an ironic gesture pointing to the film's own melodramatic sentimentality; the film's score is suspiciously similar to *Titanic*'s theme song. Whatever the implication, the *Titanic* poster breaks the film's self-containment and dreamy aura; it poignantly points to Zhang's dilemma between personal trauma and historical experience.

The ubiquitous father figure in Zhang's films is also indicative of Zhang's historical predicament. When growing up, Zhang and his peers rebelled against traditional Chinese culture and cut off ties with previous generations. In post–Cultural Revolution retrospections, they actively sought to heal the traditional culture, hence giving rise to the "roots-seeking movement," and to denunciations of their spiritual father, Mao Zedong. The desublimation of Mao nevertheless left a major void in the collective psyche of Zhang's generation. Zhang constantly seeks replacement of Mao the Father in such figures as the communist soldier in *Yellow Earth*, "My Grandpa" in *Red Sorghum* (*Hong gao liang* [1987]), Fugui in *To Live* (*Huozhe* [1994]), Zhao Benshan in *Happy Times*, or Father in *The Road Home*. These fathers are not ordinary despite their ordinary appearance and everyday struggles. For they all exist for a sublime moment in their lives, be it the moment of revolutionary success, fermentation of the best wine, or posthumous respect from former students. Patriarchal greatness reaches its peak in Zhang's representation of Qin Shihuang, who, after all, was the "first" patriarch to dream of the infinite continuation of his imperial lineage. These fathers' greatness puts them squarely in the grand narrative of Chinese history and thus qualifies them as legitimate replacements of Mao Zedong.[13]

The obsession with greatness is not unique to Fifth Generation directors; it is a transnational phenomenon shared by former socialist countries and capitalist nations alike. Russia, for example, spent $1.5 billion on renovating St. Petersburg under the premise of rejuvenating the cultural brilliance of Russia. The real motive, as Russian President Vladimir Putin disclosed in his speech on the 300th anniversary of St. Petersburg in June 2003, was to restore the glory and power that Russia possessed under Peter the Great. Russia's cold war rival, the United States, is no less obsessed with greatness. As Marjorie Garber's reading of American popular culture shows, greatness has become a master trope in contemporary American society, which lauds on a daily basis things from "great American presidents," "great American heroes," "great athletes," "great American values," "great American dreams," and "great books of Western civilization."[14] One of the key symptoms of culture, the obsession with greatness is an "ideological category, a redundancy effect,"[15] which builds into people's minds a fantasy of control, of relying on an ultimate savior who makes all problems disappear or easier to face. Interestingly, Russia's and America's obsessions with greatness share the same vision in constructing a mass utopia of modernity, which, as Susan Buck-Morss points out, oscillates between pictures of [a] dream world and of catastrophe.[16]

It is no coincidence that Garber uses the Great Wall of China as the starting point for her discussion. She cites a recent study by Arthur Waldron, who, after close examination of historical and archeological records, finds no physical evidence of the Qin Great Wall's existence and questions the alleged defensive value of the Great Wall. According to Waldron, the current Great Wall dates back to the fifteenth century, and it apparently was not built on any sites of a previous wall. Moreover, the Great Wall's symbolic status as a metonym for national unity was not established until Chinese intellectuals began to embrace the ideas preached by nineteenth-century European nationalism.[17] Garber's point is that, epitomized by the Great Wall, *greatness is but a cultural and symbolic construct*. The biggest irony in Zhang Yimou's representation of the Great Wall, of course, is his repeated emphasis that it was built by Qin Shihuang, while its origin was very much questionable. The uselessness of the Great Wall as a defensive tool and the fabrication of the Great Wall as a

long-standing symbol of China's unity are thus indicative of Zhang's entrapment by history.

The obsession with greatness is a sign of great anxieties in the age of uncertainty. In psychological terms, the fantasy of control by *someone else* inherent
in the obsession with greatness signals the ego's subordination to the superego.
The power of the superego, Freud tells us, lies behind "all the influences of the
past and of tradition," while it remains "one of the most strongly felt manifestations of reality." Freud adds: "In virtue of this concurrence, the super-ego,
the substitute for the Oedipus complex, becomes a representative of the real
external world as well and thus also becomes a model for the endeavors of
the ego. In this way the Oedipus complex proves to be—as has already been
conjectured in a historical sense—the source of our individual ethical sense,
our morality."[18] This mechanism of the ego's succumbing to the superego is behind Zhang Yimou's attempt to replace the personal experience of shock with
the "past and tradition," with historical experience, and with Qin Shihuang
the patriarchal figure.

"Genuine" Chinese Culture

The historical greatness extends to the cultural authenticity that Zhang strove
to represent in *Hero*. In an interview with *Movie View* (*Kan dianying*), China's
most popular film magazine, Zhang talked about how he intended to sell this
film to "foreigners," to entertain them while at the same time teaching them
about Chinese culture:

> I was clearly aware that I made *Hero* for foreign viewers. As soon as those
> Americans hear that Jet Li, Tony Leung, Maggie Cheung, Zhang Ziyi, and
> Donnie Yen will appear together in a martial arts film, they want to see the
> film. It wouldn't be difficult at all for us to reach the goal of opening to 2,000
> screens. . . . But I decided not to cater exclusively to their tastes. If I were to
> satisfy their tastes, I would have focused more on direct physical contact in the
> fight scenes. Instead, I decided to focus more on spiritual communication and
> less on physical contact. In fact, I wanted to lure those Americans into the
> theater before imbuing them with some ideas of genuine Chinese arts. Impress
> them a little. Give them some information. This is only the first step. There are
> things in Chinese culture that cannot be easily understood. It would be a great
> achievement if a foreigner can figure out the meaning of *yijing* (ideascape) after
> living in China for ten years. I don't expect them to understand. All I want is
> gradual influence, bit by bit. They would certainly be surprised by the way our
> martial arts are presented. Why isn't there any bodily contact? It's strange to
> them. Why do calligraphy and sword moves share the same principles? Where
> is the connection? These are things that we Chinese all take for granted. What
> I have done is sell Chinese culture with the help of the martial arts genre film.[19]

The interview bears the title "Zhang Yimou the Hero." Zhang undoubtedly perceives himself as a great cultural hero who promotes Chinese culture to the world. This Chinese culture must be at once marketable and genuine. Marketability is based on genuineness, and genuineness increases marketability.

Filmmaking is but one part of Zhang Yimou's activities as China's cultural ambassador. In 1997, he restaged Puccini's opera *Turandot* in Florence. Zhang was attracted by the opera's story, which takes place in China's Forbidden City. Unhappy with the "non-genuine" setting and with the constraints of conventional opera stage, Zhang moved the production to the *real* Forbidden City in 1998. Zhang did not have any expertise in opera, nor did he understand the Orientalist nature of this classic by Puccini, who wove Western fascinations with the Orient into a colorful tapestry of exotic material culture and unfamiliar emotive expressions. What makes Zhang's amateurish opera career unique are his insistence on "cultural authenticity" and his uncanny ability to arrange crowds in a spacious setting. And his approach has attracted attention from all over the world. Zhang's *Turandot* has since toured the world: Seoul in 2003 and Paris, Berlin, and Barcelona in 2005.

These cities chosen by Zhang have one thing in common: they have all hosted the Summer Olympics. In each of these cities, the venue for Zhang's production has been none other than the Olympic stadium. This is no coincidence. Zhang was deeply involved in Beijing's bid to host the 2008 Summer Olympics. He produced the video about Beijing that was presented to the International Olympic Committee, he directed the last eight-minute segment at the 2004 Athens Summer Olympics closing ceremony to showcase "Chinese cultural essentials," and he will direct the opening ceremony of the 2008 Beijing Olympics. The Olympics and *Turandot* are two sides of the same coin for Zhang Yimou. One side is the biggest international sports competition, which has become the primary stage for the display of nationalist melodramas; the other side is a canon in the Western civilization that has been made larger than life and reproduced as a transcultural spectacle. Together, these two sides tell an ambitious tale of *competition of marketable and copyrightable cultural spectacles* on the international stage.

In order for *Turandot* and the Olympics to be accepted internationally, the locations are most crucial. Where these cultural products take place, where they are produced, and where they are staged are key elements in the consumption of these events based on "genuine" local colors. Zhang Yimou is particularly sensitive to the importance of locations. He chose to shoot the scenes in *Hero* at the most popular tourist destinations. These sites are popular not only because they showcase natural splendor but also because they preserve significant historical memories and symbolize ethnic harmony.

Figure 1.3. Dunhuang, *Hero*.

The spectacular scenes of the formidable Qin army's attack on the Zhao capital, for instance, were shot in the sandstorms of Dunhuang in Gansu Province (fig. 1.3). Situated in the middle of the Gobi Desert and dubbed a jewel on the Silk Road, Dunhuang is known for its numerous caves that once housed tens of thousands of Buddhist canons and murals. Most of the Buddhist treasures were plundered by the British archeologist Sir Aural Stein in the early twentieth century and are now preserved in the British Museum. Dunhuang thus was made into a symbol standing for China's past suffering from Western imperialism and serving as a live textbook for nationalism and patriotism. Another spot, the Euphrates poplar forest in Inner Mongolia, is where the fight scene between Flying Snow and Moon takes place. Zhang chose the Euphrates poplar simply for its magnificent yellow foliage (fig. 1.4). But in contemporary Chinese culture, *huyang* (barbarian poplar), the Chinese term for Euphrates

Figure 1.4. Huyang Foliage, *Hero*.

Figure 1.5. Jiuzhaigou, *Hero.*

poplar, has a special significance in discourses of ethnic unity, for the tree is most treasured by the Uighur and the Mongol. "The most beautiful tree" is how *huyang* is affectionately rendered in the Uighur language. Another shooting spot, Jiuzhaigou (literally, "the valley of nine Tibetan villages"), hidden in the deep forests on the border between Sichuan Province and Tibet, is yet another symbol of Chinese ethnic unity between the Tibetans and the Han (fig.1.5).

The most extraordinary or, rather, incoherent element of *Hero* is the ease with which its protagonists traverse the vast distance among these three spots and the Qin palace. One minute Nameless is in the Zhao capital; the next minute he is fighting Broken Sword in Jiuzhaigou, which is thousands of miles away. Of course, Zhang would explain this in terms of the film's nature as a fantasy. The actual sites of shooting also should not be equated with the stage setting in the film. But the irony is that these sites are too famous and recognizable to be neglected as fictitious places for the filmic fantasy. Zhang also must rely on these actual sites' cultural connotations to convey his message in the phrase *tianxia*.

One of the contemporary cultural trends, as David Harvey points out in his notion of the "time-space compression," is "annihilation of space by time." This means that global distance under advanced capitalism is no longer significant, for the all-encompassing power of global capital has rendered human subjects' rootedness in historical time and geographical place irrelevant to profit making.[20] Increasingly infiltrated by global capital, China is no exception to this process of compressing time and space. In actual practice, however, time and space are reified in order to emphasize their *Chinese* specificities, as in the cases of Dunhuang, the Euphrates poplar forest, and Jiuzhaigou. Although the result of reification is homogenization and elimination of differences,

Chineseness is established as a marker of locality and authenticity in contrast to globality, insinuating China's historical defiance against the West. This is where the ultimate dilemma of *Hero* is: on the one hand, space is compressed to create an impression of the unity of Chinese sovereignty and culture; on the other hand, the consumption of culture extends to the consumption of the film itself in the international market, where the Chineseness with all its historical baggage resists interpretation and lighthearted entertainment. Bearing witness to this dilemma is none other than the phrase *tianxia*, which simultaneously denotes an ambition to join the world market and contradictions inherent to the cultural logic of this market.

From Ideascape to Sinascape

The most "genuine" feature of Chinese culture that Zhang intends to promote in *Hero* is China's poetic tradition best summed up by the phrase *yijing*, that is, ideascape. A highly abstract notion, "ideascape" conveys a poetic sense of the harmony between the human mind and the surrounding nature, which is always already tinged with human emotions and is thus not subject to codes of verisimilitude (fig.1.6). Zong Baihua, one of the pioneers of modern Chinese aesthetics, uses the analogy of an empty pavilion in the middle of mountains and lakes to describe ideascape.[21] The emptiness of the pavilion paradoxically functions to indicate the presence of human activity in nature and thereby makes the pavilion the converging point for the breathing and spiritual movement of the mountains and lakes. Zhang must have grasped the essence of this poetic picture. He chose to shoot a pavilion in the middle of a lake surrounded by the mountains of Jiuzhaigou (fig. 1.7). With the dead body

Figure 1.6.   Ideascape, *Hero*.

Figure 1.7. Pavilion in the Middle of a Lake, *Hero.*

of Flying Sword lying in the pavilion, Broken Sword and Nameless fight each other to pay tribute to her. The water is as still and smooth as the surface of a mirror; Flying Snow seems to have returned to nature. Any disturbance would be an insult to the dead. The two men thus engage in a quiet and dancelike fight, until they are broken off by a drop of water falling on the face of Flying Snow. A lavishly ornamental display of sentimentality has acquired poetic meanings in the mutual containment between movement and stillness.

Other scenes designed to convey ideascape include the fight between Sky and Nameless on the chess terrace. The black and white *go* pieces, the drumbeat, the Peking opera aria, the Chinese zither played by a blind old man, the imagined fight between the two that is more breathtaking than the real fight, and the water dripping from the tiled roof all point to a perfect combination of things uniquely Chinese with an aura of antiquity and spirituality. The same combination is also clearly visible in the notion of hiding sword moves in brush-pen calligraphy and in Nameless's amazing display of the quickness of his sword when he cuts loose the piles of bamboo books in the library.

Zhang's practice seems to be typically self-Orientalizing. On the one hand, he insists on presenting things that are ostensibly "Chinese"; on the other hand, he also doubts "foreign" audiences' ability to understand his rendering of ideascape. When a cross-cultural visual representation is made solely as a spectacle, not a symbolic unit that is decipherable and understandable, it inevitably becomes an object of exotic imaginations and also *a form of encryption*. Complications arise, however, if the very idea of ideascape is not always indigenously Chinese. First formulated by Zong Baihua and Wang Guowei in the early twentieth century, ideascape was able to replace many theoretical paradigms in traditional Chinese poetics. It is crucial to the relationship between subject and object, focusing on how the object is tinged by the subject's feelings. This is much easier to grasp than the "nonscientific" traditional Chinese terminology that requires not so much logical reasoning as artistic epiphany and totalizing imagination. Ideascape marked the beginning of modern Chinese aesthetics, which relies heavily on the terminology of European philosophy concerning the clear divide between subject and object. It turns out that ideascape is not a Chinese term but a result of China's coming into contact with Enlightenment rationalism.[22] Although traditional Chinese poetry can be appropriately interpreted in terms of ideascape, the very interpretation, including the desire to come up with definitive interpretations, is already a *foreign* idea.

Zhang Yimou's use of ideascape is one of the manifestations of sinascape. Key to sinascape is Chinese filmmakers' clear awareness of the transcultural gaze upon the representation of Chineseness. Facing the gaze, they tend to adjust the cinematic representation in such a way as to either emphasize the authenticity of the represented culture or pose questions against their own cultural practices. Ideascape is Zhang Yimou's response to the transcultural gaze, but its own problematic nature undermines Zhang's emphasis of cultural authenticity.

There is an inherent dialectic in sinascape due to the tension between "sina" and "scape." Chineseness and cinema contradict each other, for ethnic spectacles in electronic images conceal the historical process of the discursive practice of ethnic identity; they also define each other under the logic of transnationalism, for cinema's universal appeal is stamped by cultural specificities, while cinema's visual immediacy destabilizes cultural homogeneity. "Idea" and "scape" interact with each other in the same way. When ideas of an authentic Chinese culture are transformed into cinematic representations, the authenticity is simultaneously questioned and confirmed. Some features of Chinese culture, while difficult to describe in linguistic terms, are in particular revealed in "cinematic-scape." The Chinese poetic expressions, for instance, find their visual equivalence in modern cinema's "movement-image" and "time-image," which, as defined by Gilles Deleuze, respectively convey the intermediate nature of movement from point A to point B and the eternal fluidity of time between point A and point B.[23] Stillness and movement, geographical distance and emotive intimacy, immediate presence and representational intermediacy are all classical motifs of Chinese poetry that are vividly rendered into visual expressions in Zhang Yimou's brilliant colors, spectacular scenery, choreographed movements hinged on psychological time, and, ironically, Zhang's ideas about what an authentic Chinese cinema should be.

Christopher Doyle, *Hero*'s director of cinematography, makes a comment that, in an uncanny way, sums up my arguments: "The greatest thing about this film is that it turns linguistic ideas into visual expressions and conveys poetic meanings through the communications of colors."[24] From "idea" to "scape," and from "sina" to "scape," *Hero* indeed has reached a high level of cinematic aesthetics. The achievement, in the meantime, must rely on a spectacular display of a homogenized Chinese culture. This culture is copyrightable because it is encrypted in codes of authenticity.

There Is No Thief under the Heavens

Before bringing this chapter to a close, I must mention Feng Xiaogang's 2004 "New Year film" *A World without Thieves*. On the surface, there is nothing in common between this film and *Hero*. Feng's comedy in his trademark mixture of cynicism and lyricism is set in the contemporary world. Moral order has collapsed under the ubiquitous pursuit of wealth and hedonism. Thieves, in every sense of the term, are everywhere. A master thief, played by Hong Kong's Andy Lau, pulls off a job with the help of his girlfriend, who is portrayed by Taiwan's Rene Liu. They steal a BMW from one of the nouveau riche in Beijing and drive it all the way to Tibet to sell it. Spectacular scenery unfolds. A battle of wits and martial arts between two groups of thieves ensues. In the end, love, trust, and generosity prevail.

What intrigues me is the Chinese title of Feng's film: *Tianxia wuzei*. It does not perfectly suit the film's story. In Internet blogs, many Chinese viewers interpret the title to convey a moral idealism in the age of moral degeneracy. But, despite its feel-good ending, what the film really implies is the pointlessness of good deeds. Andy Lau dies in the end for turning against the other thieves. Considering Feng's biggest concern as a filmmaker is piracy, a form of stealing, I have to believe that there is an irony in the title that points not to the film's content but to the rampant film piracy. Also noticeable is the phrase *tianxia*, which, as I have observed above, is of the utmost importance to the theme of *Hero*. Feng has been notorious for satirizing people whom he knows in real life. His previous "New Year film," *Cell Phone* (*Shou ji*), was accused of libel by a famous Chinese TV talk show host who even filed a lawsuit. It is very likely, I believe, that the *tianxia* in *Tianxia wuzei* is a play on Zhang Yimou's central motif in *Hero*. Even if Feng's title were completely unrelated to *Hero*, Feng would have loved to take a jab at Zhang at every possible occasion. After all, these two are the biggest box office draws in China. Their producers, Zhang Weiping and the aforementioned Wang Zhongjun, are the biggest private investors and thus rivals in the Chinese film industry. If Zhang Yimou had yet to have a clear awareness of copyright competitions at the time he made *Hero*, Feng has always been driven by name brands. From *Hero's tianxia* to Feng Xiaogang's *tianxia*, twenty-first-century Chinese cinema is quickly learning to be a major player in the international copyright competition.

Notes

1. See the LG *jixian yundong* bulletin board (http://www.lgactionsports.com.cn/bbs/dispbbs.asp?BoardID=11&ID=1190&page=1) for the interview with Zhang Weiping on August 24, 2004 (accessed January 21, 2006).

2. See Reuters News, "US Could Take China to WTO on Piracy, Says Zoellick," May 17, 2005.

3. Disney's Miramax repeatedly postponed the film's release in the United States even after Zhang Yimou gave in to its demands and cut the length of the film from two hours to ninety minutes. The postponement was purportedly related to the spread of SARS (severe acute respiratory syndrome) that ravaged China, Taiwan, Hong Kong, and Toronto during the first half of 2003. Miramax also attempted to dub the film in English and to market it as *Jet Li's Hero* but met considerable resistance from the film's producers and from American audiences at test screenings. See MonkeyPeaches bulletin board (http://www.monkeypeaches.com/hero.html) (accessed January 21, 2006). The linking of the release of *Hero* to SARS indicates that a Chinese film is never perceived simply as a film but as part and parcel of the image of China. *Hero's* epic style, sublime aura, glossy cinematography, and advanced filmmaking technology apparently contradicted the recrudescent "old" image of China as a dark, dusty, dirty, disease-spreading realm awaiting Western enlightenment and modern public health management. The fear of SARS triggered a new wave of anti-Chinese sentiment, so much so that Miramax must have concluded that the timing was not right for a Chinese epic.

4. Richard Corliss, "TIME 2004 Best and Worst: Richard Corliss' Best Movies," *Time*, December 27, 2004, http://www.time.com/time/bestandworst/2004/corliss.html (accessed January 21, 2006).

5. See sina.com bulletin board (http://ent.sina.com.cn/2004-11-11/0822562035.html) for comments on *Hero* by Beijing's leading popular culture scholars (accessed January 21, 2006).

6. For a well-researched examination of Takeshi Kaneshiro's trans–East Asian appeal, see Eva Tsai, "Kaneshiro Takeshi: Transnational Stardom and the Media and Cultural Industries in Asia's Global/Postcolonial Age," *Journal of Modern Chinese Literature and Culture* 17 (Spring 2005): 100–132.

7. See "Yingxiong Zhang Yimou" ("Zhang Yimou the Hero"), an interview with Zhang Yimou, *Kan dianying* (*Movie View*) 200 (May 2003): 17–20.

8. Shujen Wang, "Recontextualizing Copyright: Piracy, Hollywood, the State, and Globalization," *Cinema Journal* 43 (Fall 2003): 28.

9. See, for instance, Jean Comaroff's book *Body of Power, Spirit of Resistance: The Culture and History of a South African People* (Chicago: University of Chicago Press, 1985).

10. Marjorie Garber, *Symptoms of Culture* (New York: Routledge, 2000), 2.

11. Jing Wang and Tani E. Barlow, eds., *Cinema and Desire: Feminist Marxism and Cultural Politics in the Work of Dai Jinhua* (New York: Verso, 2003), 22.

12. For a detailed discussion of *Not One Less*, see my article "The Pedagogical as the Political: Ideology of Globalization and Zhang Yimou's *Not One Less,*" *The Communication Review* 6 (December 2003): 327–40.

13. For the ways in which figures of the sublime were integrated into modern Chinese discourse of history and modernity, see Ban Wang, *The Sublime Figure of History* (Stanford: Stanford University Press, 1997).

14. Marjorie Garber, *Symptoms of Culture*, 2.

15. Marjorie Garber, *Symptoms of Culture*, 43.

16. Susan Buck-Morss, *Dreamworld and Catastrophe: The Passing of Mass Utopia in East and West* (Cambridge, MA: MIT Press), x–xii.

17. Arthur Waldron, *The Great Wall of China: From History to Myth* (Cambridge: Cambridge University Press, 1990).

18. Sigmund Freud, "The Economic Problem of Masochism," in *The Standard Edition of the Complete Psychological Works of Sigmund Freud*, trans. James Strachey (London: Hogarth, 1961), 19:159–70.

19. "Zhang Yimou the Hero," 19.

20. David Harvey, *The Condition of Postmodernity* (London: Blackwell, 1990).

21. Zong Baihua, *Zhongguo yishu yijing zhi dansheng* [The birth of Chinese artistic ideascape]. In *Zong Baihua quanji* [The collected works of Zong Baihua] (Hefei: Anhui jiaoyu chubanshe, 1994), 1:6.

22. See Zong-qi Cai, *Configurations of Comparative Poetics: Three Perspectives on Western and Chinese Literary Criticism* (Honolulu: University of Hawaii Press, 2002), 246.

23. My generalization does not do justice to Deleuze's complex theses. See Deleuze, *Cinema 1: The Movement-Image*, trans. Hugh Tomlinson and Barbara Habberjam (Minneapolis: University of Minnesota Press, 1986), and *Cinema 2: The Time-Image*, trans. Hugh Tomlinson and Robert Galeta (Minneapolis: University of Minnesota Press, 1989).

24. Christopher Doyle's talk is recorded on the second disc of the two-disc DVD set of *Hero*, released in region 3 format in 2003.

CHAPTER TWO

—◦◦◦—

Violence, Sixth Generation Filmmaking, and *Devils on the Doorstep*

The most productive filmmakers in early twenty-first-century China are those who belong to the "Sixth Generation." Compared to Fifth Generation directors, a cohort led by Zhang Yimou and Chen Kaige, Sixth Generation directors are much less obsessed with subjects that have overt links with "China." Mostly born in the 1960s and early 1970s, these young directors, including Zhang Yuan, Jiang Wen, Lou Ye, Wang Xiaoshuai, and Jia Zhangke, began their filmmaking careers around the early to mid-1990s. It was no coincidence that the same period marked the beginning of the postsocialist era. In the midst of rapid privatization, urbanization, and the rise of the middle class, it became easier to acquire funds for film production from channels other than state-run film studios. The increasing marketization also prepared these directors in all areas of electronic image production. Lou Ye, for instance, spent four years making TV commercials before getting a chance to direct his first feature film, *Weekend Lover* (*Zhou mo qing ren* [1995]).

Besides the economic factor, there are other factors, political and regulatory, that shaped the ways in which these directors participate in cultural activity and practice artistic expression. While Zhang Yimou and Chen Kaige have become the new darlings of China's mainstream culture, almost every Sixth Generation director experienced harsh treatment in the censorship and regulatory system. It took three years and numerous cuts, including changes of title, for Wang Xiaoshuai's *So Close to Paradise* (*Biandan, guniang* [1999]) to win permission for theatrical release. Lou Ye's *Suzhou River* (*Suzhou he* [2000]), Jiang Wen's *Devils on the Doorstep* (*Guizi lai le* [2000]), Jia Zhangke's *Hometown Trilogy* series (*Xiao Wu* [1998], *Platform* [*Zhantai*] [2000], and *Unknown*

Figure 2.1. Xiao Wu Wants to Buy the Pirated DVD *Xiao Wu, Unknown Pleasures.*

Pleasures [*Ren xiao yao*] [2002]) all achieved tremendous success in overseas art house markets and at international film festivals. None made it to Chinese movie theaters due to their violations of state regulations governing the film industry. These films nevertheless have been widely circulated within China through pirated DVDs and VCDs, another example of piracy's productiveness. Jia Zhangke even pokes fun at the piracy of his films: in *Unknown Pleasures*, the protagonist of *Xiao Wu* is a customer for pirated DVDs and chides the street hawker for not having "a copy of the highly popular film *Xiao Wu*" (fig. 2.1). The marginalized and underground position partially explains why Sixth Generation directors tend to identify with social underdogs, such as prostitutes, petty criminals, the rural emigrants termed "the floating population" in big cities, and laid-off workers from state-run industrial enterprises. Social realism thus has become the dominant style for their films. Their representation of social injustices and of widening rural-urban gaps coincides with international society's desire to unearth the "ugly truth" behind China's rosy picture of economic boom. Hence arises a double bind for these directors: on one hand, they consciously resist the tendency of self-Orientalization in Fifth Generation filmmaking, which focuses on "traditional" and "premodern" China; on the other hand, their realist representation of contemporary China's social issues continues to reinforce impressions of China's differences, of China being the violator of human rights and the dark realm of communism.

The Sixth Generation directors nevertheless have achieved cinematic breakthroughs by showing awareness of the double bind. One way for them to escape their dilemma is to reflect upon the meanings of reality and to question the very realism on which their films are made. This is the topic of the next chapter. Another way is to focus on issues of social violence. By attempting to form a critique of violence that has universal significance beyond the realm of China, these Sixth Generation directors are able to draw attention not only to their represented social injustices but also to questions regarding cinematic representation itself. They highlight through filmic images the affinity between seeing/imaging and violence, between seeking identity and excluding the other. The immediacy of the filmic image is constantly in tension with the inherent opacity of representation. The tension is now more noticeable than ever due to these directors' ever-increasing anxiety over their films' relevance to society. Insofar as the film can be understood as one of the representational forms closest to society,[1] contemporary Chinese social crises have found the most ideal outlet in these directors' films. The crises include rapid stratification, commodification of all aspects of social life, ubiquitous corruption, exploitation of the "floating people," deterioration of the environment, and urbanization that erases all traces of previous lives. The filmic representation of these crises destabilizes the logic of violence, because its overwhelming immediacy transcends the means-versus-ends rationale.[2]

Wang Xiaoshuai, Lou Ye, Jia Zhangke, Zhang Yuan, and Jiang Wen have all been focusing on issues of violence. They tend to manifest the violence of representation by challenging the previously dominant mode of cinematic representation, attacking institutionalized differentiation between legitimate state violence and illegitimate individual violence, probing the origins and problematics of Chinese modernity, and reflecting upon mechanisms of seeing. Wang Xiaoshuai's *Beijing Bicycle* (*Shiqi sui de dan che* [2001]), for example, reinvents "Camel Xiangzi," Lao She's modern *Homo economicus*,[3] in the figure of a bicycle courier from the countryside. The audience not only sees Beijing's urbanization through the subjective camera but is also left to ponder the value of labor, the human body, and the very act of seeing. Lou Ye's *Suzhou River*, a film about murder, suicide, and desperate love, goes even further, questioning the reliability of seeing as well as the camera's mechanical stare that violently tears open the layers of historical changes in the city of Shanghai. Jia Zhangke's *Platform* vividly reduplicates the enthusiastic, chaotic, and often violent process of modernization in the 1980s through the vicissitudes a small-city theatrical troupe experienced. The film brings new meanings to "the culture industry" by showing exactly how, in filmic images, aesthetics are subordinated to sociological representation. Zhang Yuan's *I Love You* (*Wo ai ni* [2003]), marking Zhang's turn to commercial films, goes deeper than its surface story of the disharmonies and violence of the married life. What is actually dissected is how language does harms, not only to interpersonal relationships, but also to filmic images that are often abruptly interrupted by arbitrary interpretations of the images.

None of these films, however, has gone as far as Jiang Wen's *Devils on the Doorstep* has in representing violence and in exposing the violence of representation. Situated in the most traumatic event to hit twentieth-century China, World War II, *Devils on the Doorstep* portrays people's mental state in the middle of violence. In this film, Jiang Wen is able to relate his thinking on the nature of violence to the discourse of modernity, restaging in a farcical fashion Lu Xun's decapitation scene. The dominance of the Great Wall in the background of the filmic images draws our attention to issues of "national character" and Chinese nation-building, the most fundamental "myth-making" of Chinese socialist ideology. All these are done through Jiang Wen's bold filmic experiments, such as the black-and-white cinematography, the claustrophobic aura, the fanatical acts, and the pastiche of motifs from old films of the 1950s and 1960s. These experiments, as I analyze in what follows, not only provide the most suitable form for Jiang Wen's examination of violence and national trauma but also call attention to the violence of representation through questioning the viewing pleasure based on masculinist aesthetics. What Jiang Wen's project ultimately suggests is that we cannot truly understand violence without considering trauma and vice versa. When understood together, trauma and violence provide a powerful tool for disrupting the notion of grand history, which, in its typically linear fashion, constructs a myth of revolutionary progression and provides legitimacy for the Chinese nation-state. While people's actual suffering and struggles are drowned in the linear history of the Chinese revolution, the history ruptured by trauma and violence rescues their suffering and shows it through the imaging power of cinema.

Devils on the Doorstep is a mixture of a comedy of errors, drama of human passions, tragedy of historical suffering, and epic of Sisyphean labors. Jiang Wen, a great actor himself, plays Ma Dasan, a strong, straight-minded, credulous, and bumbling northern peasant, reminiscent of Jiang's role in Zhang Yimou's *Red Sorghum*. The film is set in early 1945, when Dasan and his fellow villagers of Rack Armor Terrace live under the shadow of Japanese blockhouses and bunkers. Nestled between the Great Wall and a large lake, the village coexists with the Japanese in an uneasy harmony. Every morning, a Japanese naval marching band passes through the village on its way to welcoming the return of Japanese battleships. Attracted by the stirring Japanese military tunes, Chinese children line up along the road and receive candies handed out by the navy captain. Behind this eerie scene of improbable peace and idyll, Ma Dasan is enjoying his affair with a young widow. His tryst is interrupted, however, by a gun pointed at his head. The man behind the gun never reveals himself to either Ma Dasan or the audience, identifying himself only as "me." Presumably a communist guerrilla, "me" throws Dasan two sacks for safekeeping. He also orders Dasan to interrogate the "things" in the sacks before he picks them up prior to the Lunar New Year.

Inside the sacks are a Japanese soldier (Kagawa Teruyuki) and a Chinese interpreter for the Japanese. Dasan realizes the danger facing the entire village. He asks the village elders to conduct the interrogation. The scene is filled with farcical misunderstandings due to the villagers' use of classical cliché and the interpreter's deliberate mistranslation of the Japanese soldier's curse words. The New Year has passed, "me" fails to show up, and none of the area guerrillas accepts the responsibility. Dasan can no longer endure the pressure of hiding the POWs under the eyes of the Japanese. To spare Dasan, the elders vote to kill the POWs. But the executioner, who always brags about his swift and painless beheading skills, turns out to be a fraud. Dasan becomes the designated executioner. Unable to do the deed, Dasan decides to hide the captives inside the Great Wall.

The villagers do not discover Dasan's secret until August. After a heated debate, they decide to sign a pact with the POWs and send the POWs back to the blockhouse in exchange for food. The Japanese army captain agrees to reward the villagers and takes his troops to escort the food to Rack Armor Terrace. An outdoor banquet is offered by the grateful villagers. The Chinese and the Japanese suddenly become friends, drinking, singing, and laughing together. In the middle of the celebration, the army captain stands up, telling his navy colleagues that their emperor has accepted Japan's defeat and ordered all Japanese troops to surrender unconditionally. To show for the last time the spirit of the "imperial army," the previously friendly Japanese begin to massacre the villagers, killing all the men, women, and children. Ma Dasan is not among the victims, for he left the banquet early to pick up his lover from her home.

The massacre scene quickly cuts into the surrender ceremony held by the victorious Chinese Nationalists (*Kuo Min Tang* [KMT]). The Japanese are still living in their blockhouses when Ma Dasan carries out his vendetta. He chases down and stabs every Japanese soldier whom he can find. But he is quickly subdued by the KMT military police. After a public trial, the KMT general orders the Japanese to execute Ma Dasan. The chosen executioner happens to be the previously captured Japanese soldier, who repays Dasan's care and feeding by swiftly cutting off Dasan's head. The process must be satisfactory to the executed, for Dasan's head performs a legendary ritual in marveling at the executioner's skill: it spins six times, the eyes blink three times, and the

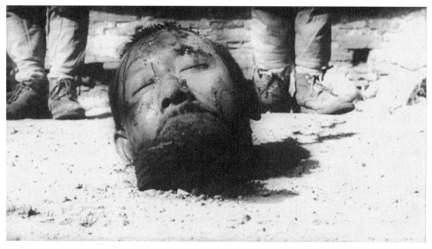

Figure 2.2.   Ma Dasan Beheaded, *Devils on the Doorstep*.

lips draw upward, forming a frozen smile. At this last moment, the previously black-and-white film turns into a full-color photo, featuring the jarring redness of Dasan's blood (fig. 2.2).

Not So Black and White

The most noticeable stylistic feature of *Devils on the Doorstep* is its black-and-white cinematography. The film stunned the audience at the 2000 Cannes Film Festival and won the Grand Jury Prize.[4] Interviews of Jiang Wen during and after the festival inevitably focused on his reasons for adopting black and white in an increasingly color-dominated contemporary cinema. Jiang gave various answers on different occasions:

1. The last and most important shot of the film is meant to be stunningly colorful and piercingly red; to achieve this effect, it is worth shooting all the previous scenes in black and white to set up the stark contrast.[5]
2. The film's cinematographer, Gu Changwei, who also worked with Jiang on *In the Heat of the Sun* (*Yangguang canlan de rizi* [1994]), had always wanted to shoot a richly textured and shadowy black-and-white film. *In the Heat of the Sun* was originally intended to be black and white.[6]
3. Jiang was unhappy with the artifice of Chinese films, which rely heavily on "native" colors and "Chinese" beauties. He jokingly pointed out that Gu Changwei was responsible for some of the films. Gu's credentials

include directing cinematography for Chen Kaige's *Farewell My Concubine* (*Ba wang bie ji* [1993]).[7]

4. To be black and white was to approximate the faded appearance of historical records. Jiang and Gu tested the effect of the cinematography by mixing together photocopied historical pictures and black-and-white pictures of the actors in costume; no one could tell the difference.[8]

In sum, according to Jiang himself, his choice of black-and-white cinematography reflects his consistent emphasis on stylistic innovations and his anti-Orientalist sentiments, criticism of Fifth Generation directors' "China anxiety," and dedication to the faithful representation of history.

The contrast between all the black-and-white scenes and the decapitation scene shot in color is the key to understanding Jiang's choice of black and white. The decapitation scene is the only subjective shot of the entire film. We are first shown how Ma Dasan's head rolls, before the perspective switches to that of the head: the surroundings are rolling. Only when the view becomes a little focused and settled do we realize that we are actually watching from the perspective of the decapitated head, which watches, from the ground level, almost amusingly how the crowd cheers at the spectacle and how Kagawa Teruyuki reports to his captain. This perspective is so bizarre and shocking that the very act of *seeing*, not the cruelty of the execution, becomes the focal point of the scene. It draws attention to these questions: Who is watching whom? Who should be the butt of the laughter? Which perspective is truer, the film audience's, the crowd's, or the head's? Which cinematographic arrangement is more reliable, the objective and black and white or the subjective and colored?

This scene resembles Lu Xun's slide-viewing experience recalled in the preface of his first short story collection, *Nahan* (Call to arms [1922]). Having seen in a newsreel how his physically strong but mentally numb compatriots cheered the beheading of a Chinese by the Japanese, Lu allegedly changed his life's goal from curing the Chinese body with Western medicine to saving the Chinese soul with realist literature. More important, this recalled experience marked the beginning of modern Chinese culture, which was founded on the "obsession with China"[9] and on the anxiety over China's well-being. Along the same vein, Jiang Wen's closing scene conveys a similar critique of the "weak," "numb," and "hungry-for-spectacle" Chinese national character.

Jiang repeatedly made references to Lu Xun. When asked about why he made a comedy out of the most tragic circumstances, Jiang compared his film with Lu Xun's "The True Story of Ah Q," the most influential account of the Chinese national character typified by the ability to turn personal humiliations into victories through deliberate renaming and misnaming. Beheaded at the end of the story, Ah Q is known for his "strategy of spiritual victory," which hinges on an act of symbolic transformation: although I am beaten by you, I am still victorious because you all are my inferior offspring in the kinship hierarchy. The most important lesson the Ah Q story has taught us, Jiang Wen contends, is that everyone is caught in Ah Q's logic: when you laugh at Ah Q, you are actually laughing at yourself because Ah Q was meant to represent every Chinese who tends to turn actual pain into symbolic triumph. When you laugh at the ignorance of Ma Dasan and his fellow villagers, Jiang Wen further implies, you have let go of your guard against graphic violence and the cruelty of war. The massacre scene was thus intended by Jiang Wen to "kick you in the groin" and wake the audience up from numbness.[10]

Lu Xun's writings on the Chinese national character epitomize what Andrew Jones has described as the "violence of representation" based on May Fourth intellectuals' unyielding faith in the powers of representation. Representation can "create a new, improved, and modern social order in a nation beset by internal crisis and Western encroachment."[11] The intellectuals privileged certain forms of representation and excluded a wide range of different voices. According to David Der-wei Wang, Lu Xun was nevertheless sophisticated and self-conscious enough to struggle with the violence of representation; hence arise the frequent confrontations between his narrator and narrative. The narrator often casts doubts on the coherence of the narrative and on the effectiveness of writing. This is why, Wang contends, beheading occurs repeatedly in Lu Xun's writings, symbolizing his obsession with representing violence for awakening the Chinese people. The beheading also symbolizes Lu Xun's struggle with the violence of representation that endorses literary realism as the only suitable mode for representing people's suffering and nationalist sentiments.[12]

Jiang Wen's subjective camera and surprising switch to color for the beheading scene add new twists to Lu Xun's motifs. On the one hand, the reaction of Ma Dasan's head to the skills of the Japanese soldier speaks volumes about Chinese peasants' naiveté, ignorance, even stupidity. The staging of this violent act apparently is intended to criticize the Chinese national character. The quirky, comical effect of the execution scene then turns the viewers' laughter toward themselves by implying the complicity of the bystanders who cheer on the execution or simply enjoy the film. On the other hand, this scene is also directed toward the conventional heroic narrative of history, which always ends with a bright note of eventual triumph and subordinates the representation of violence to certain telos in such an explicit fashion that violence is annihilated. It is modern Chinese history that is being mocked.

Jiang's assertion "no one dares to make black-and-white films nowadays except us"[13] is not accurate. Although rare, black-and-white films are still continually produced, even after the Academy of Motion Picture Arts and Sciences stopped awarding separate awards for black-and-white cinematography and color cinematography in 1966. Largely due to their innovative orientation, the recent black-and-white films are generally more thought-provoking and artistically inspiring than Hollywood color films. Examples include *Pleasantville* (1998). Not strictly a black-and-white film due to its mixture of colors and black and white, *Pleasantville* questions the seemingly innocent American nostalgia for the "family values" typified by the 1950s when television was still in black and white. A pun is played on the word "color": it refers to both color TV programming and colored people, who include not only ethnic minorities but also those who dare to be different and who are brave enough to challenge racial segregation. Because of the pun, which implies more racial commonalities ("we all want 'colors' in our life") than differences, this commercially successful film breaks the spell of the ostensibly progressive "American multiculturalism" that actually reinforces segregationism through racial stereotyping ("we are all culturally different") and disguising the increasing gaps between racial groups.[14]

The most successful example of contemporary black-and-white cinematography is undoubtedly Steven Spielberg's *Schindler's List* (1993). Spielberg chose black and white apparently because the violence of the Holocaust is too heavy and *graphic* to be represented in colors that tend to be frivolous and overly revealing. This choice is consistent with a conventional filmic technique: flashbacks of traumatic and violent memories, such as witnessing a murder, are more often than not shown in black and white. Although overused, the black-and-white flashbacks do have psychological and psychoanalytical significance in their implications that the flashbacks are not as vivid or reliable as "colored" reality and that there are always gray, thus inexplicable, areas in one's memories. Stylistically, being black and white means that there is a third color in the picture: gray, which gives the whole picture a shadowy nuance and a visual depth. To be black and white in cinematography thus means the opposite of what the phrase "black and white" denotes in terms of being clearly distinguishable, controversy free, and manifestly antagonistic. Extending the flashback technique to the entire motion picture, Spielberg has demonstrated at least two things: first, historical characters, such as Schindler, are not always as simple as "black and white," and the line between good and evil is thin. Second, there are gray areas in our traumatic memories that prohibit revisiting; we nevertheless must acknowledge their existence in the shadow of our simplistic, trouble-free recalling of the black-and-white past.

Both strategies, the metafilmic punning on color in *Pleasantville* and the complicating of black-and-white traumatic memories in *Schindler's List*, are present in *Devils on the Doorstep*. Jiang Wen mentioned on several occasions that the images of Japanese "devils" in his film are based on "their looks, as I remembered them." What he meant is not that he saw Japanese devils but that he saw Japanese devils on screen. Born in 1962, Jiang was nurtured on revolutionary films that had long molded a standard image of the Japanese devil, who hands out candies to Chinese children but is also ever ready to kill innocent Chinese. The moment the Japanese enters a village, he will be ambushed and defeated by the children, women, and grandparents, all of whom suddenly turn into highly skilled partisans. Through such films as *Tunnel Warfare* (*Di dao zhan* [1965]), *Mine Warfare* (*Di lei zhan* [1962]), and *Little Soldier Zhangga* (*Xiao bing Zhangga* [1963]), which were seen numerous times by every child and adult during the Cultural Revolution, the standard image of the Japanese devil became a source of amusement, not fear.[15] The phrase *guizi lai le* therefore, signifies the Japanese invaders' comical clumsiness and the Chinese people's heroic determination to defend their homeland. Thus arises the pun within Jiang's title: on the one hand, it literally refers to the intrusion of Japanese troops into the peaceful life of China's countryside; on the other hand, it refers to Jiang Wen's *mediated imagination* of World War II and its traumas. Since the mediation is through the war films of the 1950s and 1960s, which are mostly black and white, the punning of "devils on the doorstep" points to the making of this film in black-and-white cinematography.

Jiang Wen's film also reflects how history is not as black and white as the official version of history. In *Devils on the Doorstep*, the Japanese do not get ambushed when they come to the village searching for chickens and women; the villagers do not instantly turn into Japanese-killers either. Hatred and fear are palpable, but life goes on under the Japanese military presence. For a piece of candy, one of the innocent Chinese children in the film can inform on his friends and family; for several carts of food, the peasants can forget all about the crimes committed by the invaders. It is fitting that the story on which the film is based is titled "Shengcun" ("To survive," by You Fengwei), for the survival instinct in wartime seems to transcend hatred and national pride. *But it is precisely the survival instinct, not the nationalist sentiment, that is most revealing of the cruelty of wars and most critical of the collective violence of one nation against another.* The extreme care and caution with which Ma Dasan and his fellow villagers preserve their daily lives under the shadow of the Japanese military presence speak volumes about the fragility as well as the resilience of humanity, whose historical struggles against violence are often drowned in black-and-white versions of history that pay attention only to grand schemes of antagonism, such as class, nation, ideology, etc.

Figure 2.3.   The Japanese Rule, *Devils on the Doorstep*.

One scene in the film is revelatory. When Ma Dasan first enters the block-house to meet with the "legendary" executioner, he has to show his *liangmin zheng* (good-citizen certificate) at the gate. A primary means for controlling areas occupied by Japanese forces and their Chinese collaborators, *liangmin zheng* often appears in revolutionary films of the 1950s and 1960s for demonstrating the invaders' foolishness and communists' bravery. In *Devils on the Doorstep*, however, what we see is not Ma Dasan's defiance of the Japanese military occupation but willing acceptance of the passport-like *liangmin zheng* that both symbolically and literally makes him a subject of the Japanese imperial army. After being scrutinized and interrogated by the guards, Ma Dasan carefully puts away his *liangmin zheng* and enters the town. Signs of prosperity are everywhere: a storyteller in the plaza is celebrating Japanese rule, prostitutes are preening to attract customers, a street peddler is hawking his goods, and residents are lining up to welcome the return of the Japanese troops (fig. 2.3). The hustle and bustle is more revealing of the nihilistic nature of war violence than are direct confrontations with violence. The carefully maintained peace inside the blockhouse also indicates the inevitable affinity between violence and the state power as represented by the "good-citizen certificate."

Imagery of Trauma and Violence

The black-and-white cinematography in *Schindler's List* and *Devils on the Doorstep* certainly reveals both directors' awareness of the unusualness, if not impossibility, of the representation of trauma. It has long been debated whether trauma is representable. Some insist that trauma is irrepresentable due to its extremely private nature, despite the collective involvement of individuals in traumatic events. Bessel A. Van Der Kolk and Onno Van Der Hart argue that the traumatic memory is different from ordinary or narrative memory: the latter is a social act, but the former is inflexible and invariable. In other words, trauma cannot be placed within the schemes of prior knowledge and is not available for retrieval under ordinary conditions.[16] The distrust of narrative memory, as Ban Wang points out, often leads to the disavowal of representation. Wang writes,

> Since trauma is the shattering of cultural forms and pre-existent narrative schemes, it is [believed by some scholars of trauma to be] beyond the reach of representation. One persistent problem of trauma studies is that victims frequently feel that their experience is exclusively their own, unutterable, unsharable, and incommunicable. The trauma injures one's body and mind in a sharp stab so that no word or image can even begin to hint at the sting and intensity of the experience.[17]

If the individual trauma is not representable, then the writings of scars as collective "narratives" are merely fraudulent representations that are detrimental to true reflections on trauma. One way to get around the distrust of narrative memory, Wang suggests, is to use images to represent traumatic experience. Borrowing Robert J. Lifton's motto "We live on images," which suggests that trauma is the shattering of the inherited cultural forms that are registered through cultural imagery, Wang contends that imaging is necessary for lifting trauma "out of its invisibility and silence" and making it "a public remembrance."[18]

I mostly agree with Wang's views but not with his conclusion. Since Wang regards trauma as a singular event that has more to do with national disasters than with individual psyche, his ideas of trauma representation prioritize all forms of imaging regardless of the ideological burdens of the imagery. Thus, he praises the 1950s and 1960s Chinese revolutionary films about such national traumas as the Opium War or the Japanese invasion:

> These works have produced and transmitted more than any other medium the traumatic experience of foreign aggression and the misery of the Chinese. Sponsored by Communist ideology, the trauma was invoked to cultivate hatred and stir up patriotic passion. Yet to a mind less indoctrinated and more inclined to read against the grain, the films can offer an occasion to see how traumatic traces of history seep or break through the triumphant, heroic narrative.[19]

What Wang has failed to see in these didactic communist films are the ways in which ideology manipulates representation in order to construct a national myth of class hatred and necessary violence against enemies of revolution. The manipulation is possible due to the *non*-singular nature of trauma. Freud's original definition of trauma, dwelling on the concept *Nachträglichkeit* (deferred action), insists that the past infantile experience of trauma becomes available through a deferred act of understanding and interpretation triggered by a much later event. Ruth Leys agrees with Freud's rejection of a "straightforward causal analysis of trauma according to which the traumatic event assaults the subject from the outside," but she also argues that such outside events as war are nevertheless relevant to traumatic experiences, which should be understood not only as the working of the interior.[20] In other words, neither external traumatic shock nor internal anxiety of early castration should be excluded from our understanding of trauma. The temporal gaps between the two components of trauma leave room for false suggestion or hypnotic manipulation, which often leads to either false accusations of a nonexistent childhood traumatic event or hatred of a party held responsible for adulthood suffering.

Jiang Wen's *Devils on the Doorstep* is different from the revolutionary war films; it is, in fact, a parody of the heroic codes in those films. Ma Dasan is an antihero, worrying about his affair with a widow instead of devoting himself to restoration of national pride. So are his fellow villagers, who are too ignorant, stubborn, or selfish to come up with a feasible plan for saving the village. But their ignorance and their inability to save their own lives under the pressures of both the Japanese and the communist guerrillas lay bare the fundamental problems of violence: violence is ultimately indiscriminate and volatile, picking its victim randomly and unexpectedly so much so that the victim is left utterly defenseless; violence, endorsed by and inherent within the state, goes far beyond physical harm into the realm of psychological pressure that controls, monitors, and disciplines the human subjects of the state. We all feel for Ma Dasan, because the psychological pressure is far more difficult to bear than actual physical violence.

The revolutionary films also draw attention to violence, but they safely contain the violence in the antagonism between imperialist atrocity and revolutionary heroism. The psychological pressure of violence is annihilated by the logic of revolutionary struggle dwelling on the notion of physical battles and sublime goals. Jiang Wen's parody turns the sublime into the mundane, the physical into the psychological, and the heroic into the quotidian, so that his representation of war trauma is "infected," in Wang Ban's words, with violence as an actual and palpable force penetrating one's deepest psyche.

Only by so doing can we truly understand how the heroic narrative of history is broken through by trauma.

The Great Wall and the Modernization Projects

The heroic narrative of Chinese history finds its most compelling expression in the image of the Great Wall. The symbolism of the Great Wall is manifold: the unity of China, the resilience and diligence of the Chinese people, struggles against foreign invasions, the vast and beautiful homeland of China, intersections between China's civilized past and modernized present, etc. Among all these symbolic associations, "China" is always at the center. Nationalism is what has given the Great Wall such a prominent position in Chinese culture.

Recent examples of featuring the Great Wall in Chinese cinema include *Shadow Magic* (*Xi yang jing* [2001]), directed by Ann Hu, a Chinese businesswoman based in New York, and *Hero*, which is discussed in the previous chapter. *Shadow Magic* is about China's first encounter with cinema at the beginning of the twentieth century. Toward the end of the film, Raymond Wallace, a British fortune-seeker, and Liu Jinglun, an early specimen of "enlightened Chinese," begin their shooting of films about "local people and local scenes" along the Great Wall. Exhilarated by the beauty of the Great Wall, Wallace makes this remark to Liu: "Beautiful! What China needs is not more walls, but people like you who can bring the images of China to the world" (fig. 2.4).

Figure 2.4. "China Doesn't Need More Walls," *Shadow Magic.*

The final scenes of *Shadow Magic* and *Hero* are representative of two of the most entrenched myths about the Great Wall. First, it is commonly believed that the Great Wall was first built by Qin Shihuang and rebuilt by the Ming government on the original Qin site. The significance of such a belief lies in the sheer length of historical time that the Great Wall endured: the more ancient the wall, the more relevant it is to the notion of a unified and time-honored Chinese culture. Second, the Great Wall is so familiar to every Chinese that it has become part and parcel of the *natural* landscape of China. In other words, the Chinese normally do not think of the Great Wall as something manmade, but as an integral part of the mountains and the rivers of China that have existed for eternity. But, as I have mentioned in the previous chapter, according to a study by Arthur Waldron, the Great Wall is actually a cultural and ideological construct of modern China. The very claim that Qin Shihuang initially built the Great Wall could not be supported by archeological evidence.

Jiang Wen must have had similar doubts about both physical and symbolic myths of the Great Wall. Otherwise, he would not have deliberately chosen Xifengkou, a run-down segment of the Great Wall, as the main shooting site for the film. Xifengkou is significant in modern Chinese history; it has become a symbol of the Chinese people's heroic determination to drive out the Japanese invaders ever since the famous Xifengkou battle, in which a group of outnumbered Chinese troops fought to the death. At the foot of the Xifengkou Great Wall is Panjiakou Reservoir, another site rich in symbolic associations (fig. 2.5). A crucial part of the "Leading the Luan River into

Figure 2.5.   Japanese Warship on Panjiakou Reservoir, *Devils on the Doorstep*.

Beijing and Tianjin" project that was intended for relieving the severe water shortage in the capital area, Panjiakou Reservoir has been labeled the "Great Wall of the New Era." In fact, the "underwater Great Wall," referring to both the segment of the Xifengkou Great Wall submerged in water and the symbolism of the reservoir project, is touted as the major tourist attraction of Panjiakou. Upon closer examination, however, these two sites' symbolic significance of historical heroism and of China's modernization is very much problematic. Hiding themselves inside the Great Wall, the Chinese troops did fight heroically and successfully against the Japanese in Xifengkou. The Japanese, however, easily found a gap, moved around it, and surrounded the Chinese army before eliminating it. Xifengkou is in this sense a tragic witness to its own uselessness and to the military impotence of China not only in World War II but also for as long as the Great Wall is said to have existed. As for the "waterway Great Wall," the Luan River project is already a failure, unable to answer Beijing's desperate need for water. The expensive project now reminds people not of the great achievement of China's modernization but of the ecological disaster that relentless modernization and industrialization have wrought on northern China.

In *Devils on the Doorstep*, the Great Wall and the reservoir are indeed reminders of the humiliations China suffered during the war. That Ma Dasan hides the POWs inside the Great Wall is an act of parody and desublimation, inverting the chief function of the wall, namely, to accommodate a large number of troops. The reservoir, in the meantime, becomes an ideal port for Japanese battleships and a swimming pool for Japanese soldiers who flex their muscles as they prepare to kill the innocent and emancipated villagers. The beauty of the Great Wall and of the reservoir turns into an impressive background for the Japanese occupation of China. Due to the antiheroic nature of the film's narrative, the sense of humiliation brought by the Great Wall in the background is apparently intended not so much for inspiring national pride as for reflecting upon the symbolic construction of the Great Wall.

Coda: Sino-Japanese Relations and Transnational Reflection on Violence

Already a controversial figure in China, Jiang drew more criticism after the production of *Devils on the Doorstep*. First of all, the film was screened in Japan but not in China. Second, it was disclosed, initially by the Japanese media, that Jiang visited the Yasukuni Shrine several times before 2002.[21] The Yasukuni Shrine is Japan's national memorial, enshrining the spirits of Japanese soldiers who fell in domestic and foreign wars. It draws constant criticism from China and South Korea for housing the souls of war criminals who committed atrocities during Japan's occupation of China, Korea, and other parts of Asia in the Second World War. Frequent visits to the Yasukuni Shrine by Japan's former prime minister, Junichiro Koizumi, have been viewed as dangerous signals of the revival of Japanese ultramilitarism and the Japanese government's unwillingness to atone for war crimes committed by Japan against Asian countries. The tension was running especially high when anti-Japanese protests occurred in major Chinese cities in early 2005.

Jiang understood the seriousness of the matter. With his usual arrogance in front of the news media, he defended himself by saying that his trips were only for research purposes. Yet he mentioned on several occasions how he purchased a well-crafted Japanese sword at the shrine and how he intended to compare the meek and weak Chinese national character with the strong and masculine Japanese national character. Paying tribute to the Yasukuni Shrine revealed to a great extent Jiang's masculinist mentality and its linkage to a discourse of Chinese modernity that is based on a desire to empower the nation and to strengthen the Chinese body.

Partly due to Jiang's implicitly sympathetic portrayal of the masculinity of Japanese militarism, *Devils on the Doorstep* became a box office hit in Japan. The publication of Kagawa Teruyuki's autobiographical account of his collaboration with Jiang Wen brought further attention to the film and its production.[22] In the Japanese media and on Internet bulletin boards, the overwhelming feeling is that, compared to other Chinese films, Jiang's portrayal of Japanese soldiers is realistic and unpropagandistic and that the film is more about exposing universal human nature than about criticizing Japanese brutality. One viewer wrote:

> The prime minister will definitely not say something like "I was touched" after he watches this film. The film is a masterpiece about a war in which Japan was involved. We Japanese should appreciate that a Chinese director made such a great film. It has gone far beyond the category of "antiwar" films. It is a great film that portrays lovely yet ugly human nature, from which we have no way out.[23]

While this viewer criticizes the Japanese prime minister for neglecting the atrocities committed by the Japanese military, he or she also voices the Japanese majority opinion that regards the war as bilateral, involving both Japan and China, but not as a violent and brutal invasion deliberately and methodically planned by Japan. It is widely held in Japan that the brutality of Japanese soldiers during their occupation of China exposes the ugly side of all human nature, not something limited to the Japanese. Jiang's arrangement for the dramatic turn of events during the banquet seems to provide strong support to the theory of universal human nature.

It is unfortunate that there is no mention in the Japanese media of the irony in the massacre scene, which is accompanied by the voice-over of Emperor Hirohito's radio announcement of Japan's unconditional surrender. In the speech, Hirohito does not acknowledge Japan's defeat, nor does he convey any feeling of remorse. He says only that, if Japan does not surrender, "all of humanity will suffer." The surrender, in other words, appears to be a heroic act that sacrifices Japanese interests for the sake of humanity. The hypocrisy and the refusal to reflect on war crimes committed by Japan would have been harder to detect if the speech were not juxtaposed with the senseless killings of Chinese villagers. If the previous sections of the film are indeed about human nature, about violence, cowardice, bravery, greed, subordination, and kindness, the section juxtaposed with Hirohito's speech clearly indicates that the violent killing is premeditated, state sponsored, and executed in cold-blooded fashion. That most Japanese moviegoers fail to recognize Japanese war crimes attests to the intricacy of the violence of representation and to the frequent misinterpretation by nationalism of transnationally circulated electronic images. What Jiang Wen's film provides is a chance to reflect on both the social violence and the violence of representation in a transnational context.

Notes

1. As Adorno suggests, the film is irreducibly and inherently sociological because society projects onto the film far more directly on account of the objects than onto other forms of representation, such as painting or literature. "There can be no aesthetics of the cinema, not even a purely technological one, which would not include the sociology of the cinema." Theodor Adorno, "Transparencies on Film," in his *The Culture Industry* (New York: Routledge, 2001), 182.

2. One of the most common defenses for the use of violence is to assert necessity, emphasizing that a certain violent act is but a means to an end. The means is justified as long as the end is just. The prevalence of this argument in the contemporary world often results in acts of extreme violence such as suicide bombing, genocide, and invasion of other countries, as well as evangelical Christianity's deliberate insults to other religious beliefs. The greater the perceived cause, the more damaging the violent act. There seems to be no ending to any kind of violence as long as violence is expressed in terms of means versus ends, because the ends are open to interpretations from all perspectives and subject to ideological manipulations.

The rhetoric of means versus ends is bound in the realm of law and justice, as Walter Benjamin pointed out long ago. In Benjamin's analysis, the law is first referred to as natural law, which, "recently rekindled by Darwin's biology," "regards violence as the only original means, besides natural selection, appropriate to all the vital ends of nature." The law is also understood as positive law, which "sees violence as a product of history" instead of a product of nature. Despite their fundamental difference, both natural law and positive law are caught in the circular logic of means versus ends. Only by locating violence outside the realm of law and justice, as "pure immediate violence," Benjamin argues, can mutually independent criteria of just ends and justified means be established. Divine power always exerts such "pure immediate violence," which, precisely due to its immediacy and absoluteness, can no longer be rationalized as means serving ends. Walter Benjamin, "Critique of Violence," in his *Reflections*, ed. Peter Demetz and trans. Edmund Jephcott (New York: Schocken Books, 1978), 278. Benjamin falls short of locating where divine violence strikes, except asserting that revolutionary violence is the ultimate evidence for the possibility of unalloyed and immediate violence.

3. See Lydia H. Liu's *Translingual Practice* (Stanford: Stanford University Press, 1995), especially chapter 4 (103–27), for an insightful discussion of Xiangzi as a specimen of *Homo economicus.*

4. As a sign of the rise of Chinese cinema in the twenty-first century, the 2000 Cannes Film Festival was dominated by Chinese-language films. Besides *Devils on the Doorstep*, Wong Kar-wai's *In the Mood for Love* won two prizes, including the Technical Jury Prize and Tony Leung's best-actor award. Edward Yang won the best-director award for *Yi Yi.*

5. See Philippe Piazzo's interview of Jiang Wen for *Le Monde*, March 14, 2001. It appears in *Wo de sheyingji bu sahuang: Shengyu 1961–1970 xianfeng dianyingren dang'an* (My camera does not lie: Profiles of Chinese avant-garde filmmakers born in the 1960s), ed. Cheng Qingsong and Huang Ou (Beijing: Zhongguo youyi, 2002), 93–94.

6. See Cheng Qingsong and Huang Ou's interview of Jiang Wen in *Wo de sheyingji bu sahuang*, 75–76.

7. *Wo de sheyingji bu sahuang*, 75.

8. See Richard James Havis's interview of Jiang Wen for *Moving Picture* (http://www.filmfestivals.com/cannes_2000/official/guizi/htm [accessed January 13, 2003]).

9. This is a term used by C. T. Hsia for describing the tendency of using literature as the exclusive weapon for exposing China's suffering at the hands of Western imperialism and Chinese feudalism. C. T. Hsia, "Obsession with China," in his *A History of Modern Chinese Fiction* (New Haven: Yale University Press, 1971), 533–54. In practice, the obsession with China demanded that May Fourth intellectuals rely on so-called hard-core realism, which, as David Der-wei Wang interprets, means "a raw, even brutal exposé of Chinese misery that spurns pretensions, aesthetic or intellectual." The obsession with China has more negative than positive significance: "While this obsession has generated a moral ethos rarely seen among other national literatures, it has also enticed writers into ideological fetishism, one that makes China sanction

their unwillingness or their inability to deal with issues beyond immediate political concerns." David Der-wei Wang, "Afterword: Chinese Fiction for the Nineties," in *Running Wild*, ed. David Der-wei Wang and Jeannie Tai (New York: Columbia University Press, 1994), 253. At the core of such obsession are both nationalist sentiments and teleological attitudes toward literature.

10. *Wo de sheyingji bu sahuang*, 72–73.

11. Andrew Jones, "The Violence of the Text: Reading Yu Hua and Shi Zhicun," *Positions* 2 (Winter 1994): 593. Jones's analysis of May Fourth "representationalism" was inspired by Theodore Huters's article "Mirages of Representation: May Fourth and the Anxiety of the Real," in *Chinese Literature and the West: The Trauma of Realism, the Challenge of the (Post)Modern*, ed. Theodore Huters and Xiaobing Tang (Durham, NC: Asian/Pacific Studies Institute, 1991), 12–40.

12. David Der-wei Wang, *Fictional Realism in 20th-Century China*.

13. *Wo de sheyingji bu sahuang*, 75–76.

14. For a thorough critique of American multiculturalism, see Slavoj Žižek, *The Ticklish Subject* (New York: Verso, 2000).

15. The amusement with Japanese soldiers' "stupidity" and "vulnerability" does not fade away with the high Maoist propaganda. A recent Chinese film, *Freeze!* (*Juqi shou lai* [2005]), depicts Japanese soldiers in an even more farcical and stereotypical way. The cruelty and violence of the war are laughed away in this frivolous and lighthearted treatment of historical trauma.

16. See Bessel A. Van Der Kolk and Onno Van Der Hart, "The Intrusive Past: The Flexibility of Memory and the Engraving of Trauma," in *Trauma: Explorations in Memory*, ed. Cathy Caruth (Baltimore: The Johns Hopkins University Press, 1995), 153–60.

17. Ban Wang, "Historical Trauma in Multi-National Cinemas: Rethinking History with Trauma," *Tamkang Review* 31 (Autumn 2000), 31.

18. Wang, "Historical Trauma," 35.

19. Wang, "Historical Trauma," 36.

20. Ruth Leys, *Trauma: A Genealogy* (Chicago: University of Chicago Press, 2000), 20–21.

21. See Sohu bulletin board (http://yule.sohu.com/37/35/earticle164533537.shtml) (accessed January 19, 2006).

22. Kagawa Teruyuki, *Chugoku Miroku: "Oni ga Kita!" Satsuei Nikki* (The shadow of devils in China: Diary during the making of *Devils on the Doorstep*) (Tokyo: Kinema Jyunposha, 2002).

23. See *Japan Times* bulletin board, http://www.japantimes.co.jp/info/jtbulletinboard.htm (accessed January 3, 2005).

CHAPTER THREE

"My Camera Doesn't Lie": Cinematic Realism and Chinese Cityscape in *Beijing Bicycle* and *Suzhou River*

We are lifted out of "Realisms" by realism itself into a world of simple comparisons: for instance, are we not in search of our dignity? And does this not come to us by means of our work which is our justification and our basic worth?

—Arthur Miller, on Vittorio De Sica's *The Bicycle Thief*

People walk on the street alongside the river. They walk across the bridges. They wash their clothes and cook their food on the boats. Polluted river, floating garbage, deserted and dilapidated buildings. This is the true face of life. The opening scene of the film is like the first narrative sentence of an article. I hope this sentence can convey my true impression of Suzhou River. My camera doesn't lie.

—Lou Ye, on his film *Suzhou River*

On March 17, 2003, Sun Zhigang, a 27-year-old college graduate newly employed by a fashion design company in the city of Guangzhou, went for a stroll. He never returned home. A week later, his body turned up in a Guangzhou hospital, where an autopsy showed massive damage to his internal organs. The Guangzhou Security Bureau explained that Sun was arrested for failing to present his residence card and that he died of a sudden illness after he was transferred to the Guangzhou Custody and Repatriation Detention Center (*shourong qiansong zhan*). But it was soon disclosed through the Internet and then the official media that Sun was actually beaten to death. The public outrage spread so quickly that the government had to acknowledge the true cause of Sun's death and sentence several detention center employees to death.

Sun's death brought China's national attention to the extrajudicial detention system, which was reorganized around the early 1990s for "preserving urban beauty and neatness" by having the ability to quickly repatriate the country's floating population of migrant laborers whenever deemed necessary. Sun's case was only the tip of the iceberg. It was reported, for instance, that there was widespread police-enforced kidnapping for ransom within the detention system.[1] Under heavy criticism by international human rights activists and China's own citizens, the government finally began to address issues related to the detention system and adopt less harsh measures on repatriation. The real issue of social gaps, however, was never mentioned during the trial or in public opinion. Online discussions and public media mainly focused on Sun's identity as a well-educated up-and-comer, giving the impression that the government crackdown on detention centers would not have happened if the dead man were a real migrant laborer from the countryside. In fact, there must have been many similar cases of severe physical abuse throughout the nation's detention centers, but none of them drew any attention until the abuse happened to a college graduate.

The floating population, despite its indispensable role in providing cheap labor for China's rapid urbanization, has become the most heavily exploited in contemporary Chinese society. The migrant workers are disliked by everyone. The government is weary of their unruliness, mobility, and propensity for petty crimes; city residents regard them as untidy, dirty, and incompatible with the glowing cityscape; even their fellow villagers are often jealous of their proximity to urban wealth and culture. They are China's gypsies. While they can never become legal city residents, they or their children have been provided a way out: education as the ladder for upward mobility. In Sun's case, he was born in a small village in Hubei; college changed his fate by making him a city resident. His being beaten to death was therefore especially agonizing, not only for his friends and family, but also for a general public whose value system is deeply rooted in the rhetoric of improving one's *suzhi* (quality) through education. After all, Sun still did not manage to slough off his peasant skin; without proper identification, he was easily mistaken for his former self and suffered a tragic fate "befitting" a country rustic.

The floating population was the invisible presence in Sun's tragedy. China's dominant discourse of *suzhi* gives so much emphasis to the "after" of social ladder climbing that the "before" is deemed nonexistent, even though four out of five Chinese still live in the countryside. *Suzhi*, as Ann Anagnost defines, appeared in the new postsocialist discourses of social distinction and the discursive production of "middle class"-ness. Its sense "has been extended from a discourse of backwardness and development (the quality of the masses) to encompass the minute social distinctions defining a 'person of quality' in practices of consumption and the incitement of a middle-class desire for social mobility."[2] There are two exemplary figures in the discourse of *suzhi*: "The body · of the rural migrant, which exemplifies *suzhi* in its apparent absence, and the body of the urban, middle-class only child, which is fetishized as a site for the accumulation of the very dimensions of *suzhi* wanting in its 'other.' "[3] Significantly, both figures have become the focus of cinematic representation for contemporary Chinese filmmakers. Noteworthy examples include Zhang Yimou's *Not One Less* (*Yi ge dou bu neng shao* [1999]), Wu Wenguang's *Dance with Farm Workers* (*He min gong tiao wu* [2002]), and Wang Xiaoshuai's *So Close to Paradise* (1999) and *Beijing Bicycle* (2001). While Zhang Yimou reinforces in his film the rhetoric of social progress and upward mobility through education,[4] Wang Xiaoshuai and his fellow Sixth Generation directors draw attention to the very discourse of *suzhi*. Through representing the "awkward" body movement typical of "country bumpkins" and physical pain suffered by migrant laborers, these young directors often reveal the corporeal politics inherent of *suzhi* based on which postsocialist codes of value are established and articulated.

In this chapter, I analyze Wang's *Beijing Bicycle* and Lou's *Suzhou River*. Both films show details of contemporary urban experience through the eyes of a courier. The former is situated in Beijing, the latter in Shanghai, the two most important and best-developed metropolises in early twenty-first-century China. Both Wang and Lou insist on representing the cityscape in realist style. Lou Ye's claim that "my camera doesn't lie" has even been regarded as the collective rubric for all Sixth Generation directors, after this phrase was used as the title for both a book of interviews and a documentary about these young filmmakers.[5] The realism, however, is simultaneously undermined by the directors' obsession with figures living on the margins of the city. The real in contemporary China is most intimately related to such urban facades as skyscrapers, speed, progress, glamor, a glossy image, and a casual Westernized lifestyle. The floating population, though an inherent component of the urban picture, is supposed to remain floating, quickly passing by or being "repatriated" from the cities. Its members are not part of the realist scene, which, strictly speaking, must represent the essential, not the fleeting, moments of social life.[6] The marginal figures in Wang's and Lou's films choose to stay, to stubbornly haunt the urbanites, so much so that the urban and rural differences in value judgment are intensified. Following Ann Anagnost's reading of value and body in contemporary China, I argue in this chapter that not only the exploitation of the floating population but also the realist cinematic representation of postsocialist China is based on the classical capitalist scenario of surplus value extraction. Only by linking representation with the *suzhi* discourse and with principles of economic transaction can we begin to understand the true cause of Sun Zhigang's death: *not the physical violence but the institutionalized and symbolic exclusion of the floating population from the city that it built.*

Camel Xiangzi and the Bicycle Thief of the New Era

Beijing Bicycle tells a story of changing images: how the last remaining block of the old Beijing serves as a physical reminder of Beijing's transformation into a world inhabited only by monstrous high-rises, how the migrant laborer struggles to gain either monetary or symbolic capital by imitating the urban resident, and how Beijing's new youth manage to catch up with the latest fashions in New York or Tokyo. The film opens with an interview in which country boys with red cheeks, unkempt hair, and dirty faces are interrogated by a rude voice apparently belonging to a Beijing native. In the very next scene, their hair has been neatly cut and their faces washed. Wearing new khaki uniforms and standing beside new mountain bikes, they have been instantly transformed into sharp-looking employees of a modern fast-delivery company. As their manager proclaims, their image has become the company's image from the moment they put on the company's uniform. They must appear neat, young, energetic, and highly efficient. In other words, they must no longer look "rural," which is incompatible with Beijing's speed and urban facade. "From now on," the manager concludes, "you are all Camel Xiangzi of the New Era."

Xiangzi is one of the most memorable and best-known fictional characters in modern Chinese culture. Created by Beijing's native writer Lao She (1899–1966) in the novel *Luotuo Xiangzi* (*Camel Xiangzi* [1938]), Xiangzi has become an icon symbolizing the mentality and hardships of Beijing's lower-class citizens. Born and raised in a village, Xiangzi comes to Beijing to look for a job after losing both his parents. He quickly becomes a skillful rickshaw puller. He cares about his image, always making sure that his rickshaw is fast yet steady, like a perfect extension of his young, tall, and strong body. His simple dream of owning a rickshaw, however, is repeatedly crushed by vagabond soldiers, illnesses, political persecutions, or simple misfortune.

Beijing inhabitants often jokingly compare themselves with Xiangzi.[7] Their lighthearted comparisons, however, bespeak more dignity and pride as a Beijing resident than humiliation suffered by a migrant laborer. The true resemblance is between Xiangzi and Gui, one of the bicycle couriers in *Beijing Bicycle*. Gui is excited by his job and by the mountain bike assigned to him. He rides fast, with his head lowered against the wind, passing every bike rider on his delivery routes to fancy hotels, high-rise apartment buildings, shining office complexes, or luxurious public entertainment places. Like Xiangzi, Gui is meticulous in keeping records, dreaming about the day when he finally can have full title to the mountain bike. Just as fate would have it, the bicycle is stolen when Gui nearly achieves his goal. He loses his dignity, begging to save his job, and wandering around Beijing in tattered clothes to look for the lost bicycle. Eventually, Gui is lucky enough to find it, only to be unwittingly involved in fights among local youths, who vent their anger on his bicycle. At the end of the film, Gui, badly beaten, carries the broken bicycle on his shoulder and limply crosses the street in front of an army of bicycle riders. There is no hope for Gui. Lao She's conclusion of Xiangzi's saga seems also to speak for Gui: "Handsome, ambitious, dreamer of fine dreams, selfish, individualistic, sturdy, great Xiangzi. . . . No one knows when or where he was able to get himself buried, that degenerate, selfish, unlucky offspring of society's diseased womb, a ghost caught in Individualism's blind alley."[8]

Despite Lao She's tone of exaggeration and cynicism, Xiangzi's tragedy does have everything to do with individualism, namely, the desire for upward mobility and individual expression that came into existence during capitalism's initial phase of primitive accumulation. Heavily influenced by Charles Dickens, whose novels mostly hinge upon aspirations and unfulfilled promises of individualism,[9] Lao She saw Xiangzi as a *Homo economicus* who, as Lydia Liu puts it, mistakes "the symbol of [capital's] slavery for a promise of liberation."[10] To say that Xiangzi is a capitalist, however, is as farfetched and laden with anxieties of belated development as to say that China was once or had the potential to be a capitalist society. Fitting China's historical trajectories into Marxist phases of Western societies' linear development invalidates China's historical specificities. What Lydia Liu is able to achieve in her analysis of Camel Xiangzi is going beyond simple economic terms and understanding Lao She's writing techniques based on borrowed free indirect speech in terms of "translingual practice," through which Lao She provides self-reflexive interpretations of his own realist writing. Lao She's *Homo economicus* is therefore understood as more of a symbolic configuration of an economic being sensitive to his own image than as an awkward mimicry of Dickensian individualists.

Similar to how Lao She was both indebted to and self-reflexively critical of Dickens in cross-cultural dialogues, Wang Xiaoshuai has revealed in *Beijing Bicycle* the influence of Italian Neorealism in general and De Sica's *The Bicycle Thief* (1948) in particular. Gui resembles Xiangzi in his hopeless desire to own a bicycle; he also reminds the audience of Ricci, the everyman in postwar Rome desperately struggling for the most basic needs and failing in the most miserable yet spectacular way. The audience is led by Gui, determined and

Figure 3.1. Beijing's Street Scene, *Beijing Bicycle*.

desperate as Ricci is in finding the stolen bicycle, through a Beijing that is decentered and bewildering like a giant labyrinth. Wang Xiaoshuai's long takes, in the typical Neorealist fashion, follow Gui's eyes and create some of the most memorable moments ever produced in cinematic representations of Beijing. One of the scenes, for example, shows the various ingenious ways Beijing's common folk make use of bi- and tricycles: carrying a refrigerator on the back rack of a bicycle, with one person pushing the bicycle while another holds the refrigerator, or transporting a big armoire on a tricycle, which miraculously also carries a man who pastes himself onto the armoire to balance the entire load (fig. 3.1). Accompanied by the simple yet memorably rhythmic music, these realistic location shots give the city of Beijing a strong tinge of lyricism and nostalgia. These shots are similar to those used by De Sica, who, in Arthur Miller's words, relies on "a humane view of life" to confront yet lyricize the Rome lying in postwar ruins.[11] Both main characters, Gui and Ricci, were played by nonprofessional actors for maximum realistic effect.

While *Beijing Bicycle* resembles *The Bicycle Thief* in many aspects, including theme, style, realism, and preoccupation with cityscape, Wang Xiaoshuai nevertheless reflects on and challenges cinematic realism in his film. *The Bicycle Thief* represents the peak of high modernism, as indicated in its explicit questioning of the absurdity of life that is every bit Kafkaesque. Although one can roughly recognize the causes of Ricci's hardships in terms of wartime destruction, it is impossible to pinpoint the specific reasons for Ricci's plight. Bureaucracy, remnants of fascist propaganda, the church, superstition, the high crime rate, uneven wealth distribution, and apathy are all implicitly criticized in De Sica's film, but none is directly related to Ricci's misery. Rather, it is fate that overwhelms Ricci. This is what classical realism is about: a reality that becomes not only the setting, the aura, but also the opponent against which an individual takes action; an antagonism, not between social classes or characters, but between an individual and fate, which exists only in representations of providential chances; a truth that, instead of clarifying anything specifically truthful, forms an emotive field through which angers, frustrations, motivations, and joys are instigated, channeled, articulated, or intensified.

Ostensibly, *Beijing Bicycle* has all these realist elements: the urban milieu, Gui's disorientation in the cement jungle, his agonizing journey in finding his bicycle, his getting caught in the middle of random violence, and so on. But the appearance of another protagonist, Jian, in a transnational culture, brings the end to all these high modernist motifs. The logic of transnationalism does not necessarily make *Beijing Bicycle* postmodern, as if De Sica's classical realism becomes subject to playful parody and pastiche for the sake of purely formalistic maneuver. Rather, it highlights the transcultural circuit of exchange and brings the question of value back into realist representation, thereby providing possibilities for a critique of the realism that tends to be manipulated by various ideological ends, including that of postsocialism.

The Transnational Circuit of Value

Unlike Gui, for whom the bicycle is his livelihood, Jian and his friends need mountain bikes for recreational purposes. A 17-year-old student at a vocational school, Jian has cycling magazines and Tour de France posters beside his bed (fig. 3.2). But he does not own a good bicycle due to his family's

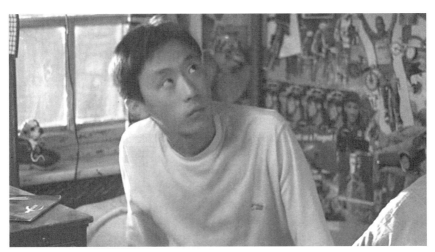

Figure 3.2. A Cycling Fan, *Beijing Bicycle*.

financial difficulties. He eventually steals his father's stashed-away cash to buy a secondhand mountain bike, which happens to be the one Gui has lost. Once Jian gains possession of the mountain bike, he is accepted by his peers. He even gains the love of a pretty female classmate. Two moments in the film signal Jian's "liberation." In the first scene, he goes with his friends to an unfinished building to perform bicycle stunts. Their joyful howling and yelling reverberate in the empty building, which overlooks an old section of Beijing, a position that foreshadows imminent changes to the once-tranquil cityscape. In the second scene, Jian escorts the girl back to her home; afterward, he rides his bicycle along a segment of Beijing's Qianhu Lake, with both hands leaving the handlebars and arms outstretched. The bicycle, it seems, brings Jian instant symbolic power.

Jian and his friends cherish not only high-end bicycles but also American youth attire, which has become a symbol of China's urban wealth and cosmopolitanism. They wear baggy pants, oversized T-shirts with English-language phrases, or cycling jerseys similar to those worn by Lance Armstrong. One teenager even wears a "FUBU" shirt (fig. 3.3). None of the teenagers is aware of the cultural coding of this American clothing, most of which is associated with street and hip-hop culture. FUBU, in particular, conveys the message of "For Us by Us," an African American slogan imparting defiance and exclusivity. Taken out of their original cultural context, these clothing items become valuable only when they are subject to mimicry. Value, in other words, is not intrinsic to transnational fashions but is rather forcibly added through intricate maneuvers based on imaging, which filters off any potentially

Figure 3.3. FUBU, *Beijing Bicycle*.

subversive content from American pop culture and makes it cross-culturally desirable and thus profitable.

The ubiquitous American pop cultural icons differentiate *Beijing Bicycle* from *The Bicycle Thief*. This is not to say that the latter does not contain reflections on cross-cultural exchanges. In fact, the poster Ricci is putting up when he loses his bicycle is a close-up picture of Rita Hayworth, one of the sex symbols produced by the Hollywood dream factory in the 1940s and 1950s. As J. Hoberman aptly points out, behind this poster is an allegory of battle for the lucrative postwar European movie market between Hollywood and Europe's national cinemas.[12] But despite the poster's prominence in the film, it does not have enough support from other similar images to form an overwhelming milieu of transnationalism. The value system of *The Bicycle Thief* is still based on an implicit reference to the Truthful, the Good, and the Beautiful. Ricci's desperation comes from the deprivation of his basic worth and respect as a universal human being. This is precisely what prompts Arthur Miller to speak of the "simple comparison" with "our own search for dignity and for the basic worth of our work."

As Anagnost's summary of Gayatri Spivak's recent thinking on the concept metaphor "value" shows, value splits into "two mutually exclusive conceptions of the subject—'Truth,' 'Beauty,' 'Goodness' ('the three value spheres: cognitive, aesthetic, ethical—the realm of cultural value'), the anchors of enduring universal values (the 'value' of the canon) on the one hand and that 'slight, contentless' thing on the other, the 'mediating . . . differential which can never appear on its own' but which enables us to see the link between living labor and the commodity in exchange."[13] What De Sica's classic emphasizes are the "enduring universal values" against which an individual or Individualist tragedy of declining fortune unfolds. By contrast, Wang Xiaoshuai's film focuses on the "slight, contentless" thing, the abstract value that can be made sense of only in terms of capital's commodification of living labor, the human body, and transnational fashion.

In *Beijing Bicycle*, there are multiple links by which the value of any of the "contentless" things can be determined. The value of the bicycle for Gui counts for 30 percent of his daily labor: he earns a 20 percent share of the profit from each delivery before the accumulation of the company's share exceeds the price of the bicycle; afterward he becomes the sole owner of the bicycle and splits the profit with the company. "This is a new management model," the snobbish manager explains to the country boys, convinced that trendy technical terms will intimidate them and disguise the exploitative nature of his arrangement. The "model" is apparently based on a transplanted Fordism, emphasizing quality, efficiency, profit, and ownership sharing for maximal surplus value extraction. That this model is "new" (denoting "Western" and "capitalist") adds both symbolic and tangible value to the exploitation of the migrant laborers. It is therefore not so much the exploitation itself as the covering up of the exploitation in desirable and "urban" articulations, those which mediate living labor and the commodity in exchange, that is the actual "contentless" thing.

For Jian, the value of the bicycle is immeasurable, in terms of peer acceptance, on the one hand and calculable on the other. The money he steals from his father is meant to pay tuition for his stepsister, who has fought through the entrance examinations to get into a highly ranked middle school. Education is the first priority in Jian's family, as in almost all Chinese families. The strange equation that links the cost of education with Jian's dream of owning a mountain bike makes explicit the inherent contradictions of the postsocialist logic based on *suzhi*: better education enhances the overall quality of the nuclear family's single child, but the eventual goal of education, which is to produce capable and hedonistic consumers for luxury items such as recreational mountain bikes, tends to trigger early commodity envy that is harmful to the improvement of *suzhi*. Such contradictions bring attention to the classical Marxist theory on surplus value extraction. The endless pursuit of surplus value, according to Marxist political economy, would push the production of commodities to such an excessive and indigestible degree that production is eventually forced to shrink to the extent of periodically generating economic crises. Of course, the *suzhi* discourse is still drastically different from the logic of primitive capital accumulation. Early commodity envy is normally integrated in the image of improved and desirable *suzhi* when the commodity assumes transnational symbolic power, which, together with China's traditional valuation of education, disguises the fact that the body of the urban single child is as much an object of exploitation as that of the migrant laborer.

The similarities between Jian and Gui are highlighted by Wang Xiaoshuai through the image of the young woman played by Zhou Xun, one of China's brightest stars. Living in a fancy apartment and constantly changing fabulous dresses, she is the target of Gui's and his country relative's voyeuristic scrutiny (fig. 3.4). Clearly aware of the male gaze, she remains arrogantly silent and makes herself even more of a spectacle with her high-heeled swagger. It turns out, however, that she herself has a rural background. Serving as a maid for a well-off Beijing family, she steals clothes from her employer and pretends to be a Beijing native when she goes out. Upon learning the "truth," Gui's relative laments: "She is no better than we are! Only if I knew, I would've . . ." The undertone is that he should have raped her when she was lying unconscious in his room after colliding with Gui's bicycle or at least treated her with contempt or frivolity "befitting" her true status.

Figure 3.4.   The Beijinger Wannabe, *Beijing Bicycle*.

Gao Ping, a character in *So Close to Paradise*, another Wang Xiaoshuai film that concerns the floating population, also distinguishes himself from his fellow villagers by dressing well, smoking brand-name cigarettes, and speaking with an urban accent. To pay for their transgression of social boundaries, Gao Ping ends up dead, and the maid played by Zhou Xun is humiliated and driven out of the city. In them Wang reveals the cruel reality of the urban-rural divide as well as the pure arbitrariness of such a divide. The unexpected conclusion from this disclosure is that the divide is easily reversible as soon as the sartorial symbols of status or other status indicators (accent, attitude, bicycle, car, house, etc.) are accordingly switched. Jian is no different from Gui without his school uniform or fancy bicycle, and Gui can become Jian after he earns enough money to buy himself a new suit and use the mountain bike only for recreation. This seems to be another one of those age-old tales of mistaken social status and identity, as often melodramatically played out in Dickens's novels. What Wang Xiaoshuai has achieved, however, is going beyond the rhetoric of individualism by linking the status symbols with the *suzhi* discourse so as to reveal the arbitrary nature of the symbols and the logic of postsocialism. Like the clothing, which adds external value to the body and disguises the exploitation of the body itself, the *suzhi* discourse relies on the attachment of value to the body of both the urban single child and the migrant laborer. Underneath the clothing and the emphasis on education and quality improvement is extraction of surplus value. Sun Zhigang's tragedy only further illuminates the most brutal aspect of the urbanization founded on the *suzhi* discourse and the consistent rendering of status symbols as desirable objects.

The equation between Jian and Gui brings questions to the very realism on which Wang Xiaoshuai relies to tell his tale of urban facade and hidden miseries. As mentioned earlier in this chapter, realism is about unearthing antagonisms behind realistic social pictures, antagonisms between different social classes, between an individual and fate, or between an individual and social institutions. Jian and Gui, as it turns out, are not enemies. They suffer equally from exploitation and the desire to live beyond their means. In contemporary Chinese cinema, when it comes to realist representation of the floating population, Zhang Yimou's Not One Less and The Story of Qiuju (Qiu Ju da guan si [1992]) immediately come to mind. In both films, there is an explicit set of antagonisms. For Wei Minzhi, the heroine in Not One Less, the antagonism is between her demand for a better life and the contempt she constantly suffers from city residents. Ironically, her frustration turns to bliss when the head of a TV station comes to her rescue. For Qiuju, it is her battle with the village chief, her demand for respect against the chief's desperate clinging to power and hierarchy. Both films seem to convey a strong sympathy with the rural population, but what Zhang's cinematic realism does is to replicate the logic of oppressor against oppressed, so much so that the oppressed can easily turn into the oppressor and that stereotypes of the peasants are regenerated and reinforced. It is not surprising, therefore, that the manager of the express delivery company compares Gui with Qiuju in a tongue-in-cheek fashion: "How come you country folks are all like the stubborn Qiuju?" Gui's relentless search for the lost bicycle is easily dismissed and mocked through this comparison. By making reference to Zhang Yimou's realist classics, Wang Xiaoshuai reveals that his concern is not the rural-urban antagonism or the battle for the bicycle between Gui and Jian but rather the fundamental contradiction between the floating population's persistent search for its proper social position and the effort to annihilate or trivialize its search in realist representation that paradoxically hints at a possible solution to "temporary" and overt antagonisms.

Laborer's Beijing versus Shanghai as a Natural Wonder

No matter how self-reflective Wang Xiaoshuai is on cinematic realism, he is still confined in the boundaries set by realism. Among Sixth Generation directors, only Lou Ye has shown radical visions that challenge all rules of realism. His statement that "my camera doesn't lie" is testimonial to his conscientious examination of realism and search for alternative forms of representation. Interests in form instead of content separate Lou Ye from the other Sixth Generation directors. He is, however, no less concerned with urgent social issues such as the floating population and the urban-rural divide. These issues are hidden in his representation of Shanghai's cityscape, which, in its unique historicity that is different from Beijing's, is equally revealing of the logic of postsocialism and transnationalism.

Lou Ye's *Suzhou River* opens with an impressive sequence about Shanghai's Suzhou River. The entire sequence is shot by handheld digital camera and from the perspective of a moving boat. The camera fades in with floating garbage on the river; then wobbling, like in an amateur video, it pans the riverbank and stops on a deserted old building being opened up and dismantled manually by a work crew. This is followed by a series of shots of the ugly and the dirty: an old and dilapidated factory, with a protruding chimney against the background of new and colorful high-rises; old barges; bridges with large cracks; boat people with dirty faces, numb complexions, and tattered clothes; etc. Before the fade-out, appearing in the remote background is the purplish fat belly of the Pearl of the Orient, symbol of Shanghai's economic takeoff since the mid-1990s (fig. 3.5). A voiceover accompanies these scenes:

> I often took the camera out to shoot the Suzhou River. All alone, I would drift on the river, from west to east, cutting through all of Shanghai. A century's worth of legends, tales, and memories and all of the garbage have accumulated here and made it the dirtiest river. But still, there are a lot of people here,

Figure 3.5. Pearl of the Orient, *Suzhou River*.

living off this river. Many people have spent their entire lives here. You can see them on the river. After a while, this river would let you see it all: the laborers, friendship, fathers and children, and loneliness. I once saw the birth of a baby on a barge. Another time I saw a girl jumping off a bridge. Yet another time I saw the bodies of a young couple being dragged out of the water by the police.

Both in cinematographic language and oral narrative, the film gives us an overwhelming impression of the Suzhou River as a waterway carrying unwanted artifacts and people at the bottom of society.

Often dubbed the "armpit of Shanghai," the Suzhou River does not provide a desirable angle for anyone seeking exciting urban pictures of Shanghai. The ideal angle is provided by the Huangpu River: on its west bank is the Bund, a stretch of Georgian structures that represents the colonial and sophisticated Shanghai; on its east bank is the Pearl of the Orient, symbolizing the new Shanghai. The Suzhou River, by contrast, has none of the Huangpu River's historical "glory" or contemporary wealth. It is the river of hard labor, it is Shanghai's sewage outlet, and it was the main gateway for millions of migrant laborers from the vast rural area surrounding the lone "island" of China's urban prosperity during much of the twentieth century. Although the Suzhou River is despised by Shanghai natives living in the "upper corner," traditionally of the foreign concessions area, it has provided livelihoods and safe haven for emigrants and the laborer class living in the "lower corner," which was the old "Chinese territory" connecting urban Shanghai with the rural areas.

Inspired by "a century's worth of legends, tales, and memories" associated with the Suzhou River, Lou Ye makes it clear from the outset that he is visually constructing an urban history that is different from the elitist's, colonialist's, or postsocialist's Shanghai. The new skyscrapers and the new TV Tower fade into the background; placed in visual prominence are the garbage and the dilapidated buildings. His urban history is therefore a history of ruins, of urban decay. Shanghai is in this way represented as a natural wonder, which irreversibly proceeds to death instead of cyclical regeneration. "It is fallen nature," as Walter Benjamin contends, that "bears the imprint of the progression of history."[14] For whenever history is seen in the light of nature, the events of history can be only *physically* and *concretely* absorbed in the setting as a picturesque field of ruins.

Comparing Shanghai with Beijing and other modern metropolises around the world, Xudong Zhang concludes that Shanghai is simultaneously of capitalist modernity and of natural history:

It is against the rural or precapitalist background of old China as a premodern swamp that the urban jungle of Shanghai was often perceived by its Chinese or Western residents as a dynamic vanguard of history, an island of civilization, and the ultimate embodiment of the true present of modernity. It is against a corrupted history that the vitality of Shanghai was seen as a force of nature, whose explosive energy and transforming power were expected to forcibly yank China—or a particular group of Chinese—out of the vicious cycle of tradition.[15]

The nostalgia prevalent in contemporary discourses about Shanghai precisely dwells on this dialectic between the spirit of modern technological advancement and the force of nature that can regulate itself and provide energy to a new round of modernization for China's economic takeoff. As Zhang further elaborates through a critique of Walter Benjamin and Theodor Adorno, the dialectic tends to be utilized for creating an urban illusion:

> The concept of natural history (*Naturgeschichte*), which in Benjamin and Theodor Adorno signals liberation from the anthropocentric iron cage of rationality, historicism, and subjectivism in order to envision a concrete history as dialectical nature, can also be employed for the opposite purpose of formulating a bourgeois—or any ruling class's—social utopia of the city as an aestheticized world of unmediated nature by means of which an alienated way of life is perpetuated. . . . Benjamin's insight that "it is the fallen nature which bears the imprint of the progression of history" often meets its post-1992 Chinese appropriation in the effort to identify the age of revolution with totalitarian control and "disastrous historical time."[16]

Zhang's argument is well founded, especially when we consider China's postsocialist logic that writes off the floating population and the uneducated as a temporary bridge to a prosperous today or future or as an unwanted stain in the beautiful and aestheticized urban picture featuring the new middle class. To say that postsocialism is based on a (mis)appropriation of Benjamin's vision of history, however, is inaccurate. For Benjamin, history is indeed petrified and in ruins, but its petrification does not lead to the "end of history" so that a new and rejuvenated history can be envisioned; rather, the petrification becomes an end in itself. It is allegory that arises from the ruins of history.

As a schema, allegory is, "in its visual character, not merely a sign of what is to be known but it is itself an object worthy of knowledge."[17] In other words, allegory points not only to the underlying significance of linguistic symbols but also to its own physical form, which, through its inherent visuality, does not so much "allegorize" as bear witness to the irreversible process of decay and fragmentation of history. The aesthetic gratuitousness of such a gesture determines that allegory has nothing in common with the postsocialist urban picture of energy, development, and youthfulness. Rather than allegory, it is symbol that is appropriated in the postsocialist picture.

The crucial differences between symbol and allegory lie in their attitudes regarding destruction. As Benjamin contends:

> Whereas in the symbol destruction is idealized and the transfigured face of nature is fleetingly revealed in the light of redemption, in allegory the observer is confronted with the *facies hippocratica* of history as a petrified, primordial landscape. Everything about history that, from the very beginning, has been untimely, sorrowful, unsuccessful, is expressed in a face—or rather in a death's head. And although such a thing lacks all "symbolic" freedom of expression, all classical proportion, all humanity—nevertheless, this is the form in which man's subjection to nature is most obvious and it significantly gives rise not only to the enigmatic question of the nature of human existence as such, but also of the biographical historicity of the individual.[18]

Symbol is constructive, representing the regenerative and cyclical power of nature, while allegory is deconstructive, emphasizing the eternally tragic ending of not only humanity but also the symbolic structure itself. To achieve redemption, symbol must dismiss and exclude the fleeting and the floating from the picture of progress and development. Hence arises the postsocialist logic that features realism based on symbol, using antagonisms of all sorts within fleeting social pictures to disguise the fundamental antagonism between the symbolic structure and the exclusion of the unwanted or the tarnished. Allegory, on the contrary, is about giving ontological significance to the fleeting and floating, which, in their concrete and material form, remain stubbornly indigestible in the symbolic world of postsocialist China. What allegory provides is not an opportunity facilitating postsocialist logic, as Xudong Zhang suggests, but a space for critiquing and defying the dominant ideology.

Lou Ye's *Suzhou River* is allegorical, because it seeks to present an urban history of decay and of ruins, to specifically target realism, to manifest the visuality inherent in the ruins, and to establish the "biographical historicity of the individual" through imagination. All these agenda are united in Lou's consistent questioning and exploring of the gap between narrative and camera-shot reality, between "I am lying" and "my camera doesn't lie."

Who's Lying? Or, *Suzhou River* as a Global MacGuffin

The narration of the opening scene in *Suzhou River* ends with an abrupt denial of all the words the narrator has just said about the river and its history: "Don't believe me. I am lying." After the title screen, the story unfolds, accompanied by the same cameraman's narrative voice. According to the voice, the narrator

Figure 3.6.　The Mermaid, *Suzhou River*.

makes a living as a videographer: "I shoot everything. Weddings, parties, even scenes of going to the bathroom or making love. However, if you don't like what I shot, you cannot complain. I have told you from the outset that my camera doesn't lie."

The videographer is hired by the owner of a bar, Happy Tavern, to make an "artistic" video of a blonde mermaid swimming in the bar's giant aquarium. He becomes obsessed with Meimei, the girl playing the mermaid (fig. 3.6). His camera follows Meimei everywhere: on streets, under neon lights, in the bar's dressing room, or inside her boathouse. Played by Zhou Xun, who also stars in *Beijing Bicycle*, Meimei, after taking off her golden wig and fish tail, appears jubilant, childish, and yet frequently melancholic. The narrator notices her mystical sadness: "Sometimes she would disappear for several days. No one knows where she has gone." Meimei shows unusual interest in Mada (motor), a motorcycle courier who obsessively asks every passerby about the whereabouts of his lost lover, Mudan (peony). Mada insists that Meimei resembles Mudan. The narrator, however, does not buy Mada's story. To prove his theory that Mada's story was made up, the narrator says that he can also create a similar story. His camera thus scans the street crowd and then fixes on a motorcycle rider, tracing him back to his past. "Maybe," the narrator says, "this was how things went for Mada."

In the narrator's story, Mada is hired to escort Mudan to her aunt's house whenever her father needs to bring a new girlfriend home. Mudan's father became rich through smuggling vodka from Eastern Europe. Mada and Mudan fall in love. But Mada's mafia friends want him to kidnap Mudan and hide her in a deserted building on the bank of the Suzhou River. It is the very same building that appeared in the opening sequence. Mudan cannot accept that her lover is her kidnapper and throws herself into the Suzhou River. Mada goes to prison, and rumors of a blonde mermaid in the river begin to spread. End of story.

"But wait," the narrator interrupts before the fade-out completely darkens the screen, "what if Mada comes back?" The screen lights up again, and we find Mada sitting in a barbershop near the Suzhou River. Having spent several years in prison, Mada comes back to search for Mudan. Upon seeing Meimei swimming as a mermaid, he is convinced that Meimei is none other than the reincarnated Mudan. Mada begins to follow Meimei around. Meimei initially feels offended. Then she is touched by Mada's persistence and by his romantic story. Eventually she falls for Mada and breaks up with the narrator. After Mada takes a beating from the owner of Happy Tavern, he seeks out the narrator, explaining that he is going away to search for the real Mudan. From a letter sent by Mada, the narrator learns that Mada does successfully find Mudan. But soon the narrator is summoned by the police to identify Mada's and Mudan's bodies from a double suicide scene. Meimei hurries to the scene as well, and she breaks down after realizing that everything Mada told her was true. Meimei chooses to vanish, leaving a note that challenges the narrator to search for her in the same way Mada searched for Mudan. The film closes with a scene in which the narrator is still adrift and shooting documentary footage on the Suzhou River. He states: "I am not searching for Meimei. You'd never know—the river might as well present me with the next story."

Based on the complex relationships among the characters, the film can be divided into three segments with three sets of characters: the narrator with Meimei until Mada appears in the background, Mada with Mudan until she plunges into the Suzhou River, and Mada with Meimei and Mudan. These segments appear to be completely independent of each other except for the resemblance between Mudan and Meimei. The most crucial linkage, however, is the motif of "lie." The narrator says that he is lying but that his camera does not lie; Meimei believes that Mada makes up the Mudan story, but the surfacing of Mudan's body confirms Mada's story, and the narrator says that he is making up the whole story about Mada's past so as to expose Mada's fabrication. Yet the most intriguing lie could very well be the *camera's*, which, in the most realistic way (the handheld camera's trembling and wobbling, the documentary representation of Shanghai's urban scenes, and the natural lighting) seems to confirm the intimate relationship between the narrator and Meimei. But the tension between the narrative voice and the camera constantly casts doubts on this relationship. Could it be that not only the stories about Mada but even the relationship between the narrator and Meimei are nothing but lies?

The doubt first arises because the narrator never appears in the film. We see only a shadow, presumably the narrator's, through the tinted glass when Meimei talks to someone, or two hands, extending from behind the camera to hold Meimei's face, or cigarette smoke, coming from behind the camera facing Meimei. Yet sometimes it is very clear that Meimei is talking to *herself* or patting hands with herself in a *mirror*. That the camera shoots from the improbable angle behind the mirror makes Meimei's monologues appear to be dialogues with the narrator. Meimei's dubious relationship with the owner of Happy Tavern also casts doubt on the narrator's assertion that he is Meimei's boyfriend. The explicitly voyeuristic nature of this ubiquitous camera thus suggests a strong possibility: there is no such person named Meimei in the narrator's life, nor is there a Mada or a romantic story about her. Meimei and Mada are only randomly selected from the street crowd by the panning camera, held by the narrator sitting on his balcony. The narrator makes up the entire story out of his own imagination stimulated by the urban hustle and bustle. With a carefully conceived plot, a narrative film is thus produced, but the camera's faithful representation is ultimately disruptive of the narrative, calling for questions about the narrative's truthfulness.

In his interview with Huang Ou and Cheng Qingsong, Lou Ye is asked about the narrator's invisibility. His answer follows: "I was hoping to gain a narrative balance. The relationship between Meimei and the videographer is both close and remote, both believable and dubious. This arrangement is precisely for questioning the rubric 'my camera doesn't lie.' I wanted to emphasize that the film is only part of the world that we see."[19] Rarely, if ever, has a mainland Chinese filmmaker been this conscientious about framing an entire film into the dialectic between the narrative as a coherent symbolic structure and the camera as a visual apparatus with a mechanism independent of the symbolic. The film thus becomes allegorical not only through its representation and ontologization of the ruins but also through its formalistic challenge to rules of Chinese cinematic realism that never allow self-questioning of the narrative mode and the realist content.

The tension between the narrative and the mise-en-scène in *Suzhou River* also provides an intriguing psychological or psychoanalytical aspect rarely seen in Chinese cinema. Focusing on the mirror image between Mudan and

Meimei, Shaoyi Sun correctly places Lou Ye's Lacanian implications in the context of cross-cultural reading of third world cinema. He argues that, in *Suzhou River*, Lou Ye establishes an "erased half," which is "to search for the possibility of constructing a speaking subject that is not only 'national' but also 'personal.' "[20] This practice is representative of Sixth Generation filmmakers' effort to do away with the "anxiety of China" and is made possible by the film's allegorical nature that brings forth the "biographical historicity of the individual."

Ironically, the film's tale of the individual and the allegorical or psychological also makes it "un-Chinese," breaking the image of "distinctive Chineseness" long cherished by some Western film critics. Its resemblance to Scorsese's *Taxi Driver*, Godard's *Breathless*, Kieslowski's *Double Life of Veronique*, and especially Hitchcock's *Vertigo*, for instance, prompted *Seattle Post-Intelligencer* reviewer William Arnold to label it a "shameless rip-off."[21] Indeed, as Jerome Silbergeld recognizes, there are striking similarities between *Vertigo* and *Suzhou River*—in both films "the 'reincarnated' heroine sits at her dressing table, lit by green and pink from the neon sign outside her window, accompanied by an undercurrent of melancholy string music."[22] There is, however, a crucial difference between the two, Silbergeld adds. While in Hitchcock films the technique of "MacGuffin" ("a gimmick that drives the plot but has little intrinsic meaning of its own and is quickly jettisoned once it has served its purpose") is instrumental, in *Suzhou River* "virtually the entire film is a MacGuffin."[23] What Silbergeld refers to is precisely Lou Ye's deliberate blurring between fact and fiction, a blurring that is not only important to the film's plot development but also crucial to a well-conceived self-reflection upon the making of the entire film.

Lou Ye himself acknowledges the imitative nature of his filmmaking but is quick to add: "When you actually enter the life of our generation, you will discover that the imitations by us who grew up in mimicry are actually ultimately original and creative."[24] What is radical in this statement is the frank acknowledgment of the mimic nature of Sixth Generation directors' filmmaking. This mimicry, however, is unique in its own right for its combination of self-reflexivity with social critique. That combination simultaneously deconstructs the mimicry itself and China's postsocialist logic, which insists on its originality in the "socialism with Chinese characteristics," a logic that is paradoxically none other than a disguised subordination to capitalism and globalization. As a transnational product itself (the film's postproduction work was finished in Germany with Karl Riedl's masterful editing), *Suzhou River* has taken full advantage of transnationalism in thinking cross-culturally about the technology of electronic imaging. The film is in this sense a "global

MacGuffin," making up, under the cross-cultural spectatorship, a story about love. The goal is to eventually discard its own sentimentality and to show real life on the Suzhou River, the real decaying Shanghai, indirectly.

Notes

1. See Susan Jakes, "Hostages of the State," *Time-Asia* 161, June 23, 2003.

2. Ann Anagnost, "The Corporeal Politics of Quality (*suzhi*)," *Public Culture* 16 (Spring 2004): 190.

3. Anagost, "The Corporeal Politics," 190.

4. See my article, "The Pedagogical as the Political: Ideology of Globalization and Zhang Yimou's *Not One Less*," *The Communication Review* 6 (Winter 2003): 327–40.

5. The book is *Wode sheyingji bu sahuang*; the documentary was made by Solveig Klaben and Katharina Schneida-Roos in 2003.

6. The paradox of realism throughout its development in nineteenth-century European literatures and in twentieth-century Chinese literature lies in its insistence on unearthing the "truth," the "undercurrent" beneath reality. The untidy and directionless reality, therefore, must be suppressed or "weeded out" in realist representation of reality. As Lydia Liu puts it, "realism performs its ideological script most effectively when that which is being legitimized through an appeal to the 'real' de-legitimizes that which it calls 'unreal'" (*Translingual Practice*, 110). For critical analyses of problems of realism in modern Chinese culture, see also Marston Anderson, *The Limits of Realism*, and David Der-wei Wang, *Fictional Realism in 20th-Century China*.

7. In the postscript to her study of *Camel Xiangzi*, Lydia Liu tells an anecdote about how Beijing's taxi drivers drew connections between themselves and Xiangzi. *Translingual Practice*, 127.

8. Lao She, *Rickshaw*, trans. Jean M. James (Honolulu: University of Hawaii Press, 1979), 249.

9. For Dickens's influence on Lao She, see David Der-wei Wang, *Fictional Realism in 20th-Century China*.

10. Lydia Liu, *Translingual Practice*, 119.

11. Arthur Miller's reading of *The Bicycle Thief* can be found on the back cover of the Criterion edition of the DVD released by Image Entertainment in 1998.

12. J. Hoberman, "Wheels of History," *The Village Voice*, September 30, 1998.

13. Anagnost, "The Corporeal Politics," 204.

14. Walter Benjamin, *The Origin of German Tragic Drama* (New York: Verso, 2003), 180.

15. Xudong Zhang, "Shanghai Nostalgia: Postrevolutionary Allegories in Wang Anyi's Literary Production in the 1990s," *Positions* 8 (Summer 2000): 367.

16. Zhang, "Shanghai Nostalgia," 372.

17. Benjamin, *The Origin of German Tragic Drama*, 184.

18. Benjamin, *The Origin of German Tragic Drama*, 166.

19. *Wode sheyingji bu sahuang,* 265.

20. Shaoyi Sun, "In Search of the Erased Half: *Suzhou River, Lunar Eclipse,* and the Sixth Generation Filmmakers of China" (paper presented at the Conference on China Pop Culture, University of Illinois at Urbana-Champaign, April 2002), 3.

21. Quoted in Jerome Silbergeld, "Hitchcock with a Chinese Face: Lou Ye's *Suzhou River," Persimmon* 8 (Summer 2002): 70.

22. Silbergeld, "Hitchcock with a Chinese Face," 70.

23. Silbergeld, "Hitchcock with a Chinese Face," 71.

24. *Wode shenyingji bu sahuang,* 270.

CHAPTER FOUR

Shaw Brothers' Old Cinema Excavated: From *Kung Fu Hustle* to *Goodbye, Dragon Inn*

In Kuching, Malaysia, there were two movie theaters near my grandparents' house. One was Capitol, which was always showing films by the Shaw Brothers Studio. The other was Audien, playing dialect films in Cantonese and Taiwanese, as well as some Tarzan and Godzilla serial films. Both theaters were surrounded by barbed wire. They were demolished probably seven or eight years ago. Today I still dream about these two theaters, especially Audien.

> —Tsai Ming-liang, on his childhood, in a 2002 interview

I saw *Dragon Inn* when I was eleven years old. A record-breaking hit, it impressed me the most among the hundreds of martial arts films I saw as a child. The sound of the vertical flute in the film made me feel for the first time the vastness and loneliness of the world of knights-errant. In other martial arts films, the characters fly around and tread freely on roofs and walls. Only King Hu's knights-errant walk the lonely path in desolate mountains. Some say King Hu chose a lonely and difficult road of filmmaking, but this is precisely what makes his films unforgettable.

> —Tsai Ming-liang, on his paying homage to
> *Dragon Inn* in *Goodbye, Dragon Inn*

Kung Fu Hustle and Shaw Brothers' Cinema

In the early twenty-first century, the only foreign-language cinema that consistently appeals to the American audience is the Chinese martial arts film.

From Ang Lee's *Crouching Tiger, Hidden Dragon* to Zhang Yimou's *Hero* and *House of Flying Daggers*, this wave of films has triggered a new fascination with Chinese martial arts and, by extension, with Chinese culture. This fascination is different from previous kung fu crazes propelled by the popularity of Bruce Lee's and Chang Cheh's films. Despite its cult-like following, the previous kung fu film tradition has been contemptuously called "chop fu," implying shabbiness reminiscent of carryout Chinese chop suey, low-tech and low-budget filmmaking befitting the shoddy Chinatown background, and an action style relying on quick strikes and frequent bodily contact. The new Chinese martial arts films by Ang Lee and Zhang Yimou are much more artistically and aesthetically elaborate, with big budgets and grand exterior scenes. They are intended for the international copyright competition, as I have discussed in chapter 1. More films of this sort are on their way to the American cinema market. Zhang Yimou's biggest rival, Chen Kaige, for instance, has recently finished the production of *The Promise* (*Wuji*), which is similar to *Hero* in theme and style. Another film, Tsui Hark's *Seven Swords* (*Qi jian*), was selected as the opening film for the 62nd Venice Film Festival and will soon be released in the United States.

Among the new martial arts films, there is a maverick, namely, Stephen Chow's *Kung Fu Hustle* (*Gong fu*), which is by far the highest-grossing Chinese film in China. It opened on April 22, 2005, in the United States to rave reviews.[1] It is a maverick film because Stephen Chow mocks everything that includes the culturally authentic and the cinematically authentic. His irreverence toward both traditional high culture and contemporary popular culture earns him the reputation as the king of *mo lei tou*, or nonsense that comes from nowhere and is seemingly irrelevant to the film's story. As A. O. Scott writes in his review of *Kung Fu Hustle* for the *New York Times* on April 8, 2005: "The movie snatches tasty morsels of international pop culture, ranging from Looney Tunes to Sergio Leone to *Airplane!*, and tosses them into a fast-moving blender." American critics and audiences consider Chow "lowbrow" because of this dizzying mixture of pop culture. However, Stephen Chow's fundamental stance of laughing at himself as a social underdog in order to expose social injustices afflicting the underprivileged turns his *mo lei tou* upside down and often reveals his most serious, "highbrow," and tragic sides reminiscent of Charlie Chaplin. Advertised in China as the kung fu film to supersede all previous kung fu films, *Kung Fu Hustle* nevertheless reveals itself, through Chow's serious side, as the inheritor of a great legacy in Chinese martial arts cinema. In the film, Chow dresses and looks like Bruce Lee before the final battle: white shirt, black pants, black cloth shoes, and long hair. The martial arts moves in the film are combinations of the best fight sequences in Bruce Lee, King Hu, and Chang Cheh films.

While influences of international pop culture and the entire martial arts film tradition are clearly visible, the more specific influences of Shaw Brothers' cinema are hard to detect for audiences not familiar with Hong Kong film history. But these specific influences are most crucial to digging beneath the obvious in order for us to truly understand Stephen Chow in particular and transnational Chinese cinema in general.

One aspect of Shaw Brothers' influence is based on Stephen Chow's fascination with Chang Cheh, the studio's greatest martial arts film director. Chang Cheh's impact on *Kung Fu Hustle* is not only highly visible in the action and in the mise-en-scène but also more deeply hidden in Stephen Chow's casting. The choice of Dong Zhihua to play Doughnut is significant in that Dong was Chang Cheh's favorite actor during Chang's final burst of creativity. A Beijing Opera actor who emigrated to Hong Kong in the 1980s, Dong played the lead role in Chang's last six films: *Great Shanghai in 1937* (1986), *Slaughter in Xian* (1987), *Across the River* (1988), *Ninja in Ancient China* (1989), *Hidden Hero* (1993), and *Shen tong* (1993). Dong was silent for a long time before Stephen Chow asked him to appear in *Kung Fu Hustle*. Rejuvenated, Dong shows some truly fantastic moves that combine power with precision and quickness.

Dong Zhihua is important to *Kung Fu Hustle*, but the most important impact of Shaw Brothers' cinema on this film is the site where all the actions take place: Pigsty Alley. *Zhulongcheng zhai* in Chinese, Pigsty Alley is not Stephen Chow's invention; instead, it is borrowed from a 1973 Shaw Brothers film, *The House of Seventy-Two Tenants* (*Qi shi er jia fang ke*). The year 1973 saw Bruce Lee's *Enter the Dragon* (*Menglong guojiang*) dominating the world's and Hong Kong's cinema markets. Surprisingly, however, *Enter the Dragon* was not that year's box office champion in Hong Kong. It was beaten out by *The House of 72 Tenants*, a situation comedy directed by Chor Yuen. Chor's film also is not an original creation; it is a remake of an eponymous film produced in mainland China in 1963 by Pearl River Studio. The mainland film itself is based on a popular Shanghai play from the 1940s.

The play, situated in a typical Shanghai *shikumen* housing complex, which accommodates many low-income households under one roof, satirizes the corruption of the Nationalist government. In the play, which is set in the mid-1940s, shortly before the communists drove the Nationalists out of Shanghai, the landlord and landlady of the complex conspire to sell their foster daughter to a corrupted policeman. In return, the policeman needs to help the landlord force out the seventy-two tenants so that the house can be sold for a hefty profit. The plan, however, is defeated by the tenants, who help the foster daughter and her lover escape. Despite its overt leftist ideology, the play is full of humorous moments due to its witty use of the Shanghainese dialect and its attention to the unexpected in the tight living space. Transplanting

Figure 4.1.   *The House of 72 Tenants.*

the play and the mainland film to 1970s Hong Kong, Chor Yuen created an unforgettable Hong Kong slum to replace Shanghai's *shikumen* house. Chor's film poignantly satirizes the bureaucracy of Hong Kong's colonial government and shows tremendous sympathy for the people struggling at the bottom of a deeply divided society (fig. 4.1).

Chor's film is a milestone in Hong Kong cinema history. First of all, its dialogue is predominantly in Cantonese. The Hong Kong cinema of the 1960s and early 1970s was dominated by Mandarin films, most of which were produced by Shaw Brothers by using talent originally from Shanghai. But, in 1973, "after a year in which no Cantonese pictures were produced, Shaw Brothers, which was still regarded as the king of the Mandarin film studios, took the lead in the revival of Cantonese by making and releasing *The House of 72 Tenants.*"[2] This was the beginning of the revival of Cantonese films in Hong Kong. Before long, Mandarin films faded into obscurity and Cantonese became the dominant language in the Hong Kong film industry.

The House of 72 Tenants is thus important to Stephen Chow for several reasons: (i) it revived the Cantonese films that Chow was accustomed to watching when he grew up; (ii) it was the best of the situation comedy or neighborhood dramas, a genre from which Chow learned his comic expressions and perfected his *mo lei tou* skills; (iii) it focuses on the underprivileged, the socially injured, and the abject, people on whom Stephen Chow pours all his sympathy and from whom Chow finds his laughs; (iv) it deliberately preserved the stage style in the original play and made the film's indoor studio set an aesthetic choice, similar to Hitchcock's theatrical nuances originating from his insistence on shooting on studio sets; and (v) it has created a most unforgettable site or sight of urban dwelling: the pigeonhole-like cohabitation, the everyday trifles, the laughter amid hardships, the unexpected arising out of banalities and routines, and the extraordinary among the most ordinary.

All these motifs in *The House of 72 Tenants* are present in *Kung Fu Hustle*. The murder scene that opens the film is situated on a clearly artificial set, visual prominence is given to ordinary life in the slum, and the ordinary is depicted as the place where the extraordinary dwells. Setting this film in prerevolutionary Shanghai, Stephen Chow also pays tribute to the original Shanghai play; he does not forget Chor's satires either. The lawlessness of the Axe Gang, which is based on the images of corrupt firemen in *The House of 72 Tenants*, as well as the corruption of the police and of the entire city bureaucratic system, makes us wonder if these are well-disguised references to contemporary China's political and economic reality.

In the midst of an unprecedented economic boom, China continues to base its development on two pillars: the capital program and the export industry. As part of the push for urbanization, China's real estate projects are quickly transforming its landscape and social life. Shanghai in particular has become China's window for showcasing urban construction that embodies modernization; it had more than three hundred skyscrapers in 2005, compared to only one in 1985.[3] Old *shikumen* slums are being demolished everywhere and replaced by fake *shikumen* structures such as the upscale New World (*Xin tiandi*) entertainment and residence project. Old tenants are driven out of their dwellings by the corrupted bureaucrats, law enforcement agents, and well-connected, powerful real estate companies; they often receive little compensation when their houses are demolished. Gangsters are often hired to attack and force out these tenants.[4] To a great extent, *Kung Fu Hustle* implicitly criticizes this trend of urban demolition, tenant intimidation, and government corruption. The neat and artificial commercial street at the beginning and the end of the film is stunningly similar to the New World complex; the Axe Gang members, in their business suits and in their ubiquity and brutality, are reminiscent of today's real estate bosses who profit through bribery and violence; and the slum, juxtaposed with the new streets, is representative of the polarized Chinese city in which the poor have nothing except support from each other.

The Shaw Theaters and Tsai Ming-liang

Stephen Chow relies on Shaw Brothers' cinema tradition to compete with the new martial arts films and to criticize the contemporary transformation of China's economy and politics. Tsai Ming-liang, a Malaysian-Chinese director based in Taiwan, also relies on the film history of Shaw Brothers for the purpose of addressing dire consequences of urbanization and modernization. These two directors have one thing in common: their penchant for and careful study of the history of world cinemas, especially that of Shaw Brothers. Both grew up watching the Shaw films and falling in love with the world of knights-errant. Unlike the work of Chow, however, Tsai's intertextual maneuvers based on the Shaw cinema are on a much more transnational scale and for a much smaller audience. A perennial international film festival winner, Tsai has art house appeal that is the opposite of Chow's popularity with all audiences. Tsai goes one step farther in integrating the Shaw cinema in his films: he not only engages with the Shaw cinema in terms of interfilmic linkages and intertextuality but also, in an autobiographical way typical of auteurism, records his own memories of the old Shaw theaters. Stephen Chow's filmmaking based on the integration of film history is meant to compete with Hollywood and to make his films Hollywoodized and thus profitable, while Tsai's strategy of integration is meant to challenge Hollywood hegemony on behalf of world cinema history. At the core of both directors' efforts is a fascination with "sites" (demolished residences and old theaters). While both have engaged in excavations of those demolished sites by paying tribute to Shaw Brothers films, Tsai Ming-liang is more conscientious in his consistent exploration of the meanings of the sites.

To understand Tsai's explorations, it is necessary to revisit the sites related to the Shaw brothers' business empire in Southeast Asia. Their enterprise in Hong Kong always centered on film production. But in Southeast Asia they focused more on actual "sites" as real estate. These sites include studios (the pre-WWII Shaw Studio at No. 8 Jalan Ampas in Singapore and the postwar Malay Film Production Limited), amusement parks (Big World and Great World), cabarets (part of the amusement parks), and office and residential projects (Shaw House and Shaw Towers in Singapore). Many of them have become or once were landmarks in Singapore, Malaysia, Indonesia, and Thailand. But no matter how grand the structures, they all began with Runmei Shaw and Run Run Shaw's effort to build film theaters throughout the Malay Peninsula. Owning theaters as a means to distribute films and as a form of real estate investment has always been the core business in Southeast Asia for Shaw Brothers.

In 1927, the Shaw brothers leased their first Singapore theater, The Empire, only because the highly protective local distributors refused to distribute the silent films produced in their Shanghai studio, Tianyi (Unique Film Productions). Using Singapore as their base, the brothers began to venture northward, setting up theaters in towns throughout Malaya so as to form their own distribution channels. They traveled to every small town, packing equipment in a van and setting up makeshift outdoor theaters wherever necessary. Sometimes they would retrofit Malay Bangsawan opera houses into crude theaters. Wherever film exhibition proved popular and profitable, they would build a permanent theater. With such a humble beginning, the Shaw theater chain in Southeast Asia expanded to 139 theaters in 1939. Many of the theaters were destroyed during the Japanese occupation. By 1965, the brothers were able to regain control of 130 theaters.[5] They were never satisfied, however. The theaters went through constant renovations to keep abreast of the latest film-projecting technology; old buildings were frequently torn down to allow space for newer and larger real estate developments. The Shaw Towers, for instance, were built on the original sites of Marlborough and Alhambra, two of the earliest movie houses in Singapore. From monaural sound to Dolby digital stereo systems, from hard benches to ergonomic leather chairs, from wooden shelters to state-of-the-art multiplexes housed in modern skyscrapers, the Shaw theaters were crucial to the modernization of entertainment and urbanization in Southeast Asia.

Because of the brothers' willingness to evolve with time, the physical sites based on the Shaw theaters have acquired rich symbolic meanings. Registered on these sites, besides modernity and urbanism, are capitalist adaptability, anxieties and insecurities associated with immigration, the ethnic and linguistic diversity of Southeast Asia, political and ideological struggles (Suharto's coup, for example, resulted in the Shaws' retreat from Indonesia in the mid-1960s), and transnational cultural production. By transnational cultural production, I refer to the Shaw Brothers' film-producing and -exhibiting activities that cross national borders on the one hand and adapt to local or national geopolitical specifics on the other. The site of the Shaw theater is in this sense a "contact zone," where various ethnicities (Chinese with vastly different geographical and linguistic backgrounds, Malays, Indians, etc.) mingle yet remain separated and where national and ethnic identities are forged through both cosmopolitanism and localism.[6] Take, for instance, Shaw Brothers' production of Malay films in the 1950s and 1960s. It was done to please Malaya political authorities and attract Malay audiences at the same time. The Shaws' Malay Film Production Limited was the sole creator of the so-called Golden Age of Malay Cinema, which fostered the stardom of such great actors as Tan Sir P. Ramlee and helped form national and ethnic identities in newly independent Indonesia and Malaysia. The multilingual practices of filmmaking and film distributing dismantled the dominance of English-language cinema in prewar Southeast Asia.[7] To truly understand Shaw Brothers' contribution to world cinema as well as to the unique formation of capitalist modernities of Southeast Asian nations, therefore, one should not overlook the importance of the old theater as both physical sites of cinema and symbolic sites of transnational cultural production.

It was not until recently that the sites of the Shaw theaters in particular and of the old theater in general began to be excavated, in the sense of being written into histories of the cinema and being evoked in debates on urbanization around the world. In terms of the history of cinema, the old theater is associated with a strong sense of nostalgia, whose objects of remembrance include not only the quaint and slow-paced way of life before electronic mass communication dramatically shrank temporal and spatial distances but also a narrative cinema of internal dramas and human feelings. Free from preoccupations with fast pacing or glossy photography, this cinema is drastically different from what David Bordwell terms "intensified continuity cinema" typical of contemporary Hollywood.[8] It is no coincidence that Roger Ebert holds his annual "Overlooked Film Festival" in the historic Virginia Theater in downtown Champaign, Illinois, which is Ebert's hometown. That theater, with its peeling ceiling, old-fashioned balcony, and outdated bathrooms, fits well with the foreign, retro, or indie films chosen by Ebert in a gesture defiant of Hollywood's "kiss kiss bang bang" blockbusters.

Besides cinema history, the old theater is also important to urban planning; it often becomes the centerpiece in America's "Main Street revitalization" projects, as showcased by the renovation of the Apollo Theater on 125th Street in the heart of Harlem. In Southeast and East Asia, the end of the twentieth century saw the erection of three of the tallest buildings in the world: Kuala Lumpur's Twin Towers, Shanghai's Pearl of the Orient, and Taipei 101. Singapore is not far behind in this competition to be higher, bigger, more urbanized, and more modern than the old industrial powers. Its latest project is to expand the renowned shopping district Orchard Road into the largest of its kind in the world. The purpose is to attract the nouveau riche from China and other Asian countries. One cannot forget, however, that Run Run Shaw used to rent a house on Orchard Road when he first arrived in Singapore and, together with Runmei Shaw, worked day and night in their Hai Seng Company, which was in the same area. The Shaw houses are long gone. The more demolitions there are in places like Orchard Road, however, the louder the voice of opposition. To demolish or to preserve, to modernize or to respect local traditions—arguments on these issues can be heard throughout Southeast and East Asian metropolises.

The oppositional voice may not be strong enough to slow down the relentless urbanization. But efforts to record the voice and to witness urban demolitions do signify the formation of an ethos different from that of demolition. Tsai Ming-liang's filmmaking has been a major part of these efforts. A transnational filmmaker based in Taiwan, Tsai consistently opposes urban demolitions and exposes alienation under postmodern urban conditions in all of his seven feature films (*Rebels of the Neon God* [1992]; *Vive l'Amour* [1996]; *The Hole* [1998]; *The River* [1997]; *What Time Is It There?* [2002]; *Goodbye, Dragon Inn* [2003]; and *The Wayward Cloud* [2005]) and one short (*The Skywalk Is Gone* [2004]). In these films, Tsai makes explicit his worldview and political and ideological orientation: pessimistic of the world's future, doubtful of capitalism's rosy picture of eternal development, resentful of commodification of human relations, and apprehensive of impending environmental catastrophes. His *Goodbye, Dragon Inn*, in particular, focuses on the old theater and evokes the cinematic history of Shaw Brothers to highlight the possibility of heterogeneity in transnational "contact zones."

Multiple personal and professional reasons prompted Tsai to make a film about an old theater. The most direct personal reason is that old Shaw theaters house Tsai's childhood memories in Malaysia. A Malaysian-Chinese, Tsai Ming-liang grew up in Kuching, a small town on the island of Borneo, which is more than 400 miles away from the Malaysian political and cultural center on the Malay Peninsula. Since the island is divided into Indonesian and Malaysian territories, and since it is geographically closer to Jakarta than to Kuala Lumpur, Borneo has strong Indonesian cultural flavors. Born in 1957, Tsai Ming-liang experienced the last six years of British colonial rule and the founding of the independent Federation of Malaysia in 1963. He also witnessed Singapore's break with the federation in 1965 as well as the anti-Chinese outbreaks after Suharto's coup in Indonesia. Eventually, he went to Taiwan for his college education and chose filmmaking as his career.

One would expect Tsai to experience culture shock upon his initial contact with Taiwan and Hong Kong. But he reminisced, "I instantly felt at home during even my very first trips to Taiwan and Hong Kong." Why? Because he had already become familiar with Taipei's or Hong Kong's cityscape and lifestyle from all the Shaw Brothers films he saw during his childhood. In fact, watching Shaw Brothers films in old theaters near his grandparents' house was one of the few entertaining memories Tsai has of his introverted and lonely childhood. Kuching had at least three theaters owned by Shaw Brothers: Capitol, Rex, and Lido. The young Tsai spent most of his childhood in these theaters. He was particularly impressed by Audien, which, also affiliated with the Shaw Brothers theater chain, could accommodate audiences of more than a thousand people. He gained much of his knowledge of the Chinese language and culture by watching Mandarin-language Hong Kong films in Capitol and Cantonese opera films in Audien.[9] Even now, he can easily recall how radiant the Shaw beauties were: Linda Lin Dai, Grace Chang (Ge Lan), Betty Loh Ti, Zheng Peipei, and Ivy Ling Po. He also vividly remembers how fascinated he was by the ancient Chinese world of knight-errantry and romantic love restaged in the films by King Hu, Li Hanxiang, and Chang Cheh.[10] And he constantly pays tribute to these films and stars in his own films. In *The Hole*, for instance, Grace Chang's old songs become crucial interludes that not only link reality with fantasy but also add fantastic colors and rhythms to the otherwise brutally dull and somber film.

Tsai's encounter with Chinese-language films is indicative of the importance of Shaw Brothers' Chinese-language film production and distribution to the ethnic identity of the Chinese diaspora in Southeast Asia. No matter how deeply rooted the Chinese communities were in their adopted countries, they still shared a belief in the continuity and homogeneity of Chinese culture, which was in no small part based on the images in Shaw Brothers films. Making Mandarin films in a Cantonese-speaking world about a nation no longer accessible under Mao's rule, Shaw Brothers' practice was already highly nostalgic and diasporic. Shot against a clearly artificial and expressionistic studio setting that includes out-of-proportion bridges, palaces, inns, waterfalls, and stretches of the Gobi Desert, most Shaw Brothers films, especially those *huangmei* opera adaptations, create an impression that Chinese communities everywhere share the same cultural heritage based on identical visual codes.[11]

Shaw Brothers' theater-building practices are certainly not immune from capital's relentless pursuit of surplus value. Although Shaw Brothers created a rich material culture for Southeast Asia, it has also single-handedly destroyed many of its own historical sites because of its insatiable appetite for profits. The unique materiality and rich symbolism of its old theaters, however, have become palimpsests, upon which layers of private and collective memories have been piled, memories that register the history of Southeast Asian cinemas and national cultures. The Shaw brothers' practice, representing a cinematic tradition different from that of Hollywood, bears witness to the transformation of Southeast and East Asian societies. The ingenuity of Tsai's cinematic vision lies not only in his remembrance of the old films made by Shaw Brothers but, more important, in his excavation of the palimpsest of the old theater layer by layer. In making references and paying homage to the films from the 1950s and 1960s and in remembering the Shaw theaters, Tsai is determined to reveal the "sites," unearth the urban palimpsest, point out how the Shaws' old theaters bridge geographical and temporal gaps, and bear witness to relentless urban destruction.

Remembering the Old Theater

In *Goodbye, Dragon Inn*, Tsai Ming-liang returns cinema to its material bases, such as actor, audience, film stock, theater, and film history as actual lived experience. Although the pure joy of moviegoing that he experienced in his childhood is pronounced dead due to the threat of Hollywood homogenization, Tsai's calling attention to the old theater suggests possibilities of preserving differences in cinema and in urbanization.

This is a film about an old theater. Facing imminent demolition, the old Taipei theater is in the middle of its last screening. What is being screened is *Dragon Inn* (*Long men ke zhan* [1967]), which was King Hu's second feature film. Hu made his first feature, *Come Drink with Me* (*Da zui xia* [1966]), for Shaw Brothers. Although *Come Drink with Me* was phenomenally successful, the differences between Hu's individualistic filmmaking philosophy and Shaw Brothers' efficient business model became apparent during the making of the film. Hu was then quickly lured away by Taiwan's Union Film (Lianbang dianying gongsi), which produced *Dragon Inn*, a work that maximized Hu's artistic creativity.[12] It is safe to say the innovations (nonlinear narrative structure, lavish exterior scenes, and extraordinary crowd fighting sequences) would not have been possible under Shaw Brothers' studio system, which emphasizes low budgets and quick production. By paying tribute to *Dragon Inn*, Tsai thus can achieve at least two goals: to remember the old theater associated with his antidemolition politics and his childhood memories based on Shaw Brothers' cinema and to justify his own idiosyncrasies, which cannot be tolerated in the big-studio system and in the increasingly Hollywoodized mode of film production.

There are seven significant characters in *Goodbye, Dragon Inn*: a ticket clerk in the old movie theater (Chen Hsiang-chi), a projectionist in the theater (Lee Kang-sheng), a Japanese tourist (Mitamura Kiyonobu), a gay man hanging out in the theater (Chen Chao-jung), a female moviegoer (Yang Kuei-mei), and two actors, Shih Chun and Miao Tien, who play themselves. Miao Tien and Shih Chun are major players in *Dragon Inn* (1967).[13] None of the audience, except Miao and Shih, seems to pay any particular attention to the film. While on the big screen Shangguan Lingfeng and Shih Chun are battling the evil imperial guards, whose leader is played by Miao Tien, each of the characters in the theater is minding her or his own business. Chen Hsiang-chi drags her crippled legs to every corner of the theater, including the staircases, the bathrooms, the storage room, and the projection room, places that moviegoers rarely get to see. As in most Tsai films, it is raining hard outside and there are leaking spots inside. Hsiang-chi seems to be checking on the leaks, but she is actually looking for the projectionist, on whom she has a crush. Hsiang-chi is not able to find the projectionist, who, played by Lee Kang-sheng, seems to leave and enter the projection room at will.

The Japanese tourist is interested in the old theater more as a tourist attraction than as a fully functional film theater. He wanders around, providing some of the most amusing episodes that punctuate the otherwise sullen film. In

Figure 4.2.   Shih Chun and Miao Tien, *Dragon Inn.*

the restroom, he bumps into two strange people, who choose the urinals next to him despite the near-emptiness of the spacious restroom. In a narrow corridor, he runs into Chen Chao-jung, who lends him a light and tells him that the theater is "haunted." There is a strong homoerotic tension between the two of them. At several occasions, they make the audience believe that they are about to kiss each other. Nothing happens, however. Having returned to his seat, the Japanese tourist notices a melon seed–cracking woman sitting behind him. Wearing heavy makeup, that woman, played by Yang Kuei-mei, quickly creates a big pile of shells by her feet. She drops one of her slippers inadvertently, so she bends over to pick it up. Yang's disappearance among rows of empty seats alarms the Japanese tourist and scares him away.

Sitting diagonally from each other are Miao Tien and Shih Chun. They are the most focused audience, since they are watching the film that brought both of them onto the big screen for the first time (fig. 4.2).

Watching the battle scenes, Shih Chun cannot help feeling melancholy and nostalgic. In a close-up, which is rare in Tsai's films, Shih Chun's eyes become teary and his lips tremble. After the screening, Shih Chun bumps into Miao Tien in the lobby. He shakes Miao's hand and calls him "Teacher Miao"; only those who are familiar with Taiwanese film history know that Miao Tien used to teach acting classes that Shih Chun took as a young apprentice.

Chen Hsiang-chi enters the empty theater to clean up. In a breathtaking long take, she shakily goes step by step, encircling the entire theater before exiting. Her footsteps are heard going farther and farther away from the main hall, but the camera stays. For almost five minutes, the camera freezes, focusing on the empty theater. This is when the theater becomes a visible character, the eighth as well as the main protagonist of the film: the unusual length of the empty shot forces the audience to observe the old theater down to every

Figure 4.3.   Emptied Theater, *Goodbye, Dragon Inn*.

detail; the theater, due to its emptiness and stillness, stares at the audience as if it has become animated and acquired agency. The shot also makes the audience aware of the awkwardness of their expectation of some sort of action to follow up on Hsiang-chi's exit (fig. 4.3).

The projectionist finally returns to the projection room. Seeing the peach-shaped fortune bun left by Chen Hsiang-chi, he rushes out and hops on his motorcycle. But she has yet to leave. After locking up the theater, she steps into the rain, leaving behind the giant movie bulletin board announcing the last showing of *Dragon Inn*.

In numerous interviews, including conversations with me, Tsai Ming-liang has provided many useful clues for watching this film. He explains that the theater, near his own apartment in Sanchong, Taiwan, is the site for one sequence in his previous film *What Time Is It There?*, in which a brief encounter prompts the character played by Lee Kang-sheng to change the Taipei time on all the clocks he sees to Paris time. In that particular sequence, the clock hanging in the lobby of an old theater is stolen by a young man, who uses it to lure Lee Kang-sheng into the men's room (fig. 4.4). During the shooting of the sequence, Tsai Ming-liang was frequently struck by how much the theater reminded him of Audien in his hometown of Kuching. The high ceilings, the numerous ceiling fans, and the seating capacity of 1,000 or more all evoked his childhood memories and his displeasure over the ubiquitous multiplexes symbolic of Hollywood power.[14] After completing *What Time Is It There?*, Tsai would often walk by the theater and chat with the owner. One day the

Figure 4.4.   Bathroom in the Old Theater, *What Time Is It There?*

owner told him that the theater was about to be demolished. Tsai immediately decided to rent the place for three months so that he could make a film about it. He also revealed that the film was originally intended to be a short. Bearing the title *Busan* (*Lingering*), it was to become the twin sister of *Bujian* (*The Missing*), directed by his favorite actor and career partner, Lee Kang-sheng. Combined together, *bujian busan* is a Chinese idiom, promising "be there or be square" when setting up a meeting. But when the compound is broken up into two words, twists occur: what is present is what lingers at the place in the form of the phantasmagoric. The promise of reunion turns out to be the return of the ghostly. Both films became so long that they had to be made into separate feature films. *The Missing* has a theme similar to that of *Goodbye, Dragon Inn* in condemning urban demolition, and it won the New Currents Award at the 2003 Pusan International Film Festival.

The theme of urban demolition links *Goodbye, Dragon Inn* with not only *The Missing* but also Tsai's consistent concern over the mindless and endless destruction of traces of previous life in contemporary urban centers. As Yomi Braester points out, one of the most significant details in Tsai's *Vive l'Amour* is its visual presentation of the bleak-looking Ta-an Forest Park, which was a highly controversial urban project in early 1990s Taipei. *Vive l'Amour* literally participated in the debate about the park "by attaching cinematic images to the urban change and associating it with the erasure of memory."[15] More important, Braester contends that *Vive l'Amour* is representative of a "poetics of demolition," a practice of "writing through erasure, building through tearing down, remembrance through amnesia, and identity formation through the unmaking of social ties."[16] Through this poetics of demolition, Tsai Ming-liang returns to the specificity of locales, which are simultaneously the material base of urban existence and sites for dialectics between remembrance and forgetting.

Goodbye, Dragon Inn is more extreme than *Vive l'Amour* or any of Tsai Ming-liang's other films. By drawing attention to cinema as the target of urban demolition, Tsai returns to the material base of not only urban existence but also film viewing and production as lived everyday experience.

There are several means by which cinema is reified as actual lived experiences in *Goodbye, Dragon Inn*. First, the film theater is defamiliarized. Instead of going to the theater to see films, we actually get to see the theater itself. The film projected on the big screen is but one part of the theater. There are other things that make the projection possible, things we normally overlook, since we do not bother to pay attention to the industry behind glossy Hollywood images. By setting the contrast between the projected and the projecting apparatus, or between fantasy and reality, Tsai restores cinema to the early "cinema of attraction," a term used by Tom Gunning for describing the lure of early cinema in not only the projected image but also the apparatus of projection.[17] In this cinema of attraction, the audience becomes intrigued by not so much the projected images as the stories hidden in the relationships among the projectionist, his machine, and his coworkers.

Second, the actors are brought back into reality. Nothing generates more dialectical intrigues between reality and filmic fantasy than scenes in which actors-as-ordinary-audience watch their own performance on the big screen. Not only are Shih Chun and Miao Tien watching their young selves of forty years ago; Yang Kuei-mei, Lee Kang-sheng, and Chen Hsiang-chi also leave the audience the impression that they are no different from their roles in Tsai's previous films. Lee Kang-sheng in particular, through his invariably emotionless face and thin, asexual body, has become an inscrutable surface, not much different from the smooth yet lifeless film stock on which all Tsai's films are made.

Third, the audiences, represented by the Japanese tourist as a film buff, become characters in this film of film. An ordinary moviegoer, Mitamura Kiyonobu was selected to perform this role because he is a devoted Tsai fan. His search for an "authentic" old film theater also hints at Taiwan's history as a colony of Japan; the main attraction of Ximenting, Taipei's famous theater district, is the largely intact Japanese architecture from the colonial period.

Last but not least, reality is clearly framed in cinematic representation. The tension between performance and performer, or between cinematic fantasy and reality, is doubled in this film of film. Normally, cinematic reality creates a peculiar illusion of immediacy through the cinematic setting in which the audience seems to have unimpeded communication with what is being screened. But Tsai's introduction of a ghostly aura breaks the cinematic illusion of immediacy, suggesting that the phantasmagoric is inherent in the real.

The Theater That Haunts and Lingers

Goodbye, Dragon Inn does not have its own score. The only music is the sound of the vertical flute from the projected film *Dragon Inn*. In the nearly empty theater, the sound of the vertical flute, which is meant to be played in desolate places, reverberates and adds a ghostly aura. Hence, the feeling of the old theater being haunted emerges. The feeling is also intensified by the ghostly aura permeating the entire film of King Hu's *Dragon Inn*. Although ghosts do not directly appear in *Dragon Inn*, the aura is generated by the inn's location in the middle of the vast Gobi Desert. When the travelers arrive at the inn after many miles of lonely struggle with the harsh nature devoid of human life, what they find is not a welcoming and warm place but a strange building that almost has a life of its own. Similar to Hitchcock's films, where the protagonists often feel that they are being watched or haunted by the building in front of them, King Hu's film reveals an unnamable fear in his characters when facing the inn.[18] The fear and apprehension peak in Shangguan Lingfeng's final approach to the inn (fig. 4.5) (fig. 4.6), when she knows that she will soon be ambushed by enemies swarming out of the beast-like building.[19] The inn is not haunted; instead, it haunts.

Figure 4.5. Shangguan Lingfeng Approaches the Inn, *Dragon Inn*.

Figure 4.6. The Ghostly Inn, *Dragon Inn*.

Ghost haunting is intimately related to nostalgia, the unwillingness to let go of the past and the desire to revisit the sites with particular significance to individuals. The revisited site, or the place where ghosts linger, is always already a contact zone. Boundaries no longer exist, be they between life and death or between nations, but the transgression indicates only the essential lack of the zone where identities are forged and simultaneously lost and where political, economic, racial, and religious confrontations are intensified. Every revisiting of this space driven by nostalgic desire rewards only a profound disappointment and melancholy that lament the irreversibility of the past or the irretrievability of the lost love object. Nostalgia functions to accumulate such disappointments to such an extent that the lack becomes visible, even physically tangible, as historical palimpsest.

In her study of the ghost film, Bliss Cua Lim points out the temporal and spatial ambiguities of the word "nostalgia": it is "from the Greek νοστος (*nostos*, return home) and αλγος (*algos*, pain or sorrow)" and became "a seventeenth-century medical term for pathological sadness or homesickness among exiles"; its "formerly spatial dimension (a longing for a place) gradually became compounded by a temporal dimension (a desire to return to a lost time)."[20] In other words, when we think of nostalgia in modern times, we usually associate it not so much with locale as with memory and the past; locale nevertheless figures prominently in nostalgia, no longer as a physical actuality but through implications associated with its glaring absence. Dissecting nostalgia in a different context, David Wang observes how nostalgia is always attached to a topographical locus, a textual coordinate that marks a lost home and exposes the nature of imagination in conjuring up images of such a home.[21] This topographical locus is precisely the site that combines physical existence with symbolic meanings. Nostalgia is in this sense always already of imagination, but such imagination is made possible only by the dialectics between the absence of a physical locale and the construction of the locale across different times. In nostalgia, therefore, locales become "'spatial palimpsests' traversed by divergent temporalities."[22] What makes ghost haunting in cinema interesting is the revisiting by the ghost of these palimpsests, revisiting that brings out the divergent temporalities in a defiant gesture against linear time and history and against modern rationality.

Goodbye, Dragon Inn ends with an old song, "Liulian" ("Lingering"), sung by the pop star Yao Li (born 1921). This song in many ways brings together almost all of Tsai Ming-liang's major motifs centered on haunting and nostalgia. The lyrics follow:

> Lingering, lingering;
> Under the moon, before the flowers.
> Lingering, lingering;
> It makes me forever remember.
> I think of the moon, I think of the flowers.
> How many reminiscences are locked in my heart.
> Half is bitterness, half is sweetness.
> Year after year all stays in my heart.[23]

Highly rhythmic and melodic, this song speaks of memory and nostalgia but without any actual object of remembrance. The physical site seems to be the most important. Only through lingering at this site can memory become possible.

There is more to this song besides its meaning that corresponds to Tsai's attachment to the physicality of remembrance. Tsai prints out the credits of the song very clearly on the big screen, apparently making sure that the audience knows not only its meaning but also the very material conditions in which it was created: " 'Liulian.' An old song from the 1960s. Sung by Yao Li. Melody by Hattori Ryoichi. Lyrics by Chen Dieyi." Tsai is well aware of the background of this song, for he also points out in his interview the importance of Hattori Ryoichi, Yao Li, and her brother Yao Min to Hong Kong cinema. Yao Li was originally from Shanghai, where, together with the likes of "Golden Throat" Zhou Xuan, she was a sensational pop star. Her song "Meigui meigui wo ai ni" ("Rose Rose I love you") was almost synonymous with colonial Shanghai's dance hall culture. She went to Hong Kong in 1949 and became one of the most recognizable singing voices on the big screen in the 1950s and 1960s. This period saw Shaw Brothers and Cathay fiercely competing with each other in order to dominate Hong Kong and Southeast Asian cinema markets. Both companies relied heavily on musicals that combine the styles of Hollywood with Chinese operas. Yao Li and Yao Min worked for both companies. Yao Min, for example, composed the score for Cathay's *The Story of Three Loves* (*Ti xiao yin yuan* [1964]) and was instrumental to the film's phenomenal success. Yao Li's voice changed with time. Her initial success in Shanghai was partially indebted to the techniques and vocal training of Russian diaspora court musicians. In the 1940s, Yao Min asked her to imitate black singers from Hollywood films that were easily available in Shanghai. Her voice thus became lower and thicker, full of jazz's lyricism. In the 1950s, however, she began to fall in love with the voice of Patti Page and developed a new hybrid style based on jazz and country music.[24]

Yao Li's career speaks volumes about the cultural interconnectedness inherent in Shaw Brothers' and Cathay's transnational cinema. Her voice is also intimately related to Tsai's personal memories, not least because she and her brother sang of Malaysia in a song called "The Beautiful Land of Malaysia." When everything goes dark after the theater is closed, only Yao Li's Patti Page-ish voice lingers in the ruins, simultaneously bearing the imprint of film history and revealing the most intimate feelings of an auteur who has far transcended the geopolitical boundaries of "Taiwan" or "Malaysia" through his constant revisiting of the old theater.

Notes

1. *Kill Bill* is another example of deviation from Ang Lee's and Zhang Yimou's new martial arts styles. Directed by Quentin Tarantino, it is certainly not a Chinese-language film, nor is it by a Chinese based in China or in Hollywood. But Tarantino has always placed himself in the lineage of great Hong Kong masters such as Chang Cheh and King Hu, and the way he pays homage to his lineage in *Kill Bill* qualifies this film as a Chinese-American hybrid (with a bit of Japanese blood). Suffice it to mention that *Kill Bill* opens with the "Shawscope" screen and music that made the film appear to be coproduced by Shaw Brothers' Studio. The same screen surely brings back memories of the golden days of the Shaw cinema in the 1960s and 1970s. *Kill Bill* is a maverick because it is a hybrid, mixing the Hong Kong kung fu tradition with the Hollywood action; it is also a mixture with an overtly Orientalist style. That style is evident, for instance, in the Japanese garden fight scene, with a distinctively postmodernist aesthetic, which exists in the pastiche, defamiliarization, and hyperbolic violence. Tarantino uses this hybridity to specifically attack the new and fashionable Chinese martial arts films. Physical contact versus no-contact swordplay, chop fu versus elaborate choreography, and hard-boiled violence versus romantic lyricism all figure; Tarantino revives Shaw Brothers' kung fu tradition with plenty of postmodern

twists in order to poke fun at and also compete with the likes of Ang Lee and Zhang Yimou. This is not to say that Tarantino focuses on only one side of the martial arts traditions. He also includes plenty of spectacular swordplay and fight choreography; in fact, Yuen Woo-ping is the action choreographer for three of the films being discussed here: *Crouching Tiger, Hidden Dragon*; *Kill Bill*; and *Kung Fu Hustle*. But Tarantino is able to mix up everything and then claims authenticity on behalf of the entire kung fu cinema tradition. This is another battle of the copyright competition. Both sides claim authenticity and legitimacy, one on behalf of the entire Chinese culture, the other on behalf of the previous transnational Chinese martial arts cinema tradition.

2. Stephen Teo, "The 1970s: Movement and Transition," in *The Cinema of Hong Kong: History, Arts, Identity*, ed. Poshek Fu and David Desser (Cambridge: Cambridge University Press, 2000), 95.

3. See the special report "China's New Revolution," *Time*, June 27, 2005, 33.

4. There are numerous examples of violence being directed at residents who are unwilling to vacate their houses. Many cases are documented at the website of Boxun (a nonprofit, nongovernmental news organization in China); see http://www.peacehall.com/ hot/chaiqian.shtml (last accessed January 21, 2006).

5. See *The Shaw Story*, officially released by the Shaw Organization, available online at http://www.shaw.com.sg/shawstory/shawstory.htm (last accessed January 21, 2006).

6. The "contact zone" is a notion brought up by Arif Dirlik in his discussion of transnationalism. For Dirlik, transnationalism understood only as crossing of borders does not do justice to the nationalist practices inherent in transnational activities. He calls attention not only to movements across national spaces but also to "the coming together of different nationalities in a compact space" enabled by the transnational; hence, he posits the notion "contact zone," which "demands boundary crossings among nationalities, and results in the forging of new identities that are not containable within a simple homogeneous idea of national culture within national boundaries policed by the nation-state." Dirlik goes on to explain: "The overdetermined culture of the contact zone is particularly conducive to the imagination of communities in a multiplicity of ways, which also mediate the imagination of the nation. In that case, 'transnationality' itself becomes a constituent of national identity." ("Transnationalism, the Press, and the National Imaginary in Twentieth Century China," *The China Review* 4, no. 1 [2004]:14–15.)

For discussions on the ways in which both cosmopolitanism and localism are essential for generating transnational identities, see Pheng Cheah and Bruce Robbins, eds., *Cosmopolitics: Thinking and Feeling beyond the Nation* (Minneapolis: University of Minnesota Press, 1998).

7. According to *The Shaw Story*, 70 percent of the films distributed through the Shaw theaters in prewar Malaya were American, while 16 percent were British and 13 percent were Chinese. The popularity and box office take of Chinese-language and Malay films surpassed those of their English-language rivals by the mid-1960s.

8. By "intensified continuity," Bordwell refers to the stylistic changes occurring in Hollywood since the 1970s. These changes are mainly based on acceleration of cutting rates: "U.S. films moved from an average shot length (ASL) of five to eight seconds in the 1970s to around three to six seconds in the mid-1990s. By the end of the 1990s, a great many films had an ASL of two to three seconds." David Bordwell, "Transcultural Spaces," in *Chinese-Language Film: Historiography, Poetics, Politics*, ed. Sheldon Lu and Emilie Yeh (Honolulu: University of Hawaii Press, 2005), 147. The implications are obvious: the pace of films has become frantically fast; technologized filmmaking (multiple cameras, heavy reliance on postproduction, digitization, etc.) has replaced inherent dramas and tensions in mise-en-scène as the dominant factor in cinema production and consumption, and the demand on theater equipment is more intense than ever.

9. My interview of Tsai Ming-liang on October 19, 2003, at the Chicago International Film Festival. See also Wen Tianxiang, *Guangying dingge: Tsai Ming-liang de xinling changyu (Frozen lights and shadows: Tsai Ming-liang's psychic field)* (Taipei: Hengxing, 2002.)

10. See *Guangying dingge*.

11. For discussion of Shaw Brothers' *huangmei* opera films, see Tan See Kam and Annette Aw, "*Love Eterne*: Almost a (Heterosexual) Love Story," in *Chinese Films in Focus: 25 New Takes*, ed. Chris Berry (London: British Film Institute, 2003), 137–43.

12. See the memoir by Sha Rongfeng, the owner of Union Film, *Bingfen dianying sishi chun: Sha Rongfeng de huiyilu* (Taipei: Guojia dianying ziliaoguan, 1994).

13. *Dragon Inn* (1967) was King Hu's second feature. The first, *Come Drink with Me (Da zui xia* [1966]), was made for Shaw Brothers. Both films were phenomenally successful; the second was an even bigger hit than the first. Although *Dragon Inn* was produced by Taiwan's Union Film (Lianbang dianying gongsi), which lured King Hu away from Hong Kong, Shaw Brothers was the biggest beneficiary, for it was able to control the film's distribution rights in Hong Kong and Southeast Asia as part of the package compensating for Hu's departure. See Sha Rongfeng, *Bingfen dianying sishi chun: Sha Rongfeng de huiyilu*.

14. For Hollywood's push for multiplexes throughout the world that would continue to benefit its dominance, see Lorenza Munoz, "Modern Movie Houses Are Sprouting Overseas," available online on the *Los Angeles Times* website, http://www.latimes.com/business/la-fi-theaters27apr27,1,7240076.story?ctrack (last accessed January 13, 2006).

15. Yomi Braester, "Taipei's Cinematic Poetics of Demolition," *Modern Chinese Literature and Culture* 15 (Spring 2003): 32.

16. Braester, "Taipei's Cinematic Poetics of Demolition," 32.

17. See Tom Gunning, "The Cinema of Attraction: Early Film, Its Spectator, and the Avant-Garde," in *Film and Theory*, ed. Robert Stam and Toby Miller (New York: Blackwell, 2000), 229–35.

18. Similar practices were already made visible in *Come Drink with Me*, in which the temple was equally important. Evildoers were depicted as demons and ghosts in their painted faces.

19. The ghostly became increasingly important to King Hu after *Dragon Inn*. *A Touch of Zen* (*Xia nu* [1971]) is based on Pu Songling's (1640–1715) famous ghost story collected in *Liaozhai zhiyi* [*Strange tales from Liaozhai*]. Although ghosts are still absent in this film about revenge and justice, Hu's oscillation between the real and the supernatural is much more evident than that in *Dragon Inn*. The film begins with a lengthy elaboration of the wilderness of the deserted fortress well before the main character, Gu Xingzhi (also played by Shih Chun), appears. Gu first states that, following Confucian teaching, one should not believe in the existence of the strange and the supernatural. But the belief quickly gives way to superstition when Gu is startled by apparitions in the fortress. Gu even pastes a Taoist incantation parchment onto the gate before he reenters the fortress. The apparition turns out to be of the heroine's making, which gives Gu the idea of using apparitions to frighten and defeat the pursuers from the corrupted imperial court. Most intriguing, Gu himself is never fully convinced again of the nonexistence of ghosts. After the massive killings following the ambush of the enemies, Gu laughs with glee when he reveals one by one the tricks and machines he disguised as ghosts during the previous night. The laughter is so excessive that he seems to be assuring himself of these devices' man-made nature. The assurance only exposes his hidden fear of the ghostly, for the very next scene shows how his laughter turns into panicked panting when he suspects that the dead are going after him. Ghosts become visible in *Legend of the Mountain* (*Shanzhong chuanqi* [1979]) and *Raining on the Mountain* (*Kongshan lingyu* [1979]). These ghosts are all trapped in the in-between world, fighting over Buddhist canons for their own salvation. The orgy between humans and demighosts reaches its climax in Hu's last film, *Painted Skin* (*Hua pi* [1993]), where a demon gives himself the title of "king of yin and yang," meaning that he is controlled by neither death (yin) nor life (yang) and holds hostage those on their way to the underworld.

20. Bliss Cua Lim, "Spectral Times: The Ghost Film as Historical Allegory," *Positions* 9 (Fall 2001): 292.

21. David Der-wei Wang, *Fictional Realism in 20th-Century China: Mao Dun, Lao She, Shen Congwen* (New York: Columbia University Press, 1992), 247–48.

22. Bliss Cua Lim, "Spectral Times: The Ghost Film as Historical Allegory," 291.

23. Translation provided by author.

24. See the interview of Tsai Ming-liang by Chang Jinn-pei in *Goodbye, Dragon Inn*, promotion brochure for the 2003 Venice Film Festival.

CHAPTER FIVE

—∿—

The Smell of the City: Memory and Hou Hsiao-hsien's *Millennium Mambo*

The screen itself is the cerebral membrane where immediate and direct confrontations take place between the past and the future, the inside and the outside, at a distance impossible to determine, independent of any fixed point.... The image no longer has space and movement as its primary characteristics but topology and time.

—Gilles Deleuze, *Cinema 2: The Time-Image*

Mia is a fervent believer in the sense of smell; her life is dependent on memories evoked by different smells.... The abyssal blue of the lake tells her that the world men have built with theories and systems will collapse, and she with her memory of smells and colors will survive and rebuild the world from here.

—Zhu Tianwen, "Fin de Siècle Splendor"

Taiwan's 2004 presidential election was closely contested and highly controversial. Not only was the result of the election questioned and legally challenged, but the strategies used by the Democratic Progressive Party (DPP) were widely criticized as divisive. Indeed, throughout the election, the right-leaning and pro-independence DPP portrayed itself as the sole representative of Taiwan and of democracy. "I love Taiwan" became the most fashionable political slogan, which implied that the "Republic of China" to which the rival KMT pledges allegiance was no longer relevant to the increasingly localized and democratized Taiwan. As a result, the animosity between ethnic groups drastically increased. Surrounding the issue of Taiwanese identity, the "local" Taiwanese residents (*benshengren*) and the post-1949 mainland emigrants (*waishengren*) blamed each other for Taiwan's social and political problems. The "local" group ended up voting mostly for the DPP, while the KMT garnered most of the emigrant group's votes.

The divisive identity politics was heavily criticized by Taiwanese intellectuals. Most notable, Hou Hsiao-hsien and Lin Huai-min, two renowned artists with no previous interest in politics, issued a bipartisan statement advocating ethnic harmony instead of antagonism based on historical conflicts. Although their advocacy was too little and too late to reconcile the deeply divided groups, it became the foundation for a postelection group, the Democratic Action Alliance (DAA), whose platform emphasizes bringing ethnic groups together so as not to be manipulated by political parties for electoral gain.

Ironically, however, the divisive identity politics criticized by Hou and his colleagues had something to do with Hou's cinematic representation of Taiwan's historical memory and trauma. In particular, Hou's 1989 masterpiece *City of Sadness* (*Beiqing chengshi*) not only created unforgettable images of the local Taiwanese elite in its struggles against the KMT but also made popular the most important emotive expression of the DPP, *beiqing*. Translated as "sadness," *beiqing* denotes a sublime melancholy saturated in historical martyrdom. It is best captured in Lin Wen-Ching's (Tony Leung) muteness and in Lin's black-and-white photography. The images convey a strong message in that the pain of suffering renders language inadequate and that traumatic memories are better preserved in speechlessness. The frozen image becomes the means by which trauma is sublimated.

It has been noted that any major political movement or party in the modern era must have its founding trauma in order to justify revolutionary ruptures from the past. In Dominick LaCapra's words, trauma is often transformed into "a foundational experience (or event), the very basis of an existence, with the possibility that trauma will be sacralized or transvalued into the sublime."[1] The February 28 Incident undoubtedly is the DPP's founding trauma, in which the deaths of Taiwanese leaders became a symbolic martyrdom and mourning became the sublime *beiqing* that motivated Taiwan's resistance movement against the KMT's "white terror." At issue here is not whether the February 28 Incident was a conspiracy to kill members of the Taiwanese elite. Although the historical picture remains murky and interpretations of the incident vary,[2] one has every reason to believe that the KMT staged the massacre in order to gain firm control of Taiwan. My concern here, however, centers on the fact that this incident, as the founding trauma, becomes the core of contemporary Taiwanese identity politics. Key to this identity politics is the antagonization of ethnic groups: one group is held responsible for the historical trauma and is also blamed for Taiwan's lack of democracy before the lifting of martial law in 1987.

Since Hou Hsiao-hsien and his colleagues advocate ethnic reconciliation under the same neoliberal terms of democracy and ethnic harmony,[3] their efforts are doomed to fail. Worse yet, what the DAA does is to give Taiwanese a false hope that ethnic conflicts can be solved through gestures of mutual trust and forgetting historical differences. The more forgiveness and forgetting are worked into the KMT's election strategy, the more divisive Taiwan's ethnic groups are, and the more intense the military confrontation between Taiwan and mainland China becomes. The only effective way to defeat the divisive identity politics is to equally emphasize *beiqing* while dehistoricizing or rehistoricizing trauma. This requires an understanding of trauma as a universal and *constant* memory in which Taiwan's identity is formed, as well as an acknowledgment of the transhistorical nature of trauma whose effect can be recounted in generations and through localized cultural heritage. Only by so doing can the false hope brought by the neoliberal vision of universal democracy be dashed and ethnic divisions directly confronted.

Hou Hsiao-hsien's political activities have done little to ward off divisive identity politics. But his continual efforts to cinematically represent Taiwan's historical as well as contemporary *beiqing* suggest the possibility of dehistoricizing or rehistoricizing trauma and making melancholy a constant feeling suggestive of Taiwan's dilemma. Especially in his recent film *Millennium Mambo* (*Qianxi manbo* [2001]), Hou has achieved, after much exploration in all his previous films, something close to the "pure recollection" of Henry Bergson's terminology. This pure recollection emphasizes the contingency of memory that, in Taiwan's transnational urban setting and youth culture, can no longer distinguish the past from the present or future. But it is precisely this contingency that raises questions about the historical specificity of what is remembered and challenges the notion of stable memory and trauma.

Gilles Deleuze has the clearest understanding of "pure recollection" and its peculiar relationship with cinematic representation. "On each occasion," Deleuze points out, "pure recollection is in a sheet or continuum which is preserved in time. Each sheet of past has its distribution, its fragmentation, its shining points, its nebulae, in short an age."[4] We can take up position on such a sheet, locating a cluster of "shining points" that will become a vivid image or images on which we project our understanding of the relationship between our present self and the past one. Sometimes our effort of recollecting would fail, for the nebulae are on a sheet different from the one we are seeking in our sea of memories. But, as Deleuze further notes, "a third case can arise:

we constitute a continuum with fragments of different ages; we make use of transformations which take place between two sheets to constitute a sheet of transformation. . . . In this way we extract non-chronological time."[5] Shining points or fragments from different sheets of memory are mixed together in the same way that digital data are simultaneously transported through several ribbon cables inside a computer CPU on their way to be programmed into a logical whole. Unlike the digital data, however, the continuum constituted by fragments from different sheets of memory can often be false. As Deleuze says, "Sometimes we only produce an incoherent dust made out of juxtaposed borrowings; sometimes we only form generalities which retain mere resemblances. All this is the territory of false recollections with which we trick ourselves or try to trick others." It is possible and *necessary* for the work of art, especially cinematography, "to succeed in inventing these paradoxical hypnotic and hallucinatory sheets whose property is to be at once a past and always to come."[6]

The indiscernibility of the past and the present, for Bergson and Deleuze, reveals "the most fundamental operation of time": "since the past is constituted not after the present that it was but at the same time, time has to split itself in two at each moment as present and past, which differ from each other in nature, or, what amounts to the same thing, it has to split the present in two heterogeneous directions, one of which is launched towards the future while the other falls into the past."[7] This "time" is not the time that a human being has trained himself to accept under the abstract idea of succession: "time passes from point A to point B," as if time takes up positions in space and is thus identical to movement or generated by movement. Rather, this time is duration per se; it is not the movement from point A to point B but the any-instant-whatever between point A and point B. To understand this time, we must study the ways in which A is related to B and how the two points form an interactive circuit at the any-instant-whatever. If a film presents to us such a relationship, then it is a film of the "time-image," where time no longer "flows" out of movement, but movement is generated from relations and durations. A time-image is a purely optical image, where characters are presented as what they *are*, not what they *do*.

Millennium Mambo is precisely this kind of "time-image," representing memory and a post-Y2K search for the possibility of remembering, no matter how bleak the future may look. Although a political critique is completely absent from this film, *Millennium Mambo* links memory to "any-instant-whatever" and uses a unique cinematic language—long take, depthless cinematography, etc.—to allegorize the constancy of *beiqing*, of melancholy. Hou Hsiao-hsien does manifest in this film a desire to reunite the ethnic groups in a utopia of youth culture. This desire, however, forms a tension with the time-image: the claim of historical and generational uniqueness by the youth culture is discredited when hollowed and temporally nonspecific memory becomes *constant* and *permanent*. It is in such a tension that divisive identity politics is confronted and questioned.

Millennial E-Generation

Millennium Mambo opens with a quintessential Hou-style long take. In this three-minute-long shot, Vicky, played by Shu Qi, takes big strides in a seemingly endless covered overpass, which apparently symbolizes "the passage of time" (fig. 5.1). The voice-over narrated by Vicky herself is set at some time around the year 2011, as if Vicky's personal experiences at the turn of the millennium are flashbacks. The present, in other words, is already the past in this film.

The voice-over then ushers us into Taipei's nightlife made alive by Vicky and her young friends. Drinking, partying, dancing, and puffing soft drugs, the pub crowd acts as if there were no tomorrow. Vicky has a boyfriend, Ah Hao, played by Duan Junhao, a nonprofessional actor. Together, Vicky and Ah Hao have escaped the provincial town of Keelung and have been living on the money Ah Hao stole from his father. Ah Hao deliberately ruined his health in order to dodge the draft. He becomes addicted to methamphetamines, while Vicky decides to make a living as a stripper. Jealous of Vicky's financial independence, Ah Hao turns increasingly abusive, constantly checking Vicky's

Figure 5.1. Shu Qi in the Tunnel of Time, *Millennium Mambo*.

phone records or beating her. Finally, after several unsuccessful attempts, Vicky breaks up with Ah Hao.

Vicky's main patron, Brother Jack (Jack Kao), a mafia head, allows Vicky to move in with him. It is unclear whether they have a sexual relationship; the two are more often seen in everyday activities like cooking, eating, smoking, etc. Eventually Jack has to flee to Japan after his gang members run into unspecified troubles. Vicky follows Jack's instructions and goes to Japan to meet with him, but Jack has vanished. Unable to stand the silence and hopeless waiting, Vicky travels to Yubari, an old mining town on the northern island of Hokkaido. The film ends with an empty shot of Yubari's "film street," home of the Yubari International Fantastic Film Festival. Covered with snow, the banner in the center of the street reinforces the symbolism of the covered overpass at the beginning of the film: time splits here into past and future, simultaneously revoking memories of the past and rekindling hopes for the future even if the bleakness and desolation have already been ominously predicted.

With the subtitle *The Name of the Rose*, this film is supposed to be the first part of a long-term project under the collective rubric "Millennium Mambo." According to Hou Hsiao-hsien's own website (http://www.sinomovie.com), which he founded in 1999, this project consists of a series of films that take their sources from "real people, events, and things in Taipei." The goal for the entire project is to create a collective memory of the city of Taipei. There are six specific guidelines for the project:

1. Real stories: The real lives and events of urban youth are the main subject. The actors and actresses could be either professional or amateur.
2. Series structure: A leading actor or actress in one of the series might be the supporting character in another installment. All films in the project will thus be connected.
3. Multiple exchanges of time and space: The time lines in the series are exchangeable with each other; they float out of the characters' past, present, or future or from their imaginations and memories. The constant shuffling of time and space makes the series kaleidoscopic.
4. Reformation of the movies based on scenes: Since the project is an assemblage of segments, it can always be reassembled by rearranging the order of the segments. The segments can also be broadcast on unconventional media such as the Internet. Viewers can choose any film, even any segment, to create their own viewing orders.
5. Cultivation of urban memories: The project is intended for recording lives in cities and for creating memories of these cities. The places, scenes, or props in one film might repeatedly appear in other films.

6. Opportunities to participate: During the project's production process, anyone who records his or her or other people's real lives by DV or any other image recorders is offered the opportunity to present those works and participate in the project.[8]

These principles emphasize interactions between different installments in the series, between professional and amateur filmmakers, between conventional and unconventional media, and between individual recollections and collective urban memories. There is, however, a paradox inherent in these guidelines. On the one hand, Hou Hsiao-hsien places paramount importance on the real: the actors, be they professional or nonprofessional, must act real, or better yet, the segments can be directly taken from real people's real lives by handheld DVs that require minimal investment or training. On the other hand, Hou wants to "construct," "create," or "cultivate" the memories of Taipei by linking those "real" segments in a random order that can be constantly rearranged. The time line is no longer linear; past, present, and future are not only mixed together but made interchangeable.

Hou's paradox, the creation of urban memories based on "real" individual memories that are nevertheless made "unreal" through random shuffling, is indicative of the constructive and unstable nature of collective memories. To say that a city has a distinctive and collective memory, we usually refer to the city's "history," which, in the case of Taipei, can be understood in terms of linear changes: from the Japanese colonial period to the martial-law era to the post–martial law democratic era. The buildings, streets, parks, and fashions all are witnesses to the vicissitudes Taipei has undergone. People's memories are also inevitably linked with the changes of the city. There might be contingent recollections that are independent of the city's history, but the totalizing power of the city upon its residents' life and memory is always *presumed* as long as "memory" is situated in the binary of the personal versus the collective.

Hou's project description also exposes his strategies of involving the new generation of filmgoers in the production and consumption of this film. The so-called E-generation is represented in popular films such as Leon Dai's *Twenty Something Taipei* (*Taipei wan jiu zhao wu* [2002]), in which the fashionably promiscuous young professionals easily cast film culture aside: "Who would still want to watch movies nowadays?!" They presumably prefer email and instant messaging over film, or *involvement* and *interaction* over passive reception of filmic images typically beamed to an audience sitting still in the dark. Temporal and spatial differences seem nonexistent in omnipresent and omnipotent electronic communications. Claiming turn-of-millennium historical uniqueness and communications superiority over all the other generations, the

E-generation desires to be part of what it sees or consumes in much the same way as the "real" people who are protagonists of reality shows such as MTV's *The Real World*. To be interactive, therefore, is the best strategy for interesting the E-generation.

The reception of *Millennium Mambo* in Taipei testifies to the success of Hou's strategy. Huang Ting, a "twenty-something" American film school graduate, was hired by Hou to document the making of *Millennium Mambo*. Huang quickly published two books, confessing her infatuations with everything about the film: the bars at which most of the scenes were shot, Taipei nightlife, Taipei youth drug culture, etc. One of the books is fittingly titled *E shidai dianying nannu shuangren yazuo: Zoujin Qianxi manbo de Taipei buyecheng (Deluxe love seats for E-generation film people: Entering the night-less Taipei in Millennium Mambo).*[9] This book records the conversations on *Millennium Mambo* among a group of popular politicians, fashion designers, film critics, youth magazine editors, and lifestyle advisors, all invited by Hou for his PR campaign. It is full of misleading fashion statements, pseudofeminist opinions, consumerist fetishism, overt sentimentalism, and misogynistic notions, representing various aspects of bourgeois fin-de-siécle decadence disguised as "new" and transnational urbanism. For instance, Cheng Yingzhu, a "feminist" scholar, asserts that "there are clearly feminine traits in women: promiscuous, unstable, stubborn, unpredictable, and irrational."[10] Although she claims to give positive significance to these "traditionally negative notions of women" by linking the "feminine irrationality" to Taipei's "inner rhythm," she can only reinforce the misogynistic essentialization of femininity. Another speaker, known by her style name of Blue Velvet (*Lan sirong*), claims to recognize in the film's set design a fashionable display of the drugged "high" state, which reminds her of her fabulous party life in London. These "trendy" figures certainly do not belong to the twenty-something E-generation; but they are, to a great extent, creators of the millennial E-generation, whose members, despite their diverse ethnic and political backgrounds, are united in the consumer culture. At the core of this consumer culture are images of fluidity and freedom conjured up by the popular cultural producers. Huang Ting's infatuation with these figures and with the film *Millennium Mambo* is a perfect example of Hou Hsiao-hsien's participation in the making of the E-generation through creating a false impression of interactivity.

The Third Mode of Memory and the Third Time-Image

Although the E-generation is one of the film's focuses, Hou was able to create a self-reflexivity upon the camera's fetishization of the youth culture. His manipulation or maybe even creation of his audience is fully integrated into the filmic technique of *Millennium Mambo*, which, through the self-reflexivity, transcends the binary of the collective versus the personal. The possibility of a third mode of memory arises from Hou's distinctive cinematographic storytelling, which relies on the intrusion of the voice-over or even the camera itself into the pictures. As mentioned above, Vicky's voice-over instantly destabilizes the time lines in the film by making the present the already past. The entire film is framed in Vicky's telling of her stories, whose ordinariness is transformed into extraordinariness due to the enabling of the circuit of time. This film is thus a "third time-image," which, in Deleuze's taxonomy, is different from the first and second time-images that respectively concern the past and the present.

In the third time-image, "the camera is constantly reaching a before or an after in the characters which constitute the real, at the very point where story-telling is set in motion."[11] The first two time-images "essentially concerned the *order of time*, that is, the coexistence of relations or the simultaneity of the elements internal to time," whereas the third "concerns the *series of time*, which brings together the before and the after in a becoming, instead of separating them."[12] The series of time does not equal a mere accumulation or mixture of three temporal planes into an indistinguishable whole; there must be a *false* impression, or a *hypnotic* state, generated by the tension between the ostensible reliability of personal recollections and the constructedness of collective memory. The false impression is precisely the "thirdness" that is designed by ingenious film directors to lead the audience into the circuit of time in which memories with different temporal associations interact and interchange with each other.

Vicky's voice-over in the storytelling mode is not the only intrusion into the film *Millennium Mambo*. The camera, too, forces itself onto the scenes that it shoots: it constantly reminds the audience of its existence. This is another way to "reach a before or an after in the characters which constitute the real": the self-reflexivity of the making of this film in the film extends the characters into the real world in which they are being photographed. The scene of love-making between Vicky and Ah Hao, for example, easily stands out from the rest of the scenes in the film and leaves a strong impression upon the audience due not so much to the steamy sex as to the persistent protrusion of a blinking yellow light from the tangled bodies (fig. 5.2). The light is so prominently "out of place" that one must wonder what it is: it could be a street lamp or lamps, whose light is continually and rhythmically blocked by car traffic; it could be headlights, with the frequency of blinking reflecting the speed and volume of the traffic; it could very well be a light on the camera that blinks during

Figure 5.2.   The Blinking Light, *Millennium Mambo*.

operation and gets reflected in the scene that it shoots; it even uncannily resembles the irregularly blinking white spots projected on film screens between
reel changes. Whether we can precisely identify the yellow light, however,
is not important; what matters is Hou's deliberately calling attention to the
existence, at the frontal position, of something *external to* and *distracting from*
the lovemaking scene. As soon as we realize that the scene is not as closed
and self-sustainable as it appears to be, the camera comes into existence as the
very embodiment of the external that indicates the representationality of the
scene. Furthermore, the yellow light can come into our sights only through
reflection, thus indicating that, between the camera and the scene, there must
be a window. This window is precisely the manifestation of the thirdness: although unseen, it nevertheless is instrumental to the interaction between the
represented and the apparatus of representation; the virtual and the real, or
different times, become exchangeable not because the camera obliterates the
difference between representation and reality but because *the camera extends
the virtual into the real or the real into the virtual through representing its own
materiality in the film.*

Protrusions by objects at the foreground are ubiquitous in *Millennium
Mambo*, although in most cases they are not as abrupt or intrusive as the
yellow light. These objects separate the characters from the audience. Unlike
in the normal cinematography that shifts the camera's focus from the object in
the foreground to the action in the background, Hou's camera focus remains
on the characters at the far end of the visual field. The visual field thus appears shallow, and the objects become blurred. The objects, however, remain

Figure 5.3. The Monitor, *Millennium Mambo*.

obstructive of the audience's vision. These include a monitor in front of Jack's apartment. Linked to a surveillance camera, the monitor shows Vicky's apparitional presence before we can see her appearing in the background (fig. 5.3). Featured prominently too is a glass wall at the entrance of a disco pub; the wall's translucency barely allows us to make out the fight scene behind it. Our attention is also drawn to the pearl curtain in Ah Hao's apartment that separates the brightly lit living quarters from Ah Hao's room, which is permeated with blue light (fig. 5.4). And our sight stops at the candles and wine bottles

Figure 5.4. The Pearl Curtain, *Millennium Mambo*.

at which a deeply depressed and melancholy Vicky stares; we also cannot fail to notice the windshield wipers that intermittently reveal Vicky's and Jack's excited faces on the surface of the overflowing neon lights of nightly Taipei. All these shots have one thing in common: they were taken at real locations, not in studio sets. To emphasize veracity, Hou insisted on shooting the party scenes in real bars during normal hours. The crowds, except Vicky and some of her friends, were real bar patrons who most likely were not aware of the existence of a handheld camera.[13] The circumstances could not yield much depth of field, hence giving a claustrophobic aura to the film. The depthlessness of the film allows the camera, in most cases set at the frontal position, to focus only on the person at the far end of the field of vision. The protrusive objects, in the meantime, cannot help blurring. In other words, the protrusive objects at the frontal position are indeed present in the pictures; their blurredness, however, creates a tension between presence and nonpresence, so much so that the differences between the virtual and the real are also blurred.[14] As a result, the audience generates impressions or feelings of uncertainty regarding the viewing experience.

Olfactory Memory and Remembering Taipei from Afar

Hou's arrangement of the protrusion of objects from the foreground draws the audience's attention to the existence of something external to the represented world in the film. This strategy relies on the audience's *sensory memory*, or *afterimage*, which makes the audience consciously compare Hou's cinematic representation with straightforward films or the lived experience regarding the perception of images. In order to know that there is something visually excessive for an already complete filmic representation of a scene, the audience must have possessed coded information from previous viewing experiences of a complete filmic representation of life, such as the imagery of a couple making love. The filmic image in *Millennium Mambo*, therefore, is not strictly an image but the very embodiment of memory. As Robert G. Crowder and Frank R. Schab point out, "[W]hat sets an image apart from any memory must be that it preserves the coding format of the original experience, untransformed by any process of recoding."[15] In other words, an image strikes you as you experience it for the first time, and the experience of viewing that particular image preserves the original coding. The image can be recalled later, but the recalled image is always already an afterimage or sensory memory, since the act of recalling involves various processes of recoding. Insofar as Hou's filmic representations are constantly transformed by processes of recoding, they are not merely images but sensory memories.

Hou has long been aware of the importance of presenting in his films something beyond image or visual imagery; he seeks moments that freeze time and space precisely because these moments entail sensory memories that, when visually represented, have meanings exceeding the images themselves. He once described the lives of urban youth as ginkgo leaves: one might be saddened by their untimely falling and withering, but careful studies of each leaf in moments that freeze time and space would yield rich meanings.[16] This explains why Hou chose to depict lives of young men and women who live on the margins of society. These characters in *Millennium Mambo* are not only represented in "frozen moments" so as to accentuate sensory memories but are also seen as possessors of particular sensory senses that are different from the normal, which, paradoxically, are make-believe endorsed by the logic of consumerism. What they see, hear, or smell are not the excitement of a postmodern metropolis, excitement that is only artificially created and enhanced by modern and postmodern buildings, commercials, fashionable crowds, or saturated colors; they tend to feel exhaustion, physical and mental fatigue, aimlessness, or lack of appetite and interest. Their senses might have been blunted or overstimulated, but acknowledging the overstimulation is precisely the first step toward a meaningful resistance against what has been warned by Baudrillard as the "simulacra," the omnipresent and omnipotent media manipulation of human life in accordance with the code of postindustrial society.[17]

One of the key moments in the film is Ah Hao's sniffing at Vicky's body. At the beginning of the film, the camera follows Vicky back to the apartment she shares with Ah Hao after she takes leave of her friends at the pub. She sits down, facing the audience; her lower body is blocked by the kitchen counter. Then Ah Hao emerges from his room's profuse mass of blue light; without a word, he brushes aside Vicky's hair and begins to sniff at her neck (fig. 5.5). At first his sniffing appears to be kissing, but soon, judging from the indifference and impatience on Vicky's face when she lights up a cigarette in the middle of Ah Hao's action, we realize that this is not a moment of intimacy; Ah Hao is examining Vicky to see if she has brought back with her the scent of other men. Ah Hao begins with her neck and then gradually lowers his head until he reaches in between Vicky's legs. At this moment we can no longer tell if Ah Hao is acting out of jealousy or excitement; pathos and eros are strangely mixed together in this ritual of odor recognition. Later the same scene occurs again, but Vicky's vehement resistance hints that she has yet to be numbed by Ah Hao's abuse and that the actual sequence of the two episodes has been reversed in the film.

According to Frank R. Schab and Robert G. Crowder, odor recognition is made possible simultaneously by *episodic memory* and *generic knowledge*. By

Figure 5.5.　Sniffing, *Millennium Mambo.*

episodic memory, they refer to the mode of remembrance through association: the word "mouse," for example, is often memorized as a member of a previously presented list. By generic knowledge, they mean memories acquired through semantic definitions: "It is tested by a question such as 'What is the plural of the word mouse?'" The "learning context," that is, the time and place of acquisition, is thus "fundamental to the episodic-memory question and quite irrelevant to the generic-knowledge question."[18] If Ah Hao wants to find an alien smell on Vicky, he must first have an idea, namely, a generic knowledge of some sort, about what smells of promiscuity *are*; his examination of Vicky is in this way encoded with sexist stereotypes and biases against women. Since any olfactory recognition of a familiar odor is essentially done by the odor's name, such as banana, brands of perfume, or kinds of flower, Ah Hao's sniffing is preceded by an act of naming. He names women's infidelity or promiscuity and then tries to match what he smells with what he has named. In the meanwhile, Ah Hao's odor recognition also relies on his association, or his episodic memory, of Vicky's bodily smells with Taipei's nightlife: bars, cigarette smoke, soft drugs, alcohol, sweat from dancing, etc. He certainly cannot reduplicate any of these smells in order to tell them apart; what he recalls is the entire *olfactory event* of the Taipei nightlife or rather, the aura with which smells are associated.

　　It is the olfactory event, not the misogynist naming, that Hou emphasizes in his effort to reproduce sensory memories of Taipei. We also must note that Hou's attention to the sensory in his cinematic remembrance of Taipei most likely had much to do with his screenwriter, Zhu Tianwen. Even better known as a fiction writer than as Hou's exclusive screenwriter, Zhu has long been experimenting in her fiction with various ways to represent sensory events, including olfactory events, in the sense that her protagonists' sensory worlds are not isolated but intimately associated with Taipei's spatiotemporal coordinates. Her most memorable pieces, the stories *Chai Shifu* (Master Chai) and *Shijimo de huali* (Fin de siècle splendor) and the novel *Huangren shouji* (Notes of a desolate man),[19] all revolve around the protagonists' memories preserved in and evoked by colors and smells of the city of Taipei in various temporal settings. In particular, Vicky bears a striking resemblance to Mia, the heroine in "Fin de siècle splendor." A fashion model, Mia "is a fervent believer in the sense of smell," and "her life is dependent on memories evoked by different smells."[20] Her olfactory memory is not so much of generic knowledge as of episodic memory, for she remembers odors based on the time and place in which they occur for the first time. The fragrance of the sandalwood, for example, is associated by Mia with the spring fashion show of 1989, which was dominated by Indian subcontinental flavors. The fresh taste of peppermint herb tea, in another instance, reminds her of the 1990 summer show featuring the paleness of the seaside. Every year in Mia's adolescent life, from 1984, when she was 16, to 1990, was marked by ephemeral fashion trends in which certain smells were recorded in Mia's memories. Every trend seemed completely random and contingent, often triggered by seemingly irrelevant events, such as the record-breaking auction of Van Gogh's *Irises* in 1985 that consequently saw dominance by the colors of yellow, purple, and green. Moreover, the story was first published in 1989, but Mia in the story is already "recalling" the fashions of 1990.

Zhu's language seems to be random, too. The depictions of the colors and smells in Mia's life display an overwhelming linguistic exuberance. Behind Zhu's linguistic labyrinth there are hidden implications: the most precious memory can never be preserved by simply reduplicating it across time based on its naming or its original coding; episodic memory, due to its nature of spontaneity and contingency, is the only reliable mode for remembrance in urban conditions. What gets remembered, however, is not the original coding but the time and place of happenings instead of the happenings per se. At the end of the story, nothing can help Mia remember her ephemeral youth but roses that Mia has carefully dried before they fully bloom; these roses are witnesses to Mia's *hollowed-out* memories.

Mia feels that Taipei is the only place where she can survive. Or more accurately, it is Taipei's urban appeal that is indispensable to Mia's life. "This is her homeland: a city confederacy of Taipei, Milan, Paris, London, Tokyo, and New York."[21] Whether this city is Taipei or Tokyo is no longer important or distinguishable; what matters, on the surface of Zhu's narrative, is the circulation of fashions among these cities, and, at a deeper level, the episodic nature of these cities' urban memories. It is impossible, in other words, to remember Taipei or Tokyo if not for the contingent time and place at which memories are formed. Mia, in fact, lives in a "transnational urban" condition, by which I mean the cultural interconnectedness of the metropolises under late capitalism, a condition that enables the tension between the attempt to remember each historically distinctive city and the impossibility of such remembrance due to the destabilization of generic knowledge about each city. The result of this tension is the prevalence of episodic memory, a memory that is emptied of the object of remembering and is hinged upon random times and places in which the memory is produced.

Taipei can still be remembered, although not based on collective memories of its dwellers, but only from afar. Mia and her friends have to climb up Mount Yangming to notice that Taipei is but a mirage in the desert; she also has to take a trip away from Taipei only to hurry back with the realization that she can survive only in the spectacles within this mirage. Taipei can be appreciated and remembered only from afar, because distance ensures the realization of its illusive nature and consequentially the urge to cling onto the episodic memories before the mirage disappears. Ah Yao, the protagonist of *Notes of a Desolate Man*, travels to Tokyo frequently, almost ritualistically, so as to remember his fleeing youth and his romantic attachment to the city of Taipei and his homosexual friends.[22]

Looking at the present as if it were ten years ago, Vicky acts according to the same logic that drives Mia: the time and space of memorable happenings must be distilled and crystallized as much as roses must be dried before they come into full bloom. This is most likely the reason that the movie is titled *The Name of the Rose*, referring to the desire to preserve the roses (youth) at their most tender moments. Vicky also has to take a trip away from Taipei. In contrast to the scenes in Taipei, which are always set in the dark, the shots of Japan are mostly taken in bright sunshine. But Vicky continues to be aimless, becoming more melancholy than she was in Taipei. The visit to Yubari in a snowstorm seems to have cheered her up, for the happy face of Torajiro (the famous character played by Atsumi Kiyoshi [1929–96] in a total of forty-eight films) on the movie billboards is irresistibly contagious (fig. 5.6). Like what all the Torajiro movies have demonstrated, life is but a spontaneous journey consisting of contingent events, a journey with which Vicky undoubtedly associates herself. Taipei cannot be farther away from Vicky at this moment. But Taipei remains Vicky's home of remembrance as much as Tokyo is Torajiro's spiritual home. What makes the simpleton Torajiro a

Figure 5.6. Torajiro, *Millennium Mambo.*

Japanese household name, an everyman hero, is his uncanny ability of finding home no matter how far he has traveled and how many mishaps he suffers. Vicky, in the end, yearns to go back to Taipei while standing in the middle of the deserted film street (fig. 5.7); Taipei for her is what Tokyo is for Torajiro, namely, a place without memory but with only the times and places to which the always already-vanished memories are attached.

It is also through the reference to Torajiro that the making of this film is incorporated in the film. *Millennium Mambo* was partially produced by the

Figure 5.7. The Film Street, *Millennium Mambo.*

renowned Japanese actor-director Kitano Takeshi's Kitano Studio. Originally Hou Hsiao-hsien invited Kitano to play Jack; Kitano is adept in portraying Triad heads.[23] One of Kitano's most memorable roles is Kikujiro in *Kikujiro's Summer* (1999), a rude, violent, hypermasculine, middle-aged man possibly associated with organized crime. Kikujiro is urged by his wife to take a neighbor's child on a tragicomic journey of finding the boy's mother; in the process, Kikujiro gradually reveals his soft and sensitive side. What he finds, in the end, is a home, not for the boy but for himself, that is made up of innocent childhood memories. This role is Kitano's way to pay homage to Yamada Yoji, the director of the Torajiro films. Not only Kikujiro's childishness hidden behind his awkwardness and clumsiness, but also his name itself, is reminiscent of, if not directly derivative from, Torajiro. Although Kitano was not able to commit himself to Hou's project due to time constraints, Hou still made Torajiro an important subtext in *Millennium Mambo*.

Gilles Deleuze has made elucidating arguments on the mode of the film within the film. This mode, Deleuze contends, must be grounded on "considerations capable of giving it a higher justification, an investigation, revenge, a conspiracy, or a plot."[24] Self-reflexivity, in other words, has to be well conceived in its totality and justifiable in higher artistic and/or moralistic standards consciously sought by the artist. Because of such considerations, Deleuze further points out, "The cinema as art itself lives in a direct relation with a permanent plot [*complot*], an international conspiracy which conditions it from within, as the most intimate and most indispensable enemy." Deleuze links this "international conspiracy" to money:

> This conspiracy is that of money; what defines industrial art is not mechanical reproduction but the internalized relation with money. The only rejoinder to the harsh law of cinema—a minute of image which costs a day of collective work—is Fellini's: "When there is no more money left, the film will be finished." . . . This is the old curse which undermines the cinema: time is money. . . . In short, *the cinema confronts its most internal presupposition, money, and the movement-image makes way for the time-image in one and the same operation*. What the film within the film expresses is this infernal circuit between the image and money, this inflation which time puts into the exchange, this "overwhelming rise." The film is movement, but the film within the film is money, is time.[25]

In discussions of auteur films, the money factor is often downplayed by critics. More often than not, critics mention how an independent film achieves success with limited financial resources, while Hollywood is criticized for lavishing money on special effects and marketing, as if independent films are able to transcend the constraint of money. Deleuze tells us that, whatever the size of the budget, money matters to every film. The differences between the *auteur* film and the Hollywood blockbuster, we can infer, are not so much in the amount of money spent on the film as in the ways in which these films confront the constraint of money. The former more likely treats the money problem as inherent in modern cinema. Self-conscious efforts to turn the constraint of money into the film's plotline, therefore, are precisely what qualify films of Italian Neo-Realism and the French New Wave as "time-images" that are based on an understanding of time as duration and "any-instant-whatever," not as linear "flows" that are comparable to the running of a river or the "spending of money."

Hou's films have always had "international plots" that consciously turn funding issues into coherent aesthetic elements. *Flowers of Shanghai*, for example, was partially funded by the Japanese. To satisfy the demands of the Japanese market, Hou cast the Japanese star Hada Michiko to play the important role of Crimson. Because Hada does not speak Chinese and needed voice dubbing, Hou minimized her dialogue to the extent that she is seen almost always sitting silently across from Tony Leung, who plays Crimson's estranged lover Wang Liansheng. A forced choice, indeed, but Hada's silence fits perfectly with Hou's intention to make *Flowers of Shanghai* a representation of visual ambivalence between silence and speech, between absence and presence.[26] Hou's "international plot" is more complex in *Millennium Mambo*, as I have demonstrated in the Torajiro and Takeshi Kitano subtext as well as in Vicky's episodic memory that requires a trip away to make explicit the hallowed nature of the transnational urban memory.

The transnational capital is thus transformed by Hou Hsiao-hsien into aesthetic and thematic values. Moreover, money is one of the most obvious motifs of the film. Vicky's voice-over tells us from the beginning that her relationship with Ah Hao was going to be over as soon as she had spent New Taiwan $500,000, her entire savings earned from stripping. We know instantly, therefore, that the relationship is doomed. The "overwhelming rise" of the issues associated with money hangs above the entire film and lends it an aura of melancholy inevitability. In this context, Fellini's phrase can thus be extended as such: "When there is no more money left, the film will be finished; memory, too, will be finished." As an industrial art, the modern film confronts its inherent monetary constraints, which always and already constitute an underlying plot of its own making; as a product of transnational capital, Hou Hsiao-hsien's *Millennium Mambo* confronts its own inherent problems that empty the urban memory of the object of remembrance and hollow out transient and compressed time-space coordinates. Such confrontation is precisely what makes *Millennium Mambo* a film of time-image and of implicit reflection on identity politics.

Notes

1. Dominick LaCapra, *History in Transit: Experience, Identity, Critical Theory* (Ithaca: Cornell University Press, 2004), 115.

2. See, for example, Chen Cuilian 陳翠蓮, *Paixi douzheng yu quanmou zhengzhi: Ererba beiju de ling yi mianxiang* 派系鬥爭與權謀政治：二二八悲劇的另一面相 [Partisan struggles and power politics: The other face of the February 28 Incident] (Taipei: Shibao wenhua, 1995).

3. For the abuse of the term "democracy" for hegemonic gains, see Wendy Brown, "Neo-Liberalism and the End of Liberal Democracy," *Theory and Event* 7 (Spring 2003): 1–21.

4. Gilles Deleuze, *Cinema 2: The Time-Image*, trans. Hugh Tomlinson and Robert Galeta (Minneapolis: University of Minnesota Press, 1989), 123.

5. Deleuze, *Cinema 2*, 123.

6. Deleuze, *Cinema 2*, 123.

7. Deleuze, *Cinema 2*, 81.

8. The message was recorded at http://www.sinomovie.com/mambo/html (accessed December 15, 2002). The original wording on the website, which was in English, contains many grammatical mistakes and stylistic problems. The guidelines must have been jotted down by Hou Hsiao-hsien after brainstorming with his colleagues. I have altered some of the words and revised some sentences in my quotation in order to reduce confusion. Since the original website is no longer available, one may go to the Cannes Film Festival's official site for the clip of the 2001 press conference at which Hou repeated the same message (see http://www.festival-cannes. fr/video/video.php?langue=6002&mp=ASF&debit=h&lsttype=31029&uid=66829).

9. Huang Ting, *E shidai dianying nannu shuangren yazuo* (Taipei: Taiwan jiaochuan, 2001); the other book is *Qianxi manbo dianying biji* [Film notes of *Millennium Mambo*] (Taipei: Maitian, 2001).

10. Huang, *Shuangren yazuo*, 107–8.

11. Deleuze, *Cinema 2*, 154.

12. Deleuze, *Cinema 2*, 155. Italics are Deleuze's. For an in-depth analysis of Deleuze's three time-images and their applicability to the study of Hong Kong cinema, see Ka-Fai Yau, "3rdness: Filming, Changing, Thinking Hong Kong," *Positions* 9 (Winter 2001): 535–57.

13. See the press conference clip at the Cannes Film Festival website (http://www.festival-cannes.fr/video/video.php?langue=6002&mp=ASF&debit=h& lsttype=31029 &uid=66829 [accessed August 9, 2006]).

14. Like Lacan's famous analysis of Hans Holbein's painting *The Ambassadors*, one must take a point of view completely different from the normal viewing perspective in order to make sense of this twisted discomforting object. For an extended interpretation of Lacan's view, see Kaja Silverman, *The Threshold of the Visible World* (New York: Routledge, 1996), 175–79.

15. Frank R. Schab and Robert G. Crowder, "Introduction," in their edited volume, *Memory for Odors* (Mahwah, NJ: Lawrence Erlbaum, 1995), 2.

16. See *HHH: A Portrait of Hou Hsiao-hsien* (1996), a documentary directed by Olivier Assayas.

17. See Jean Baudrillard, *The Mirror of Production* (St. Louis: Telos Press, 1975).

18. Schab and Crowder, 3.

19. All three pieces have English translations: Michelle Yeh, "Master Chai," in *Running Wild*, ed. David Der-wei Wang (New York: Columbia University Press, 1994), 89–100; Eva Hung, "Fin de Siècle Splendor," in *The Columbia Anthology of Modern Chinese Literature*, ed. Joseph Lau and Howard Goldblatt (New York: Columbia University Press, 1995), 444–67; and Howard Goldblatt and Sylvia L. Lin, *Notes of a Desolate Man* (New York: Columbia University Press, 1999).

20. Zhu Tianwen, "Shiji mo de huali," in *Hua yi qianshen* [Flowers remembering their previous lives] (Taipei: Maitian, 1996), 201. The English translation is Eva Hung's, in *The Columbia Anthology of Modern Chinese Literature*, 444.

21. Zhu Tianwen, "Shiji mo de huali," 214; *The Columbia Anthology*, 457.

22. It should be noted that Zhu Tianwen's sister Zhu Tianxin, with whom Zhu Tianwen shares many motifs and writing styles, also wrote extensively about remembering Taipei from afar. In Zhu Tianxin's most celebrated novella, *Gudu* (The ancient capital), the protagonist is constantly disgusted by Taipei's urban sprawl, which has wiped out traces of her past and demolished places attached to her memories. Only by traveling to Japan does she begin to realize that it is impossible to revive the Taipei of her memories. The angst of eternal loss forces her to cut short her vacation and return to Taipei, only to be mistaken as a Japanese tourist at the airport by a taxi driver. Holding an old map of Taipei from the colonial period, she decides to play along with her borrowed identity and begins to explore Taipei in the eyes of a stranger. The result is an imagined excavation of the layers of Taipei from different periods. What Zhu wants to achieve, however, is not a Foucaultian "archeology" of Taipei in terms of its ever-changing power structures through historical vicissitudes; she depicts every unique house in detail extending to its exact street number so as to consciously seek remembrance of the places and times of episodic urban memories, no matter how transient they might be.

23. See Emmanuel Burdeau, "Interview with Hou Hsiao-hsien," in *Hou Hsiao-hsien*, 130.

24. Deleuze, *Cinema 2*, 77.

25. Deleuze, *Cinema 2*, 77, original italics.

26. See my article, "*Flowers of Shanghai*: Visualizing Ellipses and (Colonial) Absence," in *Chinese Films in Focus: 25 New Takes*, ed. Chris Berry (London: British Film Institute, 2003), 104–10.

CHAPTER SIX

※

Hollywood Hong Kong, *Hollywood Hong Kong*, and the Cinematic Mode of Production

Hong Kong as a Cinematic Spectacle

In the last two chapters, I discuss how Taiwanese cinema is intricately linked to Taiwan's identity politics and to Taiwan's historically tragic position, caught in struggles among regional and global powers. This is even truer for Hong Kong, except that the causal link might be reversible for Hong Kong's situation: Hong Kong's cinema is not merely a response to its historically ambivalent identity; it might be as well a generator of Hong Kong's identity. Could it be possible that Hong Kong as we normally *see* and *understand* it is produced in and through cinema? This question is what I attempt to answer in this final chapter. In discussing Hong Kong cinema, Poshek Fu and David Desser make this observation:

> Hong Kong presents a theoretical conundrum. The accepted model of a national cinema seems hardly to apply to the Hong Kong situation—a Chinese community [previously] under British rule, a cinema without a nation, a local cinema with international appeal. Perhaps a postmodern model is more appropriate—a transnational cinema, a cinema of pastiche, a commercial cinema, a genre cinema, a self-conscious, self-reflexive cinema, ungrounded in a nation, multiple in its identities.[1]

Indeed, multiplicity seems to be the most important characteristic of Hong Kong cinema. Its transnational and hybrid nature generates tremendous energy, making it one of the most important cinematic traditions outside Hollywood. More important, Hong Kong cinema "presents a theoretical

133

conundrum," destabilizing the existing categories such as Hollywood, Chinese cinema, or national cinema.

The line between Hollywood and Hong Kong seemed further blurred after John Woo, Jackie Chan, Chow Yun-fat, and Jet Li, among others, "invaded" Hollywood in the mid-1990s. The convergence of Hong Kong and Hollywood cinemas in turn reveals the transnational nature of Hollywood, which has always been able to digest outside influences and attract well-trained world filmmakers so as to maximize profit.

There is one problem, however, in overemphasizing the multiplicity of Hong Kong cinema. If we insist that Hong Kong cinema is not grounded in nation, even if "nation" only narrowly refers to the actual institutions and symbols of sovereignty, we will overlook the importance of "China," in the sense of both geographical and sovereign entities, to Hong Kong cinema. We might fail to see that Hong Kong cinema retains a peculiar relationship with China that can best be described as "unattached attachment," seemingly distanced but actually related in all areas. China always looms large in Hong Kong's collective identity as well as in its cinema during both the colonial period and the posthandover period. Although Hong Kong cinema has managed not to be influenced by mainland China's overt political propaganda, Chinese nationalism has never been absent from it. Examples abound. Shaw Brothers films tend to create a false sense of homogeneity in representing Chinese culture to a transnational audience. More recently, Tsui Hark's immensely popular *Once Upon a Time in China* series has not only inherited Chang Cheh's strategy of pitting Han Chinese against Manchu occupiers but also further reinforced modern China's antagonistic vision, which depicts all foreign visitors at the turn of the twentieth century as agents of Western imperialism. Dr. Sun Yat-sen's nation-founding slogan ("Topple the Manchus, restore the Han order, and drive away the foreign invaders" [*fanqing fuming, quchu dalu*]), continues to reverberate in Cantonese popular culture, despite communist China's effort to include ethnic minorities in the mainstream Han culture. Hong Kong cinema in general has distanced itself from communist China, but it remains "Chinese" in the sense that it is based largely on images of Chinese landscape and Chinese culture. It was even more "Chinese" than mainland Chinese cinema when the latter concerned itself with class warfare instead of Chinese culture from 1949 to 1979. Of course, there are definitely many "non-Chinese" elements in Hong Kong cinema. The strong Southeast Asian and South Asian flavors, among others, are the most obvious examples of Hong Kong cinema's hybridity. These flavors do not prevent "China" from becoming an essential motif in Hong Kong cinema; the more hybrid Hong Kong cinema is, the more Chineseness—the constructed images and imaginations of what China *ought to* be like—it reveals.

Due to the success of Hong Kong cinema as well as its inherent Chineseness, Hong Kong becomes synonymous with the Oriental and all things Chinese in Hollywood. To scholars of cinema and to Asian audiences, Hong Kong cinema might appear to be transnational, hybrid, and multifaceted, but to Western audiences Hong Kong cinema is singularly Chinese and Oriental. The biggest irony is that the more successful the Hollywood career of Jackie Chan and his likes, the more cinematically exotic and different Hong Kong becomes. This vicious circle results in Hong Kong's insubstantiality, in the sense that Hong Kong is viewed not as a place inhabited by modern people who have their shares of everyday struggles and feelings not much different from Westerners' but as a place existing solely as a *cinematic spectacle*, a site where fights between gangsters and policemen break out (*Police Story* and *Rush Hour*), romances between Caucasian men and Asian women unfold (*Chinese Box*), the cold war continues (*Tomorrow Never Dies*), or exotic treasure vanishes (*Tomb Raider II*).

Every geographical entity in the world has its immediate associations based on the locale's cultural background and historical specificities. Hong Kong is no exception. But in contrast to places such as New York and Paris, whose immediate associations are combinations of distinctive urban facade and historically unique material life,[2] what Hong Kong immediately evokes is almost always a cinematic sequence: a bird's-eye view of the breathtaking skyline of Victorian Bay cuts into a mid-range shot of a typically crowded Hong Kong street lined with store signs and ends with a close-up of a Western face previously obscured in the crowd.

In a much-quoted discussion of the peculiarity of Hong Kong culture, Ackbar Abbas terms it the "culture of disappearance," in the sense that Hong Kong as a cinematic subject becomes invisible since it is caught in binarisms such as East and West or tradition and modernity. The more transnational Hong Kong culture becomes, the more possible the old binarisms resurface in cinematic representations of Hong Kong. Abbas points out:

> The binarisms used to represent Hong Kong as a subject give us not so much a sense of déjà vu, as the even more uncanny feeling of what we might call the *déjà disparu*: the feeling that what is new and unique about the situation is always already gone, and we are left holding a handful of clichés, or a cluster of memories of what has never been.[3]

This passage has often been cited in a tongue-in-cheek fashion, which results in repeated confirmation that Hong Kong's is a culture of disappearance, postmodern pastiche, and postcolonial in-betweenness. What has been overlooked is Abbas's implication that Hong Kong culture is closely related to

cinematic representation and that Hong Kong is doubly represented since it
is always seen through cinematic lenses. Abbas falls short only of putting it
in a more provocative fashion: *Hong Kong is nothing but a cinematic product.*
The very reason that Hong Kong exists in the globalized world is its being
represented in transnational cinema that continues to reinforce old binarisms
to the extent that China or the Orient is forced to remain opaque, representa-
tionally impenetrable, and dangerously alluring. As far as the cultural logic of
globalization is concerned, the real, breathing, inhabited Hong Kong would
not have existed were it not associated with the glamorous, the mysterious,
and the cinematically transient.

Among contemporary Hong Kong filmmakers, the only one who recognizes Hong Kong's nature as a cinematic product is Fruit Chan (Chen Guo),
although self-reflexivity of cinematic production itself abounds in films by
Wong Kar-wai (*2046* [2005]), Johnny To (*Fulltime Killer* [2001]), and Stanley
Kwan (*Center Stage* [1992]), among many others. Fruit Chan not only reflects
upon the making of film in his films; he pushes contingency to the extreme
so that boundaries between filmmaking and reality are no longer distinguishable. Moreover, he touches upon the very condition of filmmaking, that of the
mode of production indicative of the mechanisms of global capital. He also
makes Hong Kong's link with China explicit on the level of everyday life in
order to show that Chineseness is part and parcel of transnational Hong Kong
cinema. Below I discuss some of Fruit Chan's films, hoping to further elucidate
the implications of Hong Kong as a cinematic product and the mechanism of
the cinematic mode of production.

Chance and the Cinematic Mode of Production

The first thing one would notice in Fruit Chan's films is a consistent surrealist
style. At the beginning of *The Longest Summer* (*Qu nian yan hua te bie duo*
[1998]), which is about the summer of 1997 and the handover, a boy becomes
curious about a passenger on a subway train. He looks at the face of that
passenger. Much to his surprise, he literally can see through it: there is a round
hole through each cheek, as if the face has been penetrated by a sharp object
(fig. 6.1). Although it is revealed at the end of the film that the hole is caused
by a bullet, the sense of absurdity and improbability still lingers. This moment
is surrealist because the juxtaposition of fragments faithful to reality defies
rules of realism and logical reasoning. The very emptiness most improbably
located in the middle of an otherwise normative imagery indicates a nihilistic
nature typical of surrealism whose radicalism comes precisely from its nihilism.
We can find more surrealist moments in *Hollywood Hong Kong* (*Xiang gang you*

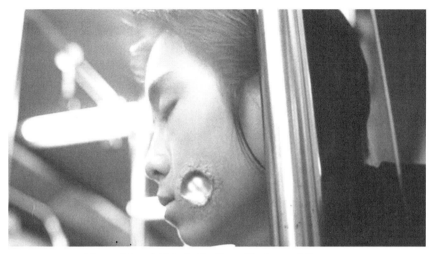

Figure 6.1. A Hole in the Face, *The Longest Summer*.

ge hao lai wu [2002]), a film about a mainland prostitute swindling money from Hong Kong slum dwellers in order to make it to the United States. When the young pimp Huang Zhiqiang has his chopped-off right hand reconnected by an underground doctor from the mainland, he finds out that it is someone else's hand. The head of a tiger tattooed on his right arm is now connected to the tail of a snake tattooed on the wrong hand (fig. 6.2). This is a play with the idiom "tiger's head and snake's tail," hinting at a lack of sexual endurance. It is also a

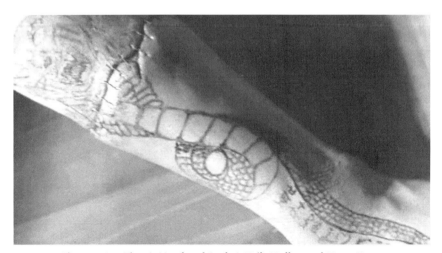

Figure 6.2. Tiger's Head and Snake's Tail, *Hollywood Hong Kong*.

specimen of the "exquisite corpse," the underlying principle of surrealism that randomly puts together body parts into an incoherent whole intended for an experience of reception so disorienting that the conventional assumption of art's decipherability and coherence is problematized. Randomness, or chance, is crucial in both examples.

In Peter Burger's classical study of the theory of the avant-garde, he emphasizes the importance of chance to classical Surrealism. According to Burger, there is an ideological implication in the Surrealist interpretation of the category of chance, which "does not lie in the attempt to gain control of the extraordinary but in the tendency to see in chance something like an objective meaning."[4] This interpretation is ideological because it submits "to an experience whose characteristic quality and value are its purposelessness,"[5] so much so that it forms a protest against means-end rationality, thus against bourgeois society and, by extension, sociality as such. The ultimate dilemma of Surrealism, however, also lies in its fundamental purposelessness or nihilism, for chance must be produced as an "event" in a collaborated sociality before it can be fully integrated into the unpredictability of daily life. The accidental is easily turned into the arbitrary in the conflict between the production of art as a social event and art itself in its purposelessness.

What makes Fruit Chan's surrealist style different from classical Surrealism is precisely his ability to disentangle himself from the inherent conflict in Surrealism. Chan treats chance as it is made possible only by cinema as a mode of production. To put it simply, chance is not produced in Chan's films; it serves as the mise-en-scène in which Chan's stories of social underdogs and acute posthandover social problems of Hong Kong unfold. Like classical Surrealist work, Chan's films form a critique of the capitalist society. But there is a crucial difference: Chan's critique seeks to unearth the inherent visuality in transnationalism. The hole in the face does not have a clear cause-and-effect relationship with what happens *next* in *The Longest Summer*, for there is no clear indication about the time sequence or whether the entire film is a flashback. There seems to be a match between the hole in the face and the shooting scene near the end of film. But one can also argue that the entire story, about the ex-Chinese soldiers in the British garrison, about their bank robbery, and about the sequence of shooting in the face, is the result of imagining what has caused the inexplicable hole.

The technique Fruit Chan used to produce this film also speaks volumes about the ways in which chance produced this film, not the other way around. Over and over again, fireworks are lit up over Hong Kong and become the most important setting for this film, therefore explaining the title *Qu nian yan hua te bie duo* (literally, "There were a lot of fireworks last year"). But the fireworks were not arranged by Fruit Chan for the purpose of making this film; they were *real* fireworks set off to celebrate a series of "historical" events leading up to the climax of the handover ceremony on June 30, 1997. The most interesting thing is that these fireworks scenes were not edited into Fruit Chan's film as a historical backdrop, nor were they used as documentaries juxtaposed with the dramatic scenes in the film. Rather, they were part of the scene in which the actors and actresses mingled with real fireworks spectators and played their roles according to the script. These shots are different from location shots or docudramas, for the real historical events of Hong Kong's handover are not only the stage setting but also integral parts of the film's plot. In other words, Fruit Chan timed his production with the celebrations and literally wrote the fireworks into his script. The whole film is in this sense a "live" movie. The scripted performances went along with the chance happenings of those events, and there was no second take. The line between chance and filmic production is thus blurred. Who produced whom? Instead of the Surrealist insistence on finding the objective meaning despite the clear realization that no meaning exists independent of a human communication nexus, Fruit Chan lets his films become the products of the objective meaning caught in the aporia between contingencies and prearranged historical happenings. There are multiple implications in such an arrangement: first of all, the massive celebrations were every bit as dramatic, scripted, and arbitrary as the cinematic dramatic sequences; second, by extension, the historically significant, even history itself, is very much a media and dramatic event; third, the individual body, with all of its extensions and associations (experience, movement, sexuality, symbolism, and historical contingencies) is both the producer and product of cinema.

These implications bring our attention to cinema as a dominant mode of production in the contemporary world. The term "cinematic mode of production" is coined by Jonathan Beller, who uses it to suggest that "cinema and its succeeding, if still simultaneous, formations, particularly television, video, computers and internet, are deterritorialized factories in which spectators work, that is, in which they perform value-productive labor." Beller argues:

> In the cinematic image and its legacy, that gossamer imaginary arising out of a matrix of socio-psycho-material relations, we make our lives. This claim suggests that not only do we confront the image at the scene of the screen, but we confront the logistics of the image wherever we turn—imaginal functions are today imbricated in perception itself. Not only do the denizens of capital labor to maintain themselves as image, we labor in the image. The image, which pervades all appearing, is the *mise-en-scène* of the new work.[6]

The ubiquity of the cinematic image means that not only our understanding of everything around us is mediated by imagery but also that our body has been reconfigured in such a way that the bodily function of seeing is now given the uttermost importance for it has the biggest value-extraction potential. We labor when we watch commercials, trigger pop-ups while surfing the net, or enjoy virtual sex on the Internet. We are also monitored closely about what we watch. *To see is to labor.* As Beller aptly puts it, "This world is not virtual in the sense that it is make-believe or pretend, but virtualized by virtue of becoming bereft of its traditional standards, properties and proportions, all of which have been geographically, temporally, perceptually and proprioceptually transformed by media capital."[7]

To Beller, Oliver Stone's 1994 film *Natural Born Killers* is able to show how the money-driven image envelops consciousness. This film is normally understood as a satire of the violence-ridden American media. But if we look at it in terms of the cinematic mode of production, we should realize that Mickey and Mallory's shooting rampage is not only a media event by feeding into and feeding on the O. J. Simpson type of media frenzy but also and more important a product of cinematic image: the way they drive into movie screens, the way the scenery changes on the window of their motel room, and the way Mallory's sexual abuse by her father is made into an appropriation of *I Love Lucy* accompanied with canned laughs all point to the virtualization of reality. As a result, Mickey, hiding behind his cinematized red sunglasses, does not even realize the damage he has done. Mickey eventually becomes the ultimate master of the cinematic production of surplus value precisely by virtualizing and thus immortalizing himself in the video camera, which becomes the last remaining witness kept alive to tell of their feats.

It is no coincidence that *Natural Born Killers* becomes an important subtext in Fruit Chan's *Made in Hong Kong* (*Xianggang zhizao* [1997]). The title itself, in a self-reflexive gesture, hints that this film is about cinema, the most famous product of Hong Kong in the eyes of Westerners who, despite their glaring ignorance of real lives in East Asia or other parts of the world, have become familiar with Hong Kong's impressive skylines, crowded streets, and the so-called aesthetics of violence transferred to Hollywood by the likes of Bruce Lee, John Woo, Jackie Chan, and Chow Yun-fat. The biggest fan of Hong Kong cinema among important Hollywood figures is Quentin Tarantino, who created the story of *Natural Born Killers* by drawing on his cinematic visions, which had always been mediated through the violent Hong Kong action sequences imprinted on his mind.[8] Ironically, *Natural Born Killers*, partially produced in Hong Kong–inspired aesthetics, becomes both the model of violence and the lenses through which Zhongqiu, the protagonist of *Made in Hong Kong*, views the world around him. The movie poster of *Natural Born*

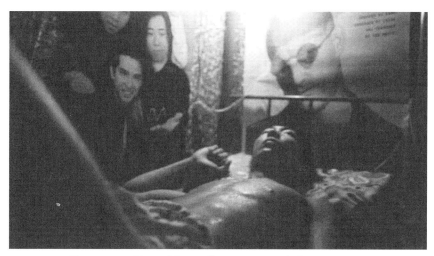

Figure 6.3.   *Natural Born Killers* Poster, Made in Hong Kong.

Killers, featuring Woody Harrelson's bald head with the infamous red sunglasses, is the main decoration over Zhongqiu's bed (fig. 6.3). When Zhongqiu dreams of the girl who has committed suicide, the camera alternates between Zhongqiu's dream and Woody Harrelson's sunglasses. The quick cutting leaves the impression that the blood in Zhongqiu's dream is seen through Harrelson's glasses, which render the blood white, not red. The white and milky blood turns out to be linked to Zhongqiu's masturbation in his dreams. Not until he realizes what he has done does the blood turn red. In this sequence, libido and violence are made interchangeable, and the interchangeability is mediated through Woody Harrelson's glasses, which are already cinematic.

Before Zhongqiu leaves his apartment to carry out his assassination assignment, he dances a *Pulp Fiction*–like dance, accompanied by techno beats. Again, the shots alternate between Woody Harrelson's poster and Zhongqiu. Having fallen into a hypnotized state under Harrelson's gaze, Zhongqiu confidently and coolly walks up to the targets, draws his gun in slow motion à la John Woo, shoots the targets, and throws away the gun. Just when we are impressed by the seamless and almost flawless action sequence, however, the film pauses for an unnoticeable second, and the entire sequence is reenacted. This time everything goes wrong. Zhongqiu is not confident, he pumps himself up by snorting cocaine, and he eventually fails in the assassination attempt. One must wonder: what sequence is the "correct" one that is supposed to be connected with the ending? Why are there two sequences while there is only one ending?

Zhongqiu's monologue after this sequence helps us understand Fruit Chan's technique in this "double sequencing." Zhongqiu says: "My father took a concubine, that was his TAKE TWO; my mother left, that was her TAKE TWO. But there is no TAKE TWO in life. All these TAKE TWOs are but the excuse of customers." His remark is made in Cantonese, except the English phrase TAKE TWO, which, as a cinematographic term, is not normally used by average Hong Kongers to express a meaning equivalent to "second chance." It is intriguing, therefore, that the phrase TAKE TWO is used at this particular juncture. What Fruit Chan wants to express here is precisely the fact that reality has been determined by the cinematic mode of production. Although there is no second chance in reality, there is nevertheless an overwhelming illusion in contemporary cosmopolitan culture that everything can be reenacted over and over again and that wrong decisions in life do not seem to be of real disastrous consequence, just like in cinema, where numerous takes can be and should be made so as to achieve perfection. The reenactments of life are exactly where the profitability of the body's sensual and visual functions can be maximized, as evident in the prevalence of reality shows that cash in on voyeurism and on the false premise that these shows are "take twos" for both the participants and the audience. Fruit Chan's idiosyncrasy lies in his consistent attempt not only to expose the inherent problematics of "take twos" but also to make them a crucial structural principle in his films. Unlike in such films as *Run Lola Run*, which focuses on contingencies of human life by rewinding the core sequence and then reenacting the sequence through ever-so-slight changes of detail, there is no rewinding in *Made in Hong Kong*. Zhongqiu's two action sequences in the same situation are so naturally and fluidly connected that one seems to be the outcome of the other. Both "take one" and "take two" generate the same result and generate each other, indicating the illusive nature of double takes and inescapability from the dominance of the cinematic mode of production. Contingency in this way becomes the mise-en-scène of this film, both productive of and produced by cinema.

There are many other ways in which Fruit Chan provides reflections on the cinematic mode of production, reflections that can help us understand both his films and the mechanisms of the cinematic mode of production, which Jonathan Beller has yet to probe. To explain how Fruit Chan renders the reflections possible, I provide a detailed analysis of *Hollywood Hong Kong* in the rest of this chapter.

Hong Kong as a (Pig) Body

Hollywood Hong Kong opens with a hilarious yet highly disturbing sequence in which the Zhu (homophone of *zhu* [pig]) family loads slaughtered hogs onto their truck. Running a pork barbecue business, the Zhus (a father and two sons) are as big and fat as hogs. Their naked upper bodies are indistinguishable from the hog carcasses that they carry. The Zhus live in Ta-hom village, a slum in the shadow of Plaza Hollywood, which is an upscale apartment complex consisting of five high-rises. A pimp named Huang Zhiqiang also lives in the village, running his escort business through the Internet. Old Zhu is Huang's customer, but both sides pretend not to know each other's identity. Huang is attracted by an online solicitation in which a girl from the mainland poses as a naughty nurse, a maid, a student, or a teacher. He meets a girl with a typical mainland name, Honghong (Little Red), who, played by Zhou Xun, the star of *Suzhou River* and *Beijing Bicycle*, completes her service to Huang in the bushes. Afterward, she drags Huang up to see Plaza Hollywood. Raising her right hand, she blocks the high-rises with her five fingers. Hollywood is her dream, she explains, and the dream is most attainable when one views the high-rises through the fingers. Besides Huang, she also gains the friendship of the youngest Zhu and seduces Zhu's father and older brother.

Plaza Hollywood appeals not only to humans but also to animals. The Zhus own a sow to ensure a reliable supply of piglets for barbecuing. Since Old Zhu's wife has run away, the pig inherits the title "Mama" and is treated as the only female member of the family. The underground mainland doctor wants to use Mama for her experiment to produce human babies through the pig's womb. "We can win the Nobel Prize," she thus persuades Old Zhu. Refusing to cooperate, Mama runs away and disappears in the labyrinthine Hollywood Plaza. She eventually comes back to Ta-hom village, with her body covered with illegible characters.

The innocent-looking Honghong turns out to be a cold-blooded mercenary. She sends blackmail letters to the three Ta-hom villagers with whom she has slept and threatens legal action because she is underage. Huang refuses to pay up. As a result, he loses his arm at the hands of gangsters hired by Honghong. Huang finally finds out that Honghong lives in an apartment in Plaza Hollywood, but his plans for revenge are interrupted by the youngest Zhu, who urges Honghong to run away. Months later, little Zhu receives a postcard from the United States. Honghong smiles at him from underneath the Hollywood sign.

There are multiple binarisms in this film between modernity and tradition, science and ignorance, human and animal, Hong Kong and the mainland, etc. But Fruit Chan does not intend to endorse either end of the binarism. All the contrasts are framed in the visual defamiliarization of the body, which is shown as cannibalistic, sexually driven, lavishly consuming, and simultaneously real and virtual. It is the visual focus on the body that prevents Hong Kong from "disappearing" despite the explicit binary contrasts. For the body becomes the

Figure 6.4.   The Pig Covered with Characters, *Hollywood Hong Kong.*

metaphor of Hong Kong, emerging from the shadow of Hollywood as both a collective experience and a figurative expression for all the dilemmas in which Hong Kong is caught.

The most visually stunning and scandalous body is that of the pig Mama. She eats human flesh: Old Zhu feeds her the flesh of a female employee from the mainland whom he has inadvertently killed. She symbolizes Old Zhu's sexual desire when Honghong turns into a pig in his dreams. She provides her womb for "scientific" research. Most significant, she turns her body into a site for signification.

As mentioned above, after Mama runs away and apparently spends some time in the high-rises of Plaza Hollywood, she comes back to the slum of Tahom village with her body covered with characters (fig. 6.4). We can recognize some of the characters, which include *Chen Guo* (Fruit Chan's name in Chinese), *Ying Huang* (the Queen of England, or Emperor Entertainment Group, a media conglomerate in Hong Kong), *Zhong Guo* (China), etc. These words all have loaded meanings that are relevant to Fruit Chan's consistent concerns over the Hong Kong–mainland relationship, Hong Kong's colonial history, or the monopolization of film and music productions by such companies as Emperor Entertainment Group, which allegedly has a mafia background.[9] But they maintain their meanings only when they are used alone. When these words are mixed up randomly, they literally become "the exquisite corpse," which was initially conceived in a word game that explores the nonsensical-ness of randomly combined words. But Fruit Chan goes beyond surrealism's emphasis on nihilism. The visual prominence of the pig's body, which is made indistinguishable from the human body throughout this film, indicates that the body is simultaneously abstracted by the process of signification. It is thus bereft of materiality and made into a physical site on which the struggles among various relationships of production are inscribed, no matter how illegible the inscriptions are. In fact, the very illegibility of the inscriptions highlights the body's materiality as the purest embodiment of value generated by the cinematic mode of production.

There is an interesting resemblance between Fruit Chan's pig and *A Case Study of Transference*, a famous installment created by the Chinese artist Xu Bing in 1994–1995. Xu Bing's work featured two breeding pigs, one whose hide was inscribed with Chinese characters and the other with English words (fig. 6.5). The two pigs made love with great abandon, while audiences were thoroughly embarrassed. The meanings of this installment were considered easily decipherable: the cultural transference of course refers to the exchanges between Chinese and Western cultures, exchanges that were historically conditioned by power relations, gender inequalities, cultural hegemonies, and so on. Only upon closer scrutiny, however, did one realize that the Chinese characters and English words were completely meaningless. The Chinese characters could very well be constructed in the way English words are created, as long as there are twenty-six strokes with each stroke functioning as a letter with phonetic, not semantic, properties that become meaningful only when

Figure 6.5. Xu Bing's *A Case Study of Transference*.

the letters are combined into semantic units. Based on the same principle, English alphabets could be used to construct Chinese characters as long as they are endowed with both phonetic and semantic properties and function as strokes and radicals. In fact, this is precisely what Xu Bing did in creating his proudest work, *New English Calligraphy*, in which Roman alphabets were used to create meaningless Chinese characters to be copied and practiced by the English-speaking audience (fig. 6.6) (fig. 6.7). What these works suggest are the arbitrariness of languages on the one hand and materiality of the meaning-making system on the other. Unknowingly, the audience members, including those who tried to decipher the meanings of these installments, had already physically become part of the works by contributing

Figure 6.6. *New English Women* from Xu Bing's *New English Calligraphy*.

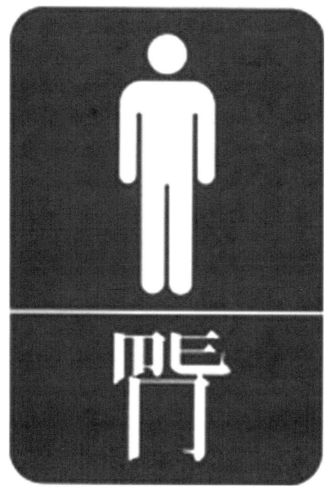

Figure 6.7.   *New English Men* from Xu Bing's *New English Calligraphy*.

their sociality in their acts of watching, practicing, feeling embarrassed, and interpreting. There is no evidence so far suggesting Fruit Chan's indebtedness to Xu Bing, but their ideas are indeed very similar. What Fruit Chan has done is to fully incorporate into his films the "situation," as in "situational arts," that gives equal importance to the abstract meaning of the artwork and the physical setting in which the audience, wittingly or unwittingly, interacts with the work. This cinematized "situation" is most clearly indicative of the cinematic mode of production: to see is to labor, since value is produced through both abstraction (in linguistic and symbolic terms) and substantiation that requires active participation of the body in the meaning-making process.

The pig Mama, therefore, becomes the most condensed symbolization of Hong Kong, which is the site for "cultural transference," namely, transnational interactions of cultures and transactions of cultures as commodity. Fruit Chan's juxtaposition of Hollywood and Hong Kong is further revealing of the mechanism of such transference. Hollywood, a symbol of the American film industry and, more narrowly, the nine-letter sign erected on Los Angeles's Hollywood Hills, becomes an actual dwelling in Hong Kong through the naming of an apartment complex as such. The impending demolition of Ta-hom village suggests that Hong Kong will soon be filled with modern high-rises built on envy and imitation of Western modernity. The symbolic power of Hollywood is turned into a value-producing real estate venture that further reinforces the dominance of the Hollywood imagery.

There is a further twist in Fruit Chan's symbolic rendering of Hollywood Hong Kong. Hiding in this story of cinematic production of the body are multiple references to *Journey to the West*, one of China's most popular classical novels. Mr. Zhu reminds the audience of Zhu Bajie, "Piggy," who is gluttonous, carnal, and undisciplined. The five high-rises of Plaza Hollywood are explicitly compared by Honghong with Mount Five Fingers, at the foot of which Monkey urinates so as to prove his power. Honghong's business transaction with Huang Zhiqiang also leaves a stain in the bushes at the foot of Plaza Hollywood. Of course, Mount Five Fingers turns out to be the transformation of Buddha's five fingers. The moral of Monkey's little adventure points to Buddha's omnipotence: no matter how far you fly (108,000 miles in Monkey's case), you will still end up in Buddha's palm. Similarly, implicit in Honghong's adventure is an affirmation of the almighty power of Hollywood. But, as the truly enlightened Buddhists will tell us through understanding the myriad transformations of Buddha, the world is illusory to the extent that even Buddha's omnipotence is no exception. Similarly, films by the likes of Fruit Chan and all the other directors discussed in this book (Zhang Yimou, Jiang Wen, Lou Ye, Wang Xiaoshuai, Tsai Ming-liang, and Hou Hsiao-hsien) have created myriad life worlds with their own local histories paradoxically guided by the cultural logics of transnationalism. From these films, we will eventually understand Hollywood's illusory nature as well as the cinematically produced simulacra that we call reality.

Notes

1. Poshek Fu and David Desser, "Introduction," in *The Cinema of Hong Kong: History, Arts, Identity*, ed. Poshek Fu and David Desser (Cambridge: Cambridge University Press, 2000), 5.

2. One needs only to consult Walter Benjamin's *The Arcades Project* (New York: Belknap Press, 2002) to get a sense of the fascination with Paris's material life. And Henry Miller's trilogy *The Rosy Crucifixion* (New York: Grove Press, 1965) is a fine example of representing New York's historically unique urbanism.

3. Ackbar Abbas, *Hong Kong: Culture and the Politics of Disappearance* (Minneapolis: University of Minnesota Press, 1997), 25.

4. Peter Burger, *Theory of the Avant-Garde* (Minneapolis: University of Minnesota Press, 1984), 66.

5. Burger, *Theory of the Avant-Garde*, 66.

6. Jonathan L. Beller, "Kino-I, Kino-World: Notes on the Cinematic Mode of Production," in *The Visual Culture Reader*, ed. Nicholas Mirzoeff, 2nd ed. (New York: Routledge, 2002), 60.

7. Beller, "Kino-I," 72.

8. The latest enterprise of Tarantino's is *Kill Bill: Vol. 1* (2003) and *Kill Bill: Vol. II* (2004), which violently take over Shaw Brothers' trademark kung fu cinema styles and wed them with Orientalist imagery to create a simultaneous celebration of violence and critique of violence as such, based on the fact that the violence is always already mediated through cinematic images.

9. *Hollywood Hong Kong* was produced by Andy Lau, a Hong Kong superstar active in acting and singing. Lau allegedly has a long history of intimidation and blackmail by Hong Kong's mafia, with which the Emperor Entertainment Group is allegedly connected. See the Sohu bulletin board (http://yule.sohu.com/19/81/article 211168119.shtml) (accessed February 12, 2006).

Postscript: Remaking East Asia

In April 2004, I invited Roy Lee to meet with the audience after a screening of *The Ring* (2002) at the University of Illinois. I had my own selfish reasons for the arrangement. Wrapping up this book about the "non-Hollywood," I felt the urgent need for a glimpse into the ways Hollywood interacts with its "other." My studies in this book are mainly from the perspective of "the other side," which I believe is necessary for a non-Eurocentric understanding of transnational visuality. References from "this side," however, can only further our understanding of the mechanisms of transnationalism. Overemphasis on multidirectional, instead of unidirectional, flows of cultural production can be misleading. If all cultural productions were interconnected, deterritorialized, and freely exchanged, then Hollywood would have been dispersed and would have lost its special interests deeply rooted in American hegemony. The biggest irony is that the more transnational national cinemas become, the more dominant Hollywood is. Only through a balanced inquiry of both the cultural interconnectedness and the continuously uneven development of world cinema can we understand how transnationalism has shaped an increasingly bipolarized world.

Roy Lee was the most appropriate source for my inquiry. Surprisingly humble and pleasant, Roy Lee nevertheless exuded a calm and confidence that befitted his status as a rising star among Hollywood power brokers. A second-generation Korean American, Lee can easily relate his success to transnationalism: getting a good American education, going to law school, becoming a professional with a respectable, stable income, and utilizing his East Asian background when opportunities strike. He discovered and then introduced the Japanese film *Ringu* (1998) to DreamWorks, which agreed to buy the re-make rights from *Ringu*'s director, Nakata Hideo, for $1.2 million. Directed by Gore Verbinski, the remake cost DreamWorks another $40 million, a hefty amount for any East Asian film but a meager figure compared to the typical cost of $100 million to $250 million for a Hollywood summer blockbuster. The film proved to be a phenomenal success, raking in $130 million domestically and $230 million worldwide. Ironically, *Ringu*, which was the highest-grossing Japanese film, made $6.6 million in Japan, while its remake, *The Ring*, earned $8.3 million in only the first two weeks on the Japanese market.[1] The success of *The Ring* gave Roy Lee instant credibility, which resulted in a series of remakes of East Asian films. Nakata continued to march into Hollywood, having two more of his films remade: *Dark Water* (2002 [Japan] and 2005 [United States]) and *Chaos* (1999 [Japan] and in production [United States]). He was also asked to direct *The Ring 2*, the sequel to *The Ring*. Another Japanese filmmaker, Shimizu Takashi, found similar success: he directed *The Grudge* (2004), the remake of *Ju-on: The Grudge* (2000–2003), a series of direct-to-video Japanese thrillers he developed. *The Grudge* was as profitable as *The Ring*, dominating the box office for three consecutive weeks in late October 2004. Overall, the number of East Asian remakes by Hollywood since 2002 is stunning. Suffice it to mention *Shall We Dance* (1997 [Japan] and 2004 [United States]), *My Sassy Girl* (2001 [Korea] and in production in the United States), *My Wife Is a Gangster* (2001 [Korea] and in production in the United States), *Infernal Affairs* (2002 [Hong Kong] and 2006 [United States; under the title, *The Departed*]), and *The Eye* (2003 [Hong Kong] and in production in the United States). Most of these films were or are being produced by Roy Lee, who is now fittingly dubbed the "king of remakes."

Hollywood has a long history of remaking commercially successful foreign films. Previous remakes were mostly based on European films, but there were East Asian precedents as well. Kurosawa's *The Seven Samurai* (1954), for example, was remade as a Western, *The Magnificent Seven* (1960). None of the previous remaking trends, however, could match the current fashion of remaking East Asian films for scale, intensity, publicity, or profit. There are various explanations of this phenomenon, but every explanation has in various degrees been rebutted. Some attribute the trend to East Asia's rich supernatural tradition as represented in the eighteenth-century Japanese short-story collection *Tales of Moonlight and Rain* (*Ugetsu Monogatari*), part of which became the base for the acclaimed film *Kwaidan*, made by Kobayashi Masaki in 1964. Indeed, there is a certain aura in Japanese ghost fiction and films, filled with women's grudges against men who deserted or injured them. Unlike most ghost stories in the West, which seek moments of shock and harmless thrills, the

Japanese ghost stories tend to allow the aura to linger, permeate, or literally haunt the audience rather than shock and thrill it. But there is another side to the contemporary Japanese ghost films. As John Chua aptly points out in his PhD dissertation on the horror film as a genre, what makes *Ringu* adaptable is its already Americanized features: the American suburban lifestyle, the strong-minded yet vulnerable female as the "final girl," unambiguous sexuality, and thrilling yet unthreatening horror. These features met DreamWorks' demand to make *The Ring* a profitable PG-13 film instead of an R-rated film, which is almost synonymous with box office disaster. Chua further notes that Nakata's *Ringu* was already a remake of a 1995 film that is much darker, horrifying, and sexually ambiguous. The biggest difference is in the gender identity of the ghost:

> Sadako, the victim-turned-ghost who kills those people who have seen her apparition, is revealed in the original story to be a hermaphrodite. She becomes a ghost because a doctor rapes her, then kills her upon discovering her dual sexuality. The original story also suggests that Sadako telepathically motivates her rapist to kill her, a different if not politically incorrect idea to incorporate within American narratives. This frank sexual ambiguity and erotic violence, described relatively graphically as flashbacks in the novel and shown onscreen in the first movie adaptation, would be much too vivid for mainstream American audiences.[2]

Without ambiguity, be it psychological or sexual, there would not have been aura. After all, aura is something that cannot be safely contained or explained away in modern rationality, something that one can vaguely feel but can hardly locate or identify.[3] If there is ever an "aura" in Japanese ghost films, it is self-consciously filtered out in Nakata's and Shimizu's remakes. In this sense *Ringu* was already Hollywoodized before it was remade into *The Ring*.

Since the current remaking trend includes not only the horror genre but also comedy and action films, the linkage between the East Asian supernatural aura and the success of remakes is further disputable. Some have attempted other explanations. Mark Cousins, for example, contends that the art of commercial cinema has been perfected in the hands of the East Asian disciples of Hollywood:

> *Dark Water*, *The Eye* and *The Ring* films—also being updated in the US—unnerved Hollywood because they beat it at its own game. They found new, subtle, inventive ways of doing what producers in southern California have spent a century perfecting: jangling audiences' nervous systems.[4]

The "new, subtle" ways Cousins refers to include slow building of tension, hinting at unseen horrors, and using sound more evocatively. Cousins is right in suggesting that the current remaking trend should not be regarded as an isolated phenomenon: East Asian cinema's creative imitation of Hollywood is based on East Asia's long history of film industries whose accumulation of talents and artistic expressions is finally being recognized and exploited.

We must note, however, that there is a profound Orientalism in Cousins's enthusiasm in the recent success of East Asian cinema. "Each of the latest new wave of Asian films," Cousins comments, "is highly decorated, tapestry-like, with an emphasis on detail, visual surface, colour and patterning, and centered on a woman, or feminized men."[5] What Cousins has in mind are such films as Zhang Yimou's *Hero* and *House of Flying Daggers*, Wong Kar-wai's *2046*, and Koreeda Hirokazu's *Nobody Knows* (2004). To Cousins, these films display a collective "Asian aesthetic"—exotic, erotic, feminine, seductive, and decorative—that makes Asian films attractive to American audiences through either direct theatrical releases in North America or remakes. We can certainly put a positive spin on Cousins's assertion, emphasizing that the attractiveness of the "Asian aesthetic" paradoxically exposes the inherent racial or sexual discrimination and the tendency to exoticize the *other* in Hollywood cinema. But the critique of Hollywood's "othering" strategy only reinforces and endorses Cousins's generalization, which is not correct in the first place. *Asian cinema is not exclusively feminine.* Suffice it to mention Kitano Takeshi's stoicism, John Woo's "aesthetics of violence," Chow Yun-fat's coolness in his trademark gun-wielding image, Hou Hsiao-hsien's masculine heroism, and Jiang Wen's worship of revolutionary sublime. These directors and actors have either entered Hollywood or become darlings of film festivals. If we follow Cousins's generalizing logic, shall we say Hollywood has been masculinized by East Asian films?

There is another major problem in Cousins's argument: he speaks indiscriminately of popular East Asian films and Hollywood remakes of East Asian films, while the differences between these two forms of film cannot be bigger. East Asian films star East Asian performers who speak in their native tongues. The requirement of subtitling makes these films a mainstay in North American art theaters, with the rare exception of *Crouching Tiger, Hidden Dragon*, *Hero*, and Takeshi Kitano's *Zatoichi* (2004). The remakes, on the other hand, rely on the star power of non-Asian actresses and actors such as Naomi Watts (*The Ring* and *The Ring Two*), Sarah Michelle Gellar (*The Grudge*), Richard Gere and Jennifer Lopez (*Shall We Dance*), and Matt Damon and Leonardo DiCaprio (*The Departed*, remake of *Infernal Affairs*), who speak English and stay comfortably in American or Americanized East Asian settings. The most ironic arrangement is in *The Grudge*, which, despite the setting in Japan, stars *Buffy's* Sarah Michelle Gellar as an expatriate American social worker. As Roy Lee told me, Andy Lau, a megastar in Hong Kong, wanted a role, however minor, in the remade *Infernal Affairs*, but it simply was not possible to insert an Asian face in the scenes of Boston mafia. From the original to the remake, the switch of ethnicity should not be overlooked. Inherent in the switch is ethnic stereotyping, if not outright racism, in a country that ironically is made up of multiple ethnicities. *What has been remade is not only the story but also ethnicity.* While the originals are ethnically specific, albeit Hollywoodized, representations, the remakes are completely severed from the original ethnic soil and become solely the product of Hollywood. The remakes, therefore, have nothing to do with the supernatural aura, the long development of East Asian cinemas, or the peculiarly "Asian" aesthetic based on cultural and ethnic specifics.

The question remains unanswered: why has remaking East Asian films become such a popular trend at the turn of the millennium? Conversations with Roy Lee yielded several interesting clues from which I finally was able to draw a conclusion. First of all, Lee mentioned several times that he did not have a particular interest in Asian horror films. All he saw was market potentials. If East Asian remakes become no longer profitable, he would easily switch to other venues for his film productions. Second, Lee emphasized repeatedly how cheap it was to make films in East Asia. East Asian filmmakers were all happy to sell the remake rights to Hollywood, for the fee paid by Hollywood studios (albeit a small portion of the cost of remaking the pictures) would most likely recoup what they originally spent on making the films. Third, Lee did not need to search hard for profitable East Asian films. The films came to him: filmmakers sent him videos, and they even asked him to read their scripts before their films went into production. It is thus not exaggerating to say that many East Asian films aiming at commercial success now have a built-in "remaking mentality" that self-consciously measures themselves against the Hollywood standard. Fourth, all of the originals of Lee's films had been tested well in East Asian cinema markets: *The Ring, The Grudge, The Sassy Girl*, and *Infernal Affairs* were megahits in East Asia. Lee's trust in the testing effect of East Asian markets reveals an assumption that North America and East Asia share the same patterns of consumption. Cinema consumption used to follow a unidirectional trail of popularity: whatever proved successful in North America would surely be welcomed in East Asia as long as those countries opened their markets to Hollywood. Now, thanks to transnationalism, the trail has traffic from both directions: whatever proved successful in East Asia would most likely succeed in North America as long as the original ethnicity is changed to that of Caucasian.

Having considered all important factors, we can now conclude that the current remaking fad corresponds to East Asia's new status as the world's production center. As much as computer chips, flat-panel screens, automobile parts, DVD players, and almost entire Wal-Mart inventories are increasingly being produced out of Taiwan, China, South Korea, and Japan, the film industry is slowly but steadily shifting its production to East Asia. This observation might sound outrageous for some, because Hollywood products are still mainly the result of collaborations among American corporations, directors, performers, and other supporting casts. But we must remember that film production is a long and complicated process. The big studio must begin with an idea, which is then developed into a prospectus before the studio is committed to hiring an expensive scriptwriter, who will then go through numerous rewrites before the script ever enters the production pipeline. Once the production is given the green light, everything will have to be in perfect sync in order for a film to come into existence: budgeting, casting, shooting, digital imaging, editing, and so on. A small glitch at any of the junctures could doom the entire film. Market testing of the film will then follow. Numerous test screenings will send the film back for endless changes in order to suit the audience's tastes. The premiere date will then be set, ad campaigns orchestrated, and marketing machines put in full gear. This long and arduous process of mass industrial production is why sequels, no matter how diluted they are in comparison with the originals, are continually being churned out by Hollywood factories. Through a simplified process, a sequel with a $100 million box office take is most likely more profitable and less risky than an original that grossed $150 million. The same is true for remakes. A plot full of dramatic twists is ready to be built into a successful screenplay, the mise-en-scène has been carefully laid out so that the remake's director only needs to make slight changes, and most important, the market has been tested. Remakes are potentially more profitable than sequels because the sequels can hardly improve on the originals, while the remakes, with the added value of "Hollywood" as the biggest name brand for cinema, would almost certainly surpass the originals at the box office.

Remaking is therefore Hollywood's way of outsourcing. Outsourced are the jobs of assistant producers who are the initial script screeners, the personnel involved in the scripting process, supporting crew for various details during production, the marketing team, and, increasingly, directors. Sooner or later, the unions within the Hollywood system will come to realize the outsourcing nature of remakes. But at least for now, remakes are making Hollywood leaner, stronger, more efficient, more profitable, and more dominant than ever. This is an irreversible but well-disguised trend. The changed ethnicity serves well to disguise this trend: as much as the glamor of the Hollywood star system makes people forget that cinema is a big industry, the Caucasian faces in the remakes cover up the significant contributions of East Asia as the provider of intense labor required by the film industry.

The title of *Ringu* is indicative of the gains and losses of remaking as outsourcing. Originally named *The Ring*, this original must yield the "original" title to the remake and is forced to use the Japanese transliteration of "ring" as its "authentic" title. The Japanese film industry might have gained recognition and a small share of the remake's profit, but the gain for the "native," symbolized by the letter "u" added to "ring," is precisely what has been lost: the original ethnicity, the "aura," the intellectual property, and the identity and history of the entire national film industry. How is this "loss by gaining" any different from outsourcing in the computer industry? Through outsourcing labor-intensive jobs such as software scripting, the American high-tech industry is able to sustain its remarkable growth while at the same time generating a new white-collar middle class in Shanghai and Calcutta. China and India have benefited greatly from this kind of outsourcing in terms of urbanization, Westernization, and improvement in living standards, but the gain can never compensate for the losses: failure to develop their own software industries and intellectual property, reliance on American trade policy, and exposure to the high cost of repackaged end products such as Microsoft Windows.

What does this outsourcing mean for the types of film production in transnational Chinese cinema as discussed in this book? While it is still too early to predict the implications, immediate impact has already begun to show. The success of East Asian films in North America enables Zhang Yimou to continue with his big-budget filmmaking. The lone "superstar" among Chinese film directors, Zhang is inching closer to the status of "national treasure," as evidenced by the assignment of directing an eight-minute segment for the closing ceremony of the 2004 Athens Summer Olympics and the entire opening ceremony of the 2008 Beijing Summer Olympics. He certainly desires as much attention from Hollywood as possible, but he does not need to settle for low-budget and sensationalized films ready to be remade. Holding the flag of "authentic national culture," Zhang Yimou will facilitate Hollywood outsourcing by attracting and training talent in commercial cinema while at the same time engaging in copyright competition. Zhang Ziyi's recent success is but one example. In the meantime, Zhang Yimou's young colleagues Jiang Wen, Wang Xiaoshuai, and Lou Ye are finding that the road of art film is narrowing. With talents, experience, name recognition, and readiness to collaborate with commercial cinema, they will most likely become China's Nakata Hideo and Shimizu Takashi. As for Taiwan's Tsai Ming-liang and Hong Kong's Fruit Chan, who are least likely to succumb to Hollywood homogenization, they will continue to fight their lonely and uphill battle. Their colleagues, such as Chen Kuo-fu and Johnny To, will possibly become the most avid promoters of Hollywood outsourcing.

Although Hollywoodization is irreversible, unexpected outcomes could still be possible. Facing the pressure of outsourcing, Chinese filmmakers are increasingly collaborating with the Japanese and Koreans to assert an East Asian identity. Trans–East Asian cinema, which is the topic of my next project, will become the new "in-between" space that cuts across the dynamics of transnationalism and regionalism, contests unequal power relations, generates new identities, and creates new intellectual properties.

Notes

1. These numbers were gathered from Tad Friend, "Remake Man: Roy Lee Brings Asia to Hollywood, and Finds Some Enemies along the Way," *The New Yorker*, June 2, 2003.

2. John Chua, "The Horror, the Horror: The Repetition and Compulsion of a Genre" (PhD diss., University of Illinois, 2004).

3. For Walter Benjamin, aura has to do with involuntary memory, which comes from the ocean of one's deeply hidden memories and is triggered only by sheer chance; aura is also based on the associations that "tend to cluster around the object of a perception," associations that were quickly disappearing due to the perceptive certainty in mechanical arts invented at the dawn of the modern era. Those mechanical arts include photography and cinema. See Walter Benjamin, *Reflections*, ed. Peter Demetz and trans. Edmund Jephcott (New York: Schocken Books, 1978), 186. Of course, it is possible that Benjamin did not fully realize the representational potential of the mechanical arts. But his understanding of aura provides a key to dissecting Hollywood horror films: viewers scream and peek through their fingers, not because fear is reverberating in their repressed anxieties and insecurities, but because they are secretly and joyfully embarrassed by the transference of their fear onto the mechanical shallowness in the film's predictability, conventionality, and inambiguity devoid of aura.

4. Mark Cousins, "The Asian Aesthetic," *Prospect*, no. 104 (November 2004): 2.

5. Cousins, "The Asian Aesthetic," 4.

Bibliography

Abbas, Ackbar. *Hong Kong: Culture and the Politics of Disappearance.* Minneapolis: University of Minnesota Press, 1997.

Adorno, Theodor W. "Transparencies on Film." In *The Culture Industry: Selected Essays on Mass Culture*, edited with an introduction by J. M. Bernstein, 154–61. London: Routledge, 1991.

Anderson, Marston E. *The Limits of Realism: Chinese Fiction in the Revolutionary Period.* Berkeley: University of California Press, 1990.

Ang, Ien. "To Be or Not to Be Chinese: Diaspora, Culture, and Postmodern Ethnicity." *Southeast Asian Journal of Social Science* 21 (1993): 1–19.

Appadurai, Arjun. "Disjuncture and Difference in the Global Cultural Economy." *Public Culture* 2, no. 2 (1990): 1–17.

———. *Modernity at Large: Cultural Dimensions of Globalization.* Minneapolis: University of Minnesota Press, 1996.

Armes, Roy. *Third World Film Making and the West.* Berkeley: University of California Press, 1987.

Baker, Rick, and Toby Russell. *The Essential Guide to Hong Kong Movies.* London: Eastern Heroes Publications, 1994.

Barmé, Geremie R. *In the Red: On Contemporary Chinese Culture.* New York: Columbia University Press, 1999.

Baudrillard, Jean. *The Mirror of Production.* St. Louis: Telos Press, 1975.

Befu, Harumi, ed. *Cultural Nationalism in East Asia: Representation and Identity.* Berkeley: Institute of East Asian Studies, University of California, 1993.

Beller, Jonathan L. "Kino-I, Kino-World: Notes on the Cinematic Mode of Production." In *The Visual Culture Reader*, 2nd ed., edited by Nicholas Mirzoeff, 60–85. New York: Routledge, 2002.

Benjamin, Walter. *The Arcades Project*. New York: Belknap Press, 2002.

———. "Critique of Violence." In *Reflections: Essays, Aphorisms, Autobiographical Writings*, edited by Peter Demetz and translated by Edmund Jephcott, 277–300. New York: Schocken Books, 1978.

———. *The Origin of German Tragic Drama*. New York: Verso, 2003.

———. "Theses on the Philosophy of History." In *Illuminations*, edited by Hannah Arendt and translated by Harry Zohn, 255–66. New York: Harcourt, Brace & World, 1968.

———. "The Work of Art in the Age of Mechanical Reproduction." In *Film and Criticism*, edited by Gerald Mast and Marshall Cohen, 665–81. New York: Oxford University Press, 1992.

Berry, Chris, ed. *Chinese Films in Focus: 25 New Takes*. London: British Film Institute, 2003.

———. "Chinese Urban Cinema: Hyper-Realism Versus Absurdism." *East-West Film Journal* 3, no. 1 (1988): 76–87.

———. "A Nation T (w/o) o: Chinese Cinema(s) and Nationhood(s)." *East-West Film Journal* 7, no. 1 (1993): 24–51.

———, ed. *Perspectives on Chinese Cinema*. London: British Film Institute, 1991.

Berry, Chris, and Mary Ann Farquhar. *China on Screen: Cinema and Nation*. New York: Columbia University Press, 2006.

———. "From National Cinemas to Cinema and the National: Rethinking the National in Transnational Chinese Cinemas." *Journal of Modern Literature in Chinese* 4 (January 2001): 109–22.

———. "Post-Socialist Strategies: An Analysis of *Yellow Earth* and *Black Cannon Incident*." In *Cinematic Landscape: Observations on the Visual Arts and Cinema of China and Japan*, edited by Linda C. Ehrlich and David Desser, 81–116. Austin: University of Texas Press, 1994.

Berry, Michael. *Speaking in Images: Interviews with Contemporary Chinese Filmmakers*. New York: Columbia University Press, 2005.

Bhabha, Homi. *The Location of Culture*. London: Routledge, 1994.

———, ed. *Nation and Narration*. New York: Routledge, 1990.

Bluestone, George. *Novels into Film*. Berkeley: University of California Press, 1973.

Bordwell, David. *Making Meaning: Interference and Rhetoric in the Interpretation of Cinema*. Cambridge, MA: Harvard University Press, 1997.

———. *On the History of Film Style*. Cambridge, MA: Harvard University Press, 1997.

———. *Planet Hong Kong: Popular Cinema and the Art of Entertainment*. Cambridge, MA: Harvard University Press, 2000.

———. "Transcultural Spaces: Toward a Poetics of Chinese Film." In *Chinese-Language Film: Historiography, Poetics, Politics*, edited by Sheldon Lu and Emilie Yeh, 141–62. Honolulu: University of Hawaii Press, 2005.

Bordwell, David, and Noel Carroll, eds. *Post-Theory: Reconstructing Film Studies*. Madison: University of Wisconsin Press, 1996.

Braester, Yomi. "If We Could Remember Everything, We Could Be Able to Fly: Taipei's Cinematic Poetics of Demolition." *Modern Chinese Literature and Culture* 15 (Spring 2003): 29–62.

⸻. *Witness against History: Literature, Film, and Public Discourse in Twentieth-Century China.* Stanford: Stanford University Press, 2003.

Braudy, Leo, and Marshall Cohen, eds. *Film Theory and Criticism: Introductory Readings.* New York: Oxford University Press, 2004.

Brown, Wendy. "Neo-Liberalism and the End of Liberal Democracy." *Theory and Event* 7 (Spring 2003): 1–21.

Browne, Nick, Paul G. Pickowics, Vivian Sobchack, and Esther Yau, eds. *New Chinese Cinema: Forms, Identities, Politics.* Cambridge: Cambridge University Press, 1994.

Buck-Morss, Susan. *Dreamworld and Catastrophe: The Passing of Mass Utopia in East and West.* Cambridge, MA: MIT Press, 2000.

Burger, Peter. *Theory of the Avant-Garde.* Minneapolis: University of Minnesota Press, 1984.

Cai, Zong-qi. *Configurations of Comparative Poetics: Three Perspectives on Western and Chinese Literary Criticism.* Honolulu: University of Hawaii Press, 2002.

Chan, Felicia. "Crouching Tiger, Hidden Dragon: Cultural Migrancy and Translatability." In *Chinese Films in Focus: 25 New Takes*, edited by Chris Berry, 56–64. London: British Film Institute, 2003.

Chang, Sung-sheng Yvonne. *Modernism and the Nativist Resistance.* Durham, NC: Duke University Press, 1993.

Cheah, Pheng. "Given Culture: Rethinking Cosmopolitical Freedom in Transnationalism." *Boundary 2* 24 (Summer 1997): 157–97.

Cheah, Pheng, and Bruce Robbins, eds. *Cosmopolitics: Thinking and Feeling Beyond the Nation.* Minneapolis: University of Minnesota Press, 1998.

Chen, Cuilian. *Paixi douzheng yu quanmou zhengzhi: Ererba beiju de ling yi mianxiang* [Partisan struggles and power politics: The other face of the February 28 Incident]. Taipei, Taiwan: Shibao wenhua, 1995.

Cheng, Qingsong, and Ou Huang, eds. *Wo de sheyingji bu sahuang: Shengyu 1961–1970 xianfeng dianyingren dang'an* [My camera does not lie: Profiles of Chinese avant-garde filmmakers born in the 1960s]. Beijing: Zhongguo youyi, 2002.

Ching, Leo. "Globalizing the Regional, Regionalizing the Global: Mass Culture and Asianism in the Age of Late Capital." *Public Culture* 12 (Winter 2000): 233–57.

⸻. "Yellow Skin, White Masks: Race, Class, and Identification in Japanese Colonial Discourse." In *Trajectories: Inter-Asia Cultural Studies*, edited by Kuan-Hsing Chen, 65–86. London; New York: Routledge, 1998.

Chow, Rey. *Primitive Passions: Visuality, Sexuality, Ethnography, and Contemporary Chinese Cinema.* New York: Columbia University Press, 1995.

Chua, John. "The Horror, the Horror: The Repetition and Compulsion of a Genre." PhD diss., University of Illinois, 2004.

Clark, Paul. *Chinese Cinema: Culture and Politics since 1949.* Cambridge: Cambridge University Press, 1988.

———. "Reinventing China: The Fifth-Generation Filmmakers." *Modern Chinese Literature* 5 (Spring 1989): 121–36.

Comaroff, Jean. *Body of Power, Spirit of Resistance: The Culture and History of a South African People.* Chicago: University of Chicago Press, 1985.

Comaroff, Jean, and John Comaroff, eds. *Millennial Capitalism and the Culture of Neoliberalism.* Durham, NC: Duke University Press, 2000.

Cornelius, Sheila, and Ian Haydn Smith. *New Chinese Cinema: Challenging Representations.* London; New York: Wallflower, 2002.

Cousins, Mark. "The Asian Aesthetic." *Prospect*, no. 104 (November 2004), http://www.prospect-magazine.co.uk/pdfarticle.php?id=6514.

Cui, Shuqin. *Women Through the Lens: Gender and Nation in a Century of Chinese Cinema.* Honolulu: University of Hawaii Press. 2003.

Deleuze, Gilles. *Cinema 1: The Movement-Image.* Translated by Hugh Tomlinson and Barbara Habberjam. Minneapolis: University of Minnesota Press, 1986.

———. *Cinema 2: The Time-Image.* Translated by Hugh Tomlinson and Robert Galeta. Minneapolis: University of Minnesota Press, 1989.

Desser, David. "The Kung Fu Craze." In *The Cinema of Hong Kong: History, Arts, Identity*, edited by Poshek Fu and David Desser, 19–43. New York: Cambridge University Press, 2000.

Dirlik, Arif. "Transnationalism, the Press, and the National Imaginary in Twentieth Century China." *The China Review* 4 (Spring 2004): 11–25.

Dirlik, Arif, and Xudong Zhang, eds. *Postmodernism and China.* Durham, NC: Duke University Press, 2000.

Dissanayake, Wimal. *Cinema and Cultural Identity: Reflections on Films from Japan, India, and China.* Lanham, MD: University Press of America, 1988.

———. *Colonialism and Nationalism in Asian Cinema.* Bloomington: Indiana University Press, 1994.

———, ed. *Melodrama and Asian Cinema.* Cambridge; New York: Cambridge University Press, 1993.

Dissanayake, Wimal, and Rob Wilson, eds. *Global/Local: Cultural Production and the Transnational Imaginary.* Durham, NC: Duke University Press. 1996.

Donald, Stephanie. *Public Secrets, Public Spaces: Cinema and Civility in China.* Lanham, MD: Rowman & Littlefield, 2000.

Ehrlich, Linda C., and David Desser, eds. *Cinematic Landscapes: Observations on the Visual Arts and Cinema of China and Japan.* Austin: University of Texas Press, 1994.

Featherstone, Mike. *Undoing Culture: Globalization, Postmodernism and Identity.* London: Sage, 1995.

Freud, Sigmund. "The Economic Problem of Masochism." In *The Standard Edition of the Complete Psychological Works of Sigmund Freud*, translated by James Strachey, 19: 159–70. London: Hogarth, 1961.

Friend, Tad. "Remake Man: Roy Lee Brings Asia to Hollywood, and Finds Some Enemies along the Way." *The New Yorker*, June 2, 2003.

Fu, Poshek. *Between Shanghai and Hong Kong: The Politics of Chinese Cinemas.* Stanford: Stanford University Press, 2003.

————. "Going Global: The Transnational Cinema of the Shaw Brothers Studio, 1960–1970." In *Hong Kong Cinema Retrospective Catalogue: Border Crossing in Hong Kong Cinema*, edited by Law Kar, 43–51. Hong Kong: Leisure and Cultural Services Department, 2000.

Fu, Poshek, and David Desser, eds. *The Cinema of Hong Kong: History, Arts, Identity*. Cambridge: Cambridge University Press, 2000.

Gao, Minglu, ed. *Inside Out: New Chinese Art*. Berkeley: University of California Press, 1999.

Garber, Marjorie. *Symptoms of Culture*. New York: Routledge, 2000.

Gateward, Frances, ed. *Zhang Yimou Interviews*. Jackson: University Press of Mississippi, 2001.

Giannetti, Louis. *Understanding Movies*. Englewood Cliffs, NJ: Prentice-Hall, 1990.

Giddens, Anthony. *The Consequence of Modernity*. Stanford: Stanford University Press, 1990.

Gledhill, Christine, and Linda Williams, eds. *Reinventing Film Studies*. London: Arnold, 2000.

Goldblatt, Howard, and Sylvia L. Lin, eds. *Notes of a Desolate Man*. New York: Columbia University Press, 1999.

Gunning, Tom. "The Cinema of Attraction: Early Film, Its Spectator, and the Avant-Garde." In *Film and Theory*, edited by Robert Stam and Toby Miller, 229–35. New York: Blackwell, 2000.

Hall, Stuart. "Cultural Identity and Cinematic Representation." *Framework* 36 (1989): 68–81.

Hamamoto, Y. Darrell, and Sandra Liu, eds. *Countervisions: Asian American Film Criticism*. Philadelphia: Temple University Press, 2000.

Harvey, David. *The Condition of Postmodernity*. London: Blackwell, 1990.

Henry, Michael. *The Film Business: A Legal and Commercial Analysis*. London: Longman, 1986.

Hill, John, and Pamela Church Gibson, eds. *The Oxford Guide to Film Studies*. London: Arnold; New York: Oxford University Press, 1998.

————, eds. *World Cinema: Critical Approaches*. Oxford; New York: Oxford University Press, 2000.

Hitchcock, Peter. "The Aesthetics of Alienation, or China's 'Fifth Generation.'" *Culture Studies* (London) 6 (1992): 116–41.

Hjort, Mette, and Scott MacKenzie, eds. *Cinema and Nation*. London: Routledge, 2000.

Hoberman, J. "Wheels of History." *The Village Voice*, September 30, 1998.

————. *Vulgar Modernism: Writing on Movies and Other Media*. Philadelphia: Temple University Press, 1991.

Hobsbawm, Eric. "Introduction: Inventing Traditions." In *The Invention of Tradition*, edited by Eric Hobsbawm and Terence Ranger, 1–14. Cambridge: Cambridge University Press, 1983.

Hsia, Chih-tsing. *A History of Modern Chinese Fiction*, 2nd ed. New Haven: Yale University Press, 1971.

Hu, Jubin. *Projecting a Nation: Chinese National Cinema before 1949*. Hong Kong: Hong Kong University Press, 2003.

Huang, Ting. *E shidai dianying nannu shuangren yazuo: Zoujin Qianxi manbo de Taipei buyecheng* (Deluxe love seats for E-generation film people: Entering the nightless Taipei in *Millennium Mambo*). Taipei: Taiwan jiaochuan, 2001.

Hung, Eva. "Fin de Siècle Splendor." In *The Columbia Anthology of Modern Chinese Literature*, edited by Joseph Lau and Howard Goldblatt, 444–67. New York: Columbia University Press, 1995.

Huters, Theodore, and Xiaobing Tang. *Chinese Literature and the West: The Trauma of Realism, the Challenge of the (Post) Modern*. Durham, NC: Asian/Pacific Studies Institute, 1991.

Jakes, Susan. "Hostages of the State." *Time-Asia*, June 23, 2003.

Jameson, Fredric. *The Geopolitical Aesthetic: Cinema and Space in the World System*. Bloomington: Indiana University Press, 1992.

⎯⎯⎯. *Postmodernism, or, The Cultural Logic of Late Capitalism*. Durham, NC: Duke University Press, 1991.

Jameson, Frederic, and Masao Miyoshi, eds. *The Cultures of Globalization*. Durham, NC: Duke University Press, 1998.

Johnson, Claire. "Women's Cinema as Counter Cinema." *Notes on Women's Cinema*. London: British Film Institute, 1973.

Jones, Amelia, and Andrew Stephenson. *Performing the Body/Performing the Text*. London: Routledge, 1999.

Kagawa, Teruyuki. *Chugoku Miroku: "Oni ga Kita!" Satsuei Nikki* (The shadow of devils in China: Diary during the making of *Devils on the Doorstep*). Tokyo: Kinema Jyunposha, 2002.

Kam, Tan See, and Annette Aw. "*Love Eterne*: Almost a (Heterosexual) Love Story." In *Chinese Films in Focus: 25 New Takes*, edited by Chris Berry, 137–43. London: British Film Institute, 2003.

Kaplan, E. Ann. *Psychoanalysis and Cinema*. New York: Routledge, 1990.

Kar, Law, ed. *Hong Kong Cinema Retrospective Catalogue: Border Crossing in Hong Kong Cinema*. Hong Kong: Leisure and Cultural Services Department, 2000.

Kraicer, Shelly. "Absence as Spectacle: Zhang Yimou's Hero." *Cinema Scope* 5 (Spring 2003): 9.

Kuoshu, Harry H., ed. *Celluloid China: Cinematic Encounters with Culture and Society*. Carbondale: Southern Illinois University Press, 2002.

⎯⎯⎯. *Lightness of Being in China: Adaptation and Discursive Figuration in Cinema and Theater*. New York: Peter Lang, 1999.

LaCapra, Dominick. *History in Transit: Experience, Identity, Critical Theory*. Ithaca, NY: Cornell University Press, 2004.

Lai, Tse-han, Ramon H. Myers, and Wei Wou, eds. *A Tragic Beginning: The Taiwan Uprising of February 28, 1947*. Stanford: Stanford University Press, 1991.

Larson, Wendy. "Zhang Yimou: Inter/National Aesthetics and Erotics." In *Cultural Encounters: China, Japan, and the West*, edited by Soren Clausen, Roy Starrs, and Anne Wedell-Wedellsborg, 215–26. Aarhus, Denmark: Aarhus University Press, 1995.

Lau, Jenny Kwok Wah. "Globalization and Youthful Subculture: The Chinese Sixth-Generation Films at the Dawn of the New Century." In *Multiple Modernities: Cinemas and Popular Media in Transcultural East Asia*, edited by Jenny Kowk Wah Lau, 13–27. Philadelphia: Temple University Press, 2002.

Lau, Shing-hon. *A Study of the Hong Kong Swordplay Film (1945–1980)*. Hong Kong: Urban Council, 1981.

Lee, Leo Ou-fan. *Shanghai Modern: The Flowering of a New Urban Culture in China, 1930–1945*. Cambridge, MA: Harvard University Press, 1999.

⸻. "The Tradition of Modern Chinese Cinema: Some Preliminary Explorations and Hypotheses." In *Perspectives on Chinese Cinema*, edited by Chris Berry, 6–20. London: British Film Institute, 1991.

Lent, John A. *The Asian Film Industry*. Austin: University of Texas Press, 1990.

Lev, Peter. *The Euro-American Cinema*. Austin: University of Texas Press, 1993.

Leys, Ruth. *Trauma: A Genealogy*. Chicago: University of Chicago Press, 2000.

Liao, Ping-hui. "Rewriting Taiwanese National History: The February 28 Incident as Spectacle." *Public Culture* 5, no. 2 (1993): 281–96.

Lii, Tin-zann. "A Colonial Empire: Reflections on the Expansion of Hong Kong Films in Asian Countries." In *Trajectories: Inter-Asia Cultural Studies*, edited by Kuan Hsing Chen, 122–41. London: Routledge, 1998.

Lim, Bliss Cua. "Spectral Times: The Ghost Film as Historical Allegory." *Positions* 9 (Fall 2001): 287–329.

Lin, Nianhong. "A Study of the Theories of Chinese Cinema in Their Relationship to Classical Aesthetics." *Modern Chinese Literature* 1, no. 2 (1985): 186–89.

Lin, Xiao Ping. "New Chinese Cinema of the 'Sixth Generation': A Distant Cry of Forsaken Children." *Third Text* 16 (September 2002): 261–84.

Liu, Kang. "Is There an Alternative to Capitalist Globalization? The Debate about Modernity in China." In *The Cultures of Globalization*, edited by Fredric Jameson and Masao Miyoshi, 164–91. Durham, NC: Duke University Press, 1998.

Liu, Lydia H. *Translingual Practice: Literature, National Culture, and Translated Modernity—China, 1900–1937*. Stanford: Stanford University Press, 1995.

Lloyd, Ann, ed. *The History of the Movie*. London: Macdonald Orbis, 1988.

Logan, Bey. *Hong Kong Action Cinema*. London: Titan Books, 1995.

Lu, Sheldon H. *China, Transnational Visuality, Global Postmodernity*. Stanford: Stanford University Press, 2001.

⸻, ed. *Transnational Chinese Cinemas: Identity, Nationhood, Gender*. Honolulu: University of Hawaii Press, 1997.

⸻. "Zhang Yimou." In *Fifty Contemporary Filmmakers*, edited by Yvonne Tasker, 412–18. London: Routledge, 2002.

Lu, Sheldon H., and Emilie Yeh, eds. *Chinese-Language Film: Historiography, Poetics, Politics*. Honolulu: University of Hawaii Press, 2005.

Lu, Tonglin. *Confronting Modernity in the Cinemas of Taiwan and Mainland China*. Cambridge: Cambridge University Press, 2001.

Lu, Xun. *The Complete Stories of Lu Xun*, translated by Yang Xianyi and Gladys Yang. Beijing: Foreign Languages Press, 1981.

Luxemburg, Rosa. *The Accumulation of Capital*. London: Routledge and Kegan & Paul Ltd., 1951.

Ma, Ning. "New Chinese Cinema: A Critical Account of the Fifth Generation." *Cinemaya* 2 (1988–89): 21–27.

Maltby, Richard. *Hollywood Cinema*, 2nd ed. Malden, MA: Blackwell Publishing, 2003.

Marx, Karl. *Capital: A Critique of Political Economy*, translated by Ben Fowkes. New York: Vintage Books, 1977.

Marx, Karl, and Frederick Engels. *Economic and Philosophic Manuscripts of 1844 and the Communist Manifesto*. New York: Prometheus Books, 1988.

Mayne, Judith. *Cinema and Spectatorship*. London: Routledge, 1993.

Metz, Christian. *Language and Cinema*, translated by Donna Jean Umiker-Sebeok. The Hague: Mouton, 1974.

Morris, Meaghan, Siu Leung Li, and Stephen Chan Ching-kiu, eds. *Hong Kong Connections: Transnational Imagination in Action Cinema*. Durham, NC: Duke University Press, 2005.

Mulvey, Laura. *Visual and Other Pleasures*. Bloomington: Indiana University Press, 1989.

————. "Visual Pleasure and Narrative Cinema." *Screen* 16 (Autumn 1975): 6–18.

Munoz, Lorenza. "Modern Movie Houses Are Sprouting Overseas." *Los Angeles Times*, April 27, 2005.

Neale, Steve, and Murray Smith, eds. *Contemporary Hollywood Cinema*. London: Routledge, 1998.

Nichols, Bill, ed. *Movies and Methods: An Anthology*. Berkeley: University of California Press, 1985.

Ong, Aihwa. *Flexible Citizenship: The Cultural Logics of Transnationality*. Durham, NC: Duke University Press, 1999.

Pang, Laikwan. *Building a New China in Cinema: The Chinese Left-Wing Cinema Movement, 1932–1937*. Lanham, MD: Rowman & Littlefield, 2002.

Pickowicz, Paul. "Melodrama Representations and the May Fourth Tradition of Chinese Cinema." In *From May Fourth to June Fourth: Fiction and Film in Twentieth-Century China*, edited by Ellen Widmer et al., 295–326. New York: Columbia University Press, 1993.

————. "The Theme of Spiritual Pollution in Chinese Films of the 1930s." *Modern China* 17 (January 1991): 38–74.

————. "Velvet Prisons and the Political Economy of Chinese Filmmaking." In *Urban Spaces in Contemporary China: The Potential for Autonomy and Community in Post-Mao China*, edited by Deborah Davis, Richard Kraus, Barry Naughton, and Elizabeth J. Perry, 193–220. Cambridge: Cambridge University Press, 1995.

Pratt, Mary Louise. *Imperial Eyes: Travel Writing and Transculturation*. London: Routledge, 1992.

Rapfogel, Jared. "Tsai Ming-liang: Cinematic Painter." *Senses of Cinema*, May 2002. http://www.sensesofcinema.com/contents/02/20/tsai_painter.html.

Reynaud, Berenice. "China: On the Set with Zhang Yimou." *Sight and Sound* 1 (July 1991): 26–28.

Robertson, Roland. *Globalization: Social Theory and Global Culture.* London: Sage, 1992.

Said, Edward. *Orientalism.* New York: Vintage Books, 1979.

Schab, Frank R., and Robert G. Crowder. "Introduction." In *Memory for Odors,* edited by Frank R. Schab and Robert G. Crowder. Mahwah, NJ: Lawrence Erlbaum, 1995.

Semsel, George S., ed. *Chinese Film: The State of the Art in the People's Republic.* New York: Praeger, 1987.

Semsel, George S., Chen Xihe, and Xia Hong, eds. *Film in Contemporary China: Critical Debates, 1979–1989.* New York: Praeger, 1993.

Semsel, George S., Xia Hong, and Hou Jianping, eds. *Chinese Film Theory: A Guide to the New Era.* New York: Praeger, 1990.

Shin, Thomas, and Keeto Lam. "Fruit Chan: Life and Death in the Global Cesspool." Interview with Fruit Chan. *Hong Kong Panorama 2002–2003.* Hong Kong: Leisure and Cultural Services Department, 2003.

Short, Stephen. "Neither Here nor There." *Time Asia,* March 18, 2002.

Silbergeld, Jerome. *Hitchcock with a Chinese Face: Cinematic Doubles, Oedipal Triangles, and China's Moral Voice.* Seattle: University of Washington Press, 2004.

———. *China into Film: Frames of Reference in Contemporary Chinese Cinema.* London: Reaktion Books, 1999.

———. "Hitchcock with a Chinese Face: Lou Ye's *Suzhou River.*" *Persimmon* 8 (Summer 2002): 70–73.

Silverman, Kaja. *The Threshold of the Visible World.* New York: Routledge, 1996.

Smith, Michael Peter. *Transnational Urbanism: Locating Globalization.* New York: Blackwell, 2001.

Smith, Sean. "Invasion of the Hot Movie Stars." *Newsweek,* May 9, 2005.

Solinger, Dorothy. "China's Floating Population." In *The Paradox of China's Post-Mao Reforms,* edited by Merle Goldman and Roderick MacFarquhar, 220–40. Cambridge, MA: Harvard University Press, 1999.

Stokes, Lisa Odham, and Michael Hoover. *City on Fire: Hong Kong Cinema.* London: Verso, 1999.

Tam, Kwok-kan, and Wimal Dissanayake. *New Chinese Cinema.* New York: Oxford University Press, 1998.

Tanaka, Stefan. *Japan's Orient: Rendering Pasts into History.* Berkeley: University of California Press, 1993.

Teo, Stephen. *Hong Kong Cinema: The Extra Dimension.* London: British Film Institute, 1997.

Tomlinson, John. *Globalization and Culture.* Cambridge, MA: Harvard University Press, 1977.

Tsai, Eva. "Kaneshiro Takeshi: Transnational Stardom and the Media and Cultural Industries in Asia's Global/Postcolonial Age." *Journal of Modern Chinese Literature and Culture* 17 (Spring 2005): 100–32.

Udden, James. "Hou Hsiao-hsien and the Poetics of History." *Cinema Scope* 3 (Spring 2000): 48–51.

Uhde, Jan, and Yvonne Ng Uhde. *Latent Images: Film in Singapore.* New York: Oxford University Press, 2000.

Van Der Kolk, Bessel A., and Onno Van Der Hart. "The Intrusive Past: The Flexibility of Memory and the Engraving of Trauma." In *Trauma: Explorations in Memory,* edited by Cathy Caruth, 153–60. Baltimore: The Johns Hopkins University Press, 1995.

Waldron, Arthur. *The Great Wall of China: From History to Myth.* Cambridge: Cambridge University Press, 1990.

Wang, Ban. "Black Holes of Globalization: Critique of the New Millennium in Taiwan Cinema." *Modern Chinese Literature and Culture* 15 (Spring 2003): 90–119.

———. "Historical Trauma in Multi-National Cinemas: Rethinking History with Trauma." *Tamkang Review* 31, no. 1 (2000): 22–48.

———. *The Sublime Figure of History.* Stanford: Stanford University Press, 1997.

Wang, David Der-wei. "Afterword: Chinese Fiction for the Nineties." In *Running Wild: New Chinese Writers,* edited by David Der-wei Wang and Jeannie Tai, 238–58. New York: Columbia University Press, 1994.

———. *Fictional Realism in 20th-Century China: Mao Dun, Lao She, Shen Congwen.* New York: Columbia University Press, 1992.

Wang, Jing. *High Culture Fever: Politics, Aesthetics, and Ideology in Deng's China.* Berkeley: University of California Press, 1996.

Wang, Jing, and Tani E. Barlow, eds. *Cinema and Desire: Feminist Marxism and Cultural Politics in the Work of Dai Jinhua.* New York: Verso, 2003.

Wang, Shujen. "Recontextualizing Copyright: Piracy, Hollywood, the State, and Globalization." *Cinema Journal* 43 (Fall 2003): 25–43.

Wasko, Janet. *Hollywood in the Information Age.* Austin: University of Texas Press, 1994.

Wen, Tianxiang. *Guangying dingge: Tsai Ming-liang de xinling changyu* (Frozen lights and shadows: Tsai Ming-liang's psychic field). Taipei: Hengxing, 2002.

Widmer, Ellen, and David Der-wei Wang, eds. *From May Fourth to June Fourth: Fiction and Film in Twentieth-Century China.* Cambridge, MA: Harvard University Press, 1993.

Williams, Alan, ed. *Film and Nationalism.* New Brunswick, NJ: Rutgers University Press, 2002.

Xu, Gary G. "The Pedagogical as the Political: Ideology of Globalization and Zhang Yimou's *Not One Less*." *The Communication Review* 6 (December 2003): 327–40.

———. "*Flowers of Shanghai*: Visualizing Ellipses and (Colonial) Absence." In *Chinese Films in Focus: 25 New Takes,* edited by Chris Berry, 104–10. London: British Film Institute, 2003.

Yamasaki, Sachio. *Hou Hsiao-hsien.* Tokyo: Asahi Shimbun, 1993.

Yang, Jeff. *Once upon a Time in China: A Guide to Hong Kong, Taiwanese, and Mainland Chinese Cinema.* New York: Atria Books, 2003.

Yau, Esther, ed. *At Full Speed: Hong Kong Cinema in a Borderless World.* Minneapolis: University of Minnesota Press, 2001.

Yau, Ka-Fai. "3rdness: Filming, Changing, Thinking Hong Kong." *Positions* 9 (Winter 2001): 535–57.

Yip, June. "Constructing a Nation: Taiwanese History and the Films of Hou Hsiao-hsien." In *Transnational Chinese Cinemas: Identity, Nationhood, Gender*, 139–68. Edited by Sheldon H. Lu. Honolulu: University of Hawaii Press, 1997.

Yip, June. *Envisioning Taiwan: Fiction, Cinema, and the Nation in the Cultural Imagery*. Durham, NC: Duke University Press, 2004.

Young, Robert J. C. *Colonial Desire: Hybridity in Theory, Culture and Race*. London: Routledge, 1995.

Zhang, Xudong. *Chinese Modernism in the Era of Reforms: Cultural Fever, Avant-Garde Fiction, and the New Chinese Cinema*. Durham, NC: Duke University Press, 1997.

———. "Shanghai Nostalgia: Postrevolutionary Allegories in Wang Anyi's Literary Production in the 1990s." *Positions* 8 (Summer 2000): 349–87.

Zhang, Yingjin. *Chinese National Cinema*. New York: Routledge, 2004.

———. *The City in Modern Chinese Literature & Film: Configurations of Space, Time, and Gender*. Stanford: Stanford University Press, 1996.

———. *Screening China: Critical Interventions, Cinematic Reconfigurations, and the Transnational Imaginary in Contemporary Chinese Cinema*. Ann Arbor, MI: Center for Chinese Studies, 2002.

Zhang, Yingjin, and Zhiwei Xiao. *Encyclopedia of Chinese Film*. New York: Routledge, 1998.

Zong, Baihua. *Zhongguo yishu yijing zhi dansheng* (The birth of Chinese artistic ideascape). In *Zong Baihua quanji* (The collected works of Zong Baihua), vol. 2, 326–38. Hefei, China: Anhui jiaoyu chubanshe, 1994.

Index

About the Author

A native of Nanjing, China, Gary Gang Xu 徐鋼 has a PhD from Columbia University and is presently associate professor at the University of Illinois, Urbana-Champaign. He specializes in Chinese cinema, modern Chinese fiction, criticism, and interpretative theories. He is the editor of *The Cross-Cultural Žižek Reader* (Beijing University Press, 2006) and author of numerous articles.